FRANCE DEFEATS EDC

THIS VOLUME IS SPONSORED JOINTLY BY THE
CENTER FOR INTERNATIONAL STUDIES (M.I.T.)
AND THE INSTITUT D'ÉTUDES EUROPÉENNES (PARIS).
THE FRENCH EDITION IS ENTITLED
La Querelle de la CED (Armand Colin)

FRANCE DEFEATS EDC

Edited by Daniel Lerner and
Raymond Aron

FREDERICK A. PRAEGER · NEW YORK

CONTENTS

Introduction to the American Edition

The Great Debate over a European Defense Community brought into dramatic focus the most divisive issues of the western alliance. The controversy over a supranational army—which sought to integrate forces of Benelux, France, and Italy with reconstituted contingents from a hitherto demilitarized Germany—was bound to divide political opinion within and between the western nations. No nation was so deeply divided within itself as France; no pair of allied nations so sharply out of phase as France and the United States. Yet, when the Assemblée Nationale terminated the controversy begun in 1950 by finally rejecting EDC in 1954, the divisive issues did not disappear. Indeed, the very German rearmament rejected in August was promptly accepted in December 1954 under WEU.*

The issues raised by EDC within France, and between the Franco-American partners, still divide people today and will persist in the near future. The issue of a six-nation European Community, leading through supranational institutions toward a common market, is current in the Euratom proposal for a nuclear pool. (It is not to prejudge the outcome to remind ourselves that some corpses display considerable vivacity before they give up the ghost.) Such issues persist because they are *real*—i.e., because the

* West European Union, created by the Accords of Paris, which authorized the reconstitution of an autonomous German military corps and its admission to NATO.

manner and matter of their resolution will have important (if not always predictable) consequences for every nation involved in the western system and hence for the western system as a whole. Differences on these issues can neither be settled by fiat nor explained away, for they derive from the long-term divergence of power and responsibility between France and America within the western system.

The primary American responsibility in the world arena today is for the Big War. This follows naturally from American monopoly, within the western system, of the nuclear technology by which alone the Big War can be fought—or avoided. This is an awesome power breeding an awesome responsibility. It is understandable that alongside this priority all other problems should recede to secondary status in the perspective of Washington. It is understandable, too, that Washington should cherish the aim of converting each strategic region of the world into a military sector equipped to handle its own "little wars" with maximum efficiency. The twin objective in every sector is: (1) to prevent the expansion of Soviet power by military means; (2) to prevent the military containment of Soviet power in "little wars" from chain-reacting us into the Big War. This objective is surely admirable. But conversion of others, even to righteous goals, is always a difficult process requiring subtle procedures. Whatever the virtues of NATO, MEDO, SEATO, they have exhibited no excess of subtlety. Not a few presumptive converts have resisted the straight American gospel in favor of some more congenial version of life's purposes.

EDC was an instance of this move-and-check sequence on the global checkerboard designed in Washington. Its purpose was to equip the European "continental sector" of the Atlantic alliance for concerted self-defense. Several special features in the situation of continental Europe, however, open the validity of this particular application of general American strategy to just as serious question among men of good will as among men of little faith. Among these features is the general expectation, in the Pentagon as at SHAPE, that under no presently visible conditions could a "little war" in Western Europe be prevented from unleashing the Big War. This being so, the question was bound to arise on EDC: why make this strenuous effort at converting the continent to the formal institutions of a "local sector" when it is not expected that, on the main issue, a "Little Europe" could function merely as such?

There were reasonable answers on both sides of this question, hence the French body politic was divided by it and the margin of final decision was small. Because this question also involved other questions of great poignancy for Frenchmen, the decision was shaped by more than merely reasonable estimates. To begin with, the world arena looks different seen from Paris than from Washington. France is involved in the Big War with neither the power nor the responsibility to do very much about it. This suggests the special agony of political decision in a France whose national power has receded. She remains committed in a world arena requiring "international decisions", but their execution far exceeds her independent capacity for national action. To withdraw from the arena or narrow her commitments would be to certify weakness to her adversaries. To exceed her real scope of effective decision is to invite defeat by her friends and allies.* Anybody with an easy solution to this dilemma will not last long as a politician in such a nation. The instability of French foreign policy as of internal French politics is, in this sense, "no accident".

The French rejection of EDC illustrates the difficulty of identifying, in specific cases, the international limits imposed upon the scope of national decision. A substantial number of deputies in the Assemblée Nationale voted on EDC *as if* the choice available to them was: German rearmament or no German rearmament. As was subsequently demonstrated by events, this was an error of overdefining French freedom of choice. The French decision could be imposed (if at all) only by provoking in the Atlantic Alliance a deep crisis which nobody wanted. But only after EDC was rejected did it become clear to many deputies that the alternative of *no* German rearmament had already been foreclosed by the joint Anglo-American decision that, one way or the other, Germany *would* be rearmed. The only choice left open to French policy was *which way*—EDC or NATO? In closing the EDC way, the Assemblée Nationale did not obviate German rearmament but merely made the NATO way inevitable. Four months later, when the same Assembly that rejected EDC accepted WEU, this was certified in a manner humiliating to Frenchmen with strong na-

* Since these lines were written, the Suez affair has provided a dramatic instance of their meaning.

tional feelings. Belatedly did some French opponents of EDC declare that, had they known WEU would be the result, they would rather have declared for EDC in the first place.

What did EDC propose, as compared with the autonomous German military formation aligned to NATO? The treaty begins by instituting among the six continental nations "a European Defense Community, supranational in character, consisting of common institutions, common armed Forces and a common budget" (Article 1). The principal provisions of the treaty text are analyzed in the first three chapters. Here we note that the proposed "common institutions" of EDC were modelled closely upon those of the European Coal-Steel Community, which, having been accepted by France, might be presumed to be relatively non-controversial. However, in the EDC context, French criticism of institutions creating armed forces not under the supreme political authority of a constituted state became one spearhead of attack upon the treaty. Further, the allocation of these "common Forces" became a center of controversy—as creating national troop units in a Germany without any, and suppressing national units (through integration) in a France with some and a need for more. Finally, the operation of a "common budget" which could exercise major impact upon the economy of each member nation without regard to the political consequences terrified some sections of the business and political elites.

With such a formidable array of doubt and distrust against its major provisions, the treaty was bound to intensify old dissensions and provoke new ones among the French politicians responsible for its fate. Only two parties weathered the storm intact: The Communists voted with their customary unanimity against the treaty, the MRP (Catholic party) voted with near-unanimity for the treaty. Every other party from the Socialists on the Left to the Gaullists on the Right was sharply divided. Indeed, these two parties turned out, when the final votes were tallied, to have played the decisive role. The internal evolution within and between the French parties was shaped by their dissensions over EDC (see chapters 7 and 8).

And so an idea born in France died in France. The intervening four-year controversy left its mark upon all concerned. The Western allies, who had scheduled an endless series of international negotiations (see the Chronology of EDC, p. xv) and had sought to adapt the treaty to French desires, were disappointed and in some quarters enraged. The French political elite, having been put through an exceedingly tight wringer of domestic dissension and foreign pressure, were despondent and embittered. *Anticédistes*, having won the battle of EDC, promptly lost the battle of WEU. The "Europeans" sensed that for them WEU was a pyrrhic victory, which threatened to destroy their essential goal. The defeat of the Defense Community undermined the foundation of their long-term plan for achieving by stages an integrated European Community. Even that which had already been achieved in this direction seemed to be endangered—notably, the Coal-Steel Community operating at Luxembourg since 1951. A direct result of the EDC defeat was Jean Monnet's resignation from the Coal-Steel Community, whose presiding genius he had been from the start, to resume leadership of the internal French political battle to "save Europe".

The current form of this battle is Euratom, which proposes a new continental community with supranational control over nuclear resources. Euratom brings back to the center of the political stage those divisive factors which were spotlighted by EDC. After Euratom finally has been decided, there may well be new proposals —for transport pools or "green pools" (agriculture) or "white pools" (public health)—wherein the same set of factors will be regrouped and reargued. To help clarify the terms of these future debates is an underlying purpose of this book. The EDC treaty is dead, but the issues it raised remain very much alive.

The more so since the failure of the Anglo-French gambit at Suez. This abortive operation showed how dramatically the capacity for independent action by European nations has been limited in the current world arena. Its aftermath was bound to renew interest in the possibilities of a West European community of power. Events in Poland and Hungary add a new possibility that, at the level of trade, the continental nations may gain by giving institutional form to their genuine community of economic interest. Polish coal, for example, could be a boon to every fuel-hungry European nation that now fills its requirements in the dollar area. While many Frenchmen now regret EDC, in the light of these recent events, this does not mean that the six-nation supranational formula has a bright new future. It means only that the quest for a common European policy, and an unacceptable institutional housing for such a policy, is bound to occupy public attention in the near future.

This book advocates no policy. Its authors are Frenchmen who were themselves divided on EDC. M. Philip speaks with the full-throated voice of the active politician who makes no bones about his advocacy of EDC. M. Fauvet was an ardent public spokesman of *anticédisme*. Our common effort in this book is to disengage the real issues of the past controversy. In so doing, we hope to limit the influence of political utterances which merely inflame passions without solving problems. One important consequence of the EDC controversy was to disrupt Franco-American relations by exaggerating spurious differences on both sides. Our effort is rather to highlight the *genuine* differences that exist within and between the two countries. This effort springs from the belief that political rationality requires clarity on the scope and limits of decision-making. The American edition of this book appears in parallel with a French edition; together they aim at clarification of the persistent problems we must face together. It is our hope that this act of international communication will shed light without heat on the common course of the western world. We shall be content if it persuades readers on both sides of the ocean that where there is a common will there are many ways.

The book is a product of the Institut d'Etudes Européennes. This autonomous research institute in Paris, under the scientific direction of the editors, is carrying forward systematic comparative studies of the sociological foundations of European political behavior. Its several activities, including publication of this book in both countries, have been made possible by the cooperation of the Center for International Studies (M.I.T.) and the Institut d'Etudes Politiques (Sorbonne), to both of which we express our gratitude. Our special thanks are due to Madame Genevieve Auclair, who handled the difficult problems of translation with her special blend of intelligence and diligence. Our colleagues at M.I.T., Miss Martha Tucker, Mrs. Lucille Pevsner, Mr. Frank Bonilla and Professor Ithiel Pool helped to solve complicated editorial and administrative problems. Mrs. Jean Lerner exercised masterful control over manuscripts in constant transit between two continents.

D.L. AND R.A.

Cambridge, Mass.
Paris, France
March 1956

List of Abbreviations

"European" Projects and Institutions

EDC   European Defense Community, initiated by Pléven Plan

CECA   Coal and Steel Community, initiated by Schuman Plan

OEEC   Organization for European Economic Cooperation, initiated by Marshall Plan

EPU   European Payments Union, initiated by OEEC

NATO   North Atlantic Treaty Organization, known as Atlantic Alliance

SHAPE   Supreme Headquarters Allied Powers in Europe, military command established under NATO

WEU   West European Union, initiated by Accords of London and Paris

JACEUR   Joint Allied Command in Europe

French Political Parties

MRP   Mouvement Républicain Populaire (Catholic)

SFIO   Section Français de l'Internationale Ouvrière (Socialist)

RPF   Rassemblement du Peuple Français (Gaullist)

ARS   Action Républicain et Social (ex-Gaullist)

UDSR Union Démocratique et Socialiste de la Résistance (Center-Left)

RGR Rassemblement des Gauches Républicaines (Center-Left)

PCF Parti Communiste Français (Communists)

MODÉRÉS Moderate Party (Center-Right), based on small business and not prevented by their name from adopting extreme positions

PAYSANNES Peasants Party (Center-Right), based on rural land-owning population

POUJADISTES Grouping of parties formed at 1956 election and therefore non-existent during EDC period

German Political Parties

CDU Christian Democratic Union

SPD Socialist Party

FDP Free Germany Party

Miscellaneous

PRÉSIDENT Président du Conseil (Prime Minister or chief of government), as distinguished from President of the Republic (chief of state)

J.O. Journal Officiel, official record of parliamentary proceedings

ASSEMBLÉE National Assembly, controlling chamber of the French parliamentary system

Chronology of EDC

JUNE 1950   Opening of the Korean War.

SEPTEMBER 1950   New York and Washington Conferences. Unofficial proposal for a European Defense Community launched by M. René Pléven, French Prime Minister.

OCTOBER 25, 1950   The French National Assembly, rejecting any autonomous German army in its motion of confidence to the Government, accepts the principle of a European Army.

JUNE 17, 1951   Legislative elections in France; 120 Gaullists and 101 Communists (all opposed to EDC) elected to the Assembly.

DECEMBER 11, 1951   National Assembly approves creation of European Coal and Steel Community (CECA) by 376 votes (including Socialists) against 240.

FEBRUARY 19, 1952   The French National Assembly approves EDC in principle, by 327 votes against 240; but numerous conditions are imposed by the opposition.

FEBRUARY 1952   Lisbon Conference.

MAY 27, 1952   M. Pinay, Prime Minister, initials the EDC treaty.

SEPTEMBER 10, 1952   An Assembly *Ad Hoc* is constituted by the Six European Foreign Ministers with the task of drafting a European Constitution.

JANUARY 29, 1953   The EDC treaty is sent for ratification to the

National Assembly by M. Robert Schuman, Foreign Minister (M. Rene Mayer being then Prime Minister).

MARCH 1953 The Constitution drafted by the Assembly *Ad Hoc* is not taken into consideration by the Committee of European Ministers at the Rome Conference.

FROM JANUARY 1953 TO JUNE 1954 The EDC project is submitted to the several parliamentary commissions of the National Assembly for their recommendations.

APRIL 1, 1954 Marshal Juin who had declared himself opposed to EDC is relieved of his NATO posts (M. Laniel being then Prime Minister).

APRIL 3, 1954 At a ceremony at the Arch of Triumph, some demonstrators, cheering Marshal Juin (opponent of EDC) jostled M. René Pléven, Minister of National Defense and sponsor of EDC.

APRIL 25, 1954 Beginning of the Geneva Conference on the war in Indochina.

JUNE 18, 1954 Investiture of M. Pierre Mendès-France as Prime Minister. The latter entrusts two of his ministers, M. Bourgès-Maunoury and General Koenig, with finding a compromise version of EDC that will be acceptable to both its supporters and opponents.

JULY 1954 Failure of the Bourgès-Maunoury and Koenig search for a compromise.

JULY 30, 1954 Signature of the Indochinese Armistice at the Geneva Conference.

AUGUST 16, 1954 At the Brussels Conference, Mendès-France proposes his own compromise solution for differences over text of EDC treaty.

AUGUST 19, 1954 Failure of the Mendès-France compromise and of the Brussels Conference.

AUGUST 30, 1954 EDC is rejected by a vote on a preliminary motion presented by General Aumeran, deputy of Algiers, without being granted the honor of a debate.

DECEMBER 30, 1954 The Accords of Paris are ratified by the French National Assembly.

About the Contributors

ARON, RAYMOND Professor of Sociology at the Sorbonne; Scientific Committee, Institut d'Etudes Européennes; editorial writer, *Le Figaro*; author, *The Century of Total War*, *Le Grande Schisme*

FAUVET, JACQUES Political Editor, *Le Monde*; lecturer, Institut d'Etudes Politiques; author, *Les Forces Politiques de la France*

GROSSER, ALFRED Professor of History, Institut d'Etudes Politiques; author, *The Colossus Again*

HOFFMANN, STANLEY Instructor in Government, Harvard University; author, *Organisations Internationales et Pouvoirs Politiques des Etats*, *Le Mouvement Poujadiste*

LERNER, DANIEL Professor of Sociology at M.I.T.; Research Director, Institut d'Etudes Européennes; Research Associate, Center for International Studies (M.I.T.); author, *The Policy Sciences*, *The Nazi Elite*, *Sykewar*

MARCHAND, J.-J. Research Associate, Institut d'Etudes Européennes; former editor, *Le Rassemblement*; author, *La Vie aux frontières du poème*

PHILIP, ANDRÉ Professor of Economics, University of the Saar; Director, Mouvement Européen; author, *L'intégration de l'économie européenne à l'économie internationale*

STOETZEL, JEAN Professor of Social Science at the Sorbonne; Scientific Committee, Institut d'Etudes Européennes; Director, Institut Francais d'Opinion Publique; author, *Théorie des Opinions*, *Jeunesse Sans Chrysanthème ni Sabre*

THE
SETTING

1 : Historical Sketch of the Great Debate

RAYMOND ARON

Proposed in September 1950, initialed in May 1952 by M. Pinay, the EDC was finally rejected by the French National Assembly on August 30, 1954. From the initial proposal to the final defeat, four years had elapsed. In the meantime, the international situation had undergone a great change: the anxiety that had prevailed at the end of 1950 had given way during the summer of 1954 to a kind of tranquillity. International tensions had eased considerably.

Changes in France's domestic politics were no less decisive. The initiative for EDC had come from a third force government, presided over by M. Pleven and supported by a majority in which the 160 deputies of the M.R.P. played the leading role. The final decision was taken by a completely different Assembly, a government presided over by M. Mendès-France and supported by the Social Republicans (formerly the Gaullists), the Radicals and the Socialists. The so-called "European Party" in power at the early stages of the enterprise was in the opposition during the last phase.

A complete history of the EDC, with its national and international, parliamentary and diplomatic aspects, would merge into the history of French and Western policy during these four years. In the following pages, we shall outline this evolution.

On May 7, 1950, M. Schuman spectacularly launched the European coal and steel pool. This scheme marked the beginning of a new phase in French post-war diplomacy. France had tried between 1944 and 1947 to be the mediator between East and West. From 1947 to 1950 French diplomacy had faithfully but reluctantly adopted the western view. And in 1950, for the first time, she endeavoured to make her own positive contribution to European and Western reconstruction.

Instead of hindering the inevitable restoration of West Germany, the French Foreign Minister contrived a safeguard against German power by the offer of an honourable place for the Bonn Government within a United Europe. The Schuman Plan, as presented to the Council of Ministers, was in no way directed against the Soviet Union, nor designed to be a tool in the cold war. It was, however, implied that the new Europe of the Pool would be strong enough to acquire some independence from the U.S. and to encourage peaceful coexistence between the two giants.

The full meaning of this event should be clear. France no longer was seeking guarantees against Germany through reparations, dismantling of factories, controls provided by the Ruhr international office or by the Disarmament Commission; but rather was seeking security through the frame of a European system in which Germany would be admitted on terms of equality. France was stressing the importance of a supranational power and preferred to construct a new supranational Europe without Great Britain rather than a traditional international coalition with Great Britain. By insisting upon a supranational power, France took the lead for federal type of organisation restricted to the six continental nations, Holland, Belgium, Luxembourg, West Germany, Italy and France.

The opening of the Korean War, six weeks after the Schuman proposal, changed the direction of French policy. Although the Pool had been conceived in the climate of a third-force Europe, it became the symbol of the West strengthening itself against the Soviet threat. This idea became even clearer when the French government, confronted with the American demand to rearm Germany and its acceptance by all the partners of the Atlantic Treaty, tried to avoid a categorical commitment by suggesting the formation of an armament pool on the same model as the Coal and Steel Pool.

The European Army Plan (the so-called Pléven Plan) was the

result of a compromise between the hostility of the French government and Parliament towards the remilitarization of Germany and the external pressure (mainly American) for it. It was a compromise between the ministers who were most opposed to rearmament, such as M. Jules Moch, and the ministers who were resigned to the principle. The compromise was inspired by a faith and supported by a theory: a faith in the value of European unity; a theory that supranational power would be accepted as the basis for the reconstruction of Europe.

With respect to parliamentary opinion, the Pléven Plan had the following advantages: it postponed the decision, and it substituted for the brutal term "German rearmament" the subtler formula of "German participation in the defense of Europe". The notion of a "Wehrmacht" was changed to one of "German divisions in the European Army". The principle of equality was limited to the European Community, thus preventing the entry of Germany into the Atlantic Community.

This was the first phase of the EDC story: an attempt to apply the Schuman Plan method to the settlement of the problem brought up by the American demand for German rearmament. The European idea was popular. Its popularity could bring about the acceptance of the obviously unpopular remilitarization of Germany. But it was obvious, too, that this possibility was marked by the risk of the opposite result; the unpopularity of German rearmament might be carried over to the European idea.

The Pléven proposal for a European Army was received with some scepticism by the West. In Washington, some officials of the State Department and the Pentagon believed that it was just a means to gain time or a refusal hidden within an impossible project. It was decided to enter simultaneously into two negotiations, one between the Allied High Commissioners of West Germany, the other in Paris between the representatives of the Six European Governments. The texts of the High Commissioners' negotiations were not published. It seems that agreement was easy to obtain on the effective strength, the composition, and the organisation of the future German Army. (The same figure of 12 divisions is to be found in EDC as in the Paris Treaty.) But Chancellor Adenauer had pointed out that

Germany would make this contribution only on the condition that she would obtain equal rights, that is to say a War Office and admission to the Atlantic Pact. These were conditions that the French National Assembly had explicitly excluded in its Order of the Day of October 25, 1950.

The simultaneous negotiations concerning the European Army among the Six in Paris were much more difficult. Their aim was the writing of a Constitution for the European Community. But nothing could be more difficult to draft than a federal constitution because the sharing of powers between the Central authority and States must be carefully specified. No negotiator wished to declare himself favorable to a European State comparable to the Swiss or to the American State.

The pattern accepted was the very same that had been elaborated in the Coal and Steel Community Treaty: a High Authority (called the "Commissariat") which had some power of decision; an Assembly to which the Commissariat had to present an annual report; a Committee of Ministers which shared power with the Commissariat; a Court of Justice which heard appeals from the decisions of the Commissariat. But these institutions, which were easily accepted by the National Assembly for coal and steel caused strong protests when they concerned the Army. These protests expressed deep and justifiable feelings, as well as the genuine difficulties of the enterprise.

The objectives of the High Authority for the Coal and Steel Community could be only vaguely defined. They were: a single market, fair competition, optimum distribution of the means of production, full-employment, etc. But many specific questions were unanswered. Traditionally, the Army obeys a policy, and only a State can determine a policy. To which State would the Army belong and which policy would it follow? For want of a European State, the Army remained without a government and without a policy source. To overcome these difficulties, the drafters of the treaty decided that the Commissariat (similar to the High Authority of the EDC) would be responsible only for the formation, the recruitment, and the training of the European Army. The trained divisions would then be put under JACEUR, a joint European command under an American General. It was easy later to criticize an Army that had no government to fix its objectives.

The Commissariat were to act, as did the members of the High Authority, as ministers in a Federal State. But they were not directly responsible to an Assembly, since there was no Assembly elected by universal suffrage representing Europe. One could wonder about the historical or moral reality these Commissars were supposed to represent. Hence the repeated criticism refering to them as merely technocrats representing neither an elected Assembly nor an organized State.

Even beyond the constitutional plan, vigorous criticism continued. However the shares of authority were to be apportioned between the Commissars and the Committee of Ministers, there were objections. If the plan required unanimity of Ministers and Commissars, opponents denounced the clumsiness of such a mechanism, the risks of paralysis, and the impossibility of taking quick decisions in military affairs. On the other hand, opponents also denounced the transfer of sovereignty—mainly the fact that the military budget and the length of military service were no longer solely under the authority of elected national assemblies. The Commissariat did not have enough supranational power to act effectively, but it certainly had enough to offend national feelings.

In the spring of 1951, one could foresee the problems that EDC would create. The American leaders were induced to favor the European army over the German army for two reasons: (1) The French politicians convinced them that the National Assembly would never ratify formation of a national German Army. (2) The connection between the remilitarization of the Federal Republic and European Unity pleased American public opinion. Some top American leaders (including General Eisenhower) believed that the six continental nations would find an unprecedented prosperity within a federated Europe. In spite of reservations among the military and some officials of the State Department—the former anxious about the delay in forming the German divisions and doubtful about the efficiency of such a system; the latter sceptical about the possibilities of a European Federation—President Truman and Dean Acheson decided to back up the "European" party in France and the EDC project. This position was solemnly ratified in September, in Washington, at the meeting of the Foreign Ministers that followed the San Francisco Conference.

But the crisis was approaching at the very moment when French initiative began to find support in Washington, support that had been lacking at the beginning of the enterprise. The American leaders had "bought" the Pleven Plan so completely that they became its warmest propagandists. But now the idea had to be "sold" to the French Parliament.

Opposition to German rearmament was strong in the National Assembly. The formula of a European Defense Community had won over some opponents but also had created new ones. By the end of 1951, the Socialists were more willing to rally to EDC than to accept the reconstruction of a national German army, but the Gaullists had decided that a German army was preferable to the loss of French military sovereignty.

At the beginning of 1952, just before the Lisbon Conference, M. Edgar Faure, then Prime Minister, pleaded the cause of the European army and prevailed at the National Assembly. But this victory had no great significance: the vote had occurred on the principle and not on the text, which was not yet quite drafted and not known. Even this favorable vote was accompanied by numerous conditions, some of which were to become the "preliminaries". They were the ones the Socialist deputies considered as desirable: Washington's promise to maintain American troops on the continent; the close participation of Great Britain: the formation of a European political power, limited but effective for the control of the specialized agencies. In my view, however, the two last conditions were mutually exclusive: the further one went in the creation of a supranational power, the less one could count on British participation. The joining of these two conditions was a symbol of French vacillation: to reduce the risks of German rearmament, they wished the creation of a European authority; but they wanted no part of a European authority in which German dynamism would not be counter-balanced by the British presence.

Nonetheless, by its vote on the principle, the Assembly seemed to have adopted a definite position and to have set aside all other possible forms of German rearmament. The order of the day explicitly rejected the entrance into the Atlantic Pact of any State that might have territorial claims, as well as the reconstitution of a German army.

M. Pinay then succeeded M. Edgar Faure. At first rather indifferent to the European idea, he became progressively more favorable to it. He initialed the EDC treaty on May 27, 1952. But M. Robert Schuman, Foreign Minister, kept the treaty in his briefcase and only sent it to the Parliament for ratification on January 29, 1953. This delay has never been satisfactorily explained. Did the Foreign Minister intend to join a *political* community to the EDC? Or did the Quai d'Orsay think that the parliamentary climate was so unfavorable that it would be better to gain time? I cannot give an explicit answer. Whatever the reason, more than six months elapsed between the signature of the treaty and its disposition in the Assembly. These six months were rather a loss than a gain, since the situation for EDC deteriorated every month.

On the international level, little remained of the anxiety and urgency that had dominated all minds at the time of the Chinese intervention in the Korean war. Military operations had been stabilized on the Korean peninsula, and the risks of a generalization of the war were greatly reduced—in spite of the fact that the Armistice was not yet signed. The death of Stalin, the style adopted by his successors, and the conclusion of the Korean truce during the first half of 1953—all these accentuated the impression of an easing world situation and made German rearmament even less acceptable.

On the domestic level, the evolution of party relationships was no more favorable to EDC. In the Pinay government the Socialists had gone over to the opposition, and the dissident Gaullists (called A.R.S.) now belonged to the majority. But dissident as well as orthodox Gaullists remained unanimous in their opposition to EDC. From then on appeared the contradiction that was going to weigh for two years on French politics; the government majority was split. The succeeding cabinets included opponents of EDC—the A.R.S. under Pinay and the U.R.A.S. under Mayer and Laniel. Conversely, the Socialists, who were favorable to ratification, belonged to the opposition throughout this decisive period.

None of the Parties had ever been unanimous on the issue, and even the third-force governments of "Centrists" would have had the utmost difficulty in finding a majority for EDC equivalent to the majority that existed for C.E.C.A. (Coal-Steel Community). But, none of the parties which supported the earlier third-force governments was really hostile to EDC and none had made it a decisive issue in the formation of a cabinet. The entrance into the majority of precisely those parties on the right, which aimed explicitly at the defeat of EDC, transformed this situation.

The replacement of M. Robert Schuman by M. Georges Bidault in the René Mayer government was an initial success of the opponents of EDC, but it was only a symbolic success. M. Schuman had given particular attention to the German problem; above everything, he wanted to realize a Franco-German reconciliation and the rapprochement of the two States. EDC as it was understood by M. Schuman, was to bring about Franco-German understanding—the first phase of European Unity—as well as the formation of twelve German divisions.

M. Bidault followed, in principle, the same policy. He was probably convinced, after some months, that the EDC was the only means of obtaining from the National Assembly a favorable vote for the rearmament of West Germany. But when he first returned to the Quai d'Orsay, it seems that he had some doubts and some anxiety about the EDC: in giving up a part of her military sovereignty for the benefit of a European authority, would France not give up her position in the world? How could she reconcile her obligations in Asia and in Africa with her participation, even as a leader, in a European Federation? It seems that M. Bidault was, at the beginning of 1953, as anxious to slow down the movement towards a Federation of the Six as to hasten the EDC ratification.

Two additional factors made for delay: the parliamentary commissions were in no hurry to find a way and had started a long and elaborate study of the treaty; secondly, the French governments had committed themselves to negotiate the protocols of the treaty and to obtain the realisation of the "preliminaries", required by the National Assembly. To the "preliminaries" set forth in the order of the day of February 1952, M. René Mayer had added a Saar "preliminary", to settle definitely the fate of that contested territory.

The protocols to the treaty concerned mainly the relations between the French divisions of the European Army and the divisions of the French Union. The object was to maintain, as far as possible, the unity of the French Army, to facilitate the transfer of officers from one part to the other, and to leave as much freedom of action and of decision as possible to the French staff.

Two preliminaries, concerning American and British participation, had no real significance. It was known from the start that it would be impossible to obtain what the National Assembly desired, i.e. the formal promise of the U.S. to maintain her troops on the Continent for an indefinite length of time. A President is not bound by the decisions of his predecessors, and the Senate would never ratify a treaty which would fix the size of American military forces in Europe for a long period. On the other hand, the maintenance of American troops in Europe was, in any case, probable. Some officials and Congressmen in Washington had vaguely expressed a desire to substitute German forces for American; but such a decision was improbable on account of the probable psycho-political repercussions in France, in Germany and on the other side of the Iron Curtain.

British participation was excluded by the supranational character of the organisation—but that did not prevent close collaboration, the advantages of which would be even greater for Britain than for the six continental nations. The maintenance of British divisions and strategic air forces was, with or without a formal declaration, very likely to last as long as the Americans would leave an army in Europe. The main objective of British diplomacy in the new postwar form of "continental equilibrium" (historic condition of Great Britain's survival) has been to keep the Soviets out of Western Europe. To counter-balance the Soviet mass, the military presence of the U.S. on the continent also has been a necessity.

From January 1953 to August 1954 took place the greatest ideological and political debate France has known since the Dreyfus affair; its most visible stake was German rearmament, but its ultimate significance concerned the very existence of the French national state. Any attempt to sum up the debate must seem contentious, since each party mingled the pros and cons of the controversy uniting to serve its own purpose, arguments that were not always logically consistent.

The anti-EDC arguments concerned mainly German rearmament. The idea of German rearmament was known to be unpopular, so that it was to the interest of the hostile party to minimize as much as possible the importance of the rather popular European idea. They had good reasons to think that the defeat of EDC would make unacceptable any form of German rearmament. Thus, many EDC opponents who might have preferred the EDC to some other system of German rearmament concentrated their criticism on the supranational system, hoping that defeat of EDC would prevent any German rearmament.

The confusion between EDC and German rearmament was, in a degree everyone is still free to evaluate, unquestionable. EDC entailed the formation of 12 divisions of German military forces. European military integration was only realized on the army corps level, and for the Commissariat on the administrative level. Those who opposed German rearmament had good reason to denounce, behind the EDC camouflage, the revival of the *Wehrmacht*. And those who were not in principle opposed to German rearmament maintained logically that EDC was the worst method of obtaining it. Such was the meaning of the formulae "EDC revives the German Army and destroys the French Army", or "EDC rearms Germany and disarms France".

These arguments seem, at first glance, to be contradictory. If the supranational organization did not prevent the development of a German Army, why would it prevent the survival of the French Army? How could the same organization give all the opportunities to Germany and none to France? It was not impossible, however, to find arguments—some of them not without merit—that proved that the system under consideration was very advantageous for Germany, but mostly disadvantageous for France. France already had an army that the European system could throw into confusion; Germany had none. France had overseas obligations; Germany had none. The European system would cut the French Army in two parts (one European and the other French Union) without endangering the unity of the future German Army.

Generally speaking, the European system was based on equality of rights and demanded about as much from France as it did from Germany. Nobody wanted Germany to have an independent army; hence France couldn't have one either. Nobody wanted German generals to be appointed by the German government; hence the French generals should also be detached from the French government. But to demand such sacrifices from France for German restoration to full sovereignty was bound to excite criticism and indignation.

The "continental frame" of the Six was also an object of denunciation and invective. By agreeing to join her army to the continental system, France was going to bind herself closer to her former enemies than to her old friends. This solution seemed rather paradoxical: that France should again risk domination by the German Federal Republic, a more populous and industrialized country; and that she should have to face again a German-Italian coalition. Hence, the watchword "no Europe without Great Britain" gained currency, as did the slogan "no clerical Europe" (since the three promoters of the EDC idea, Schuman, de Gasperi and Adenauer, were all Christian Democrats).

Against this reasoning, the pro-EDC argument developed on several levels. Logically, the first phase should have consisted in demonstrating that German rearmament was a necessity because of the Soviet threat. In fact, the EDC partisans did not insist much on this point for several reasons. In 1954, nobody believed (on either side of the controversy), in the probability of a total war or of a Soviet aggression. If such an attack were to come, in any case, atomic power would be much more effective than a few German divisions. An extension of the Asian war seemed just as unlikely. Moreover, many believed that the risk of general war was not the real reason for German rearmament. So-called conventional weapons have still a role to play in psycho-political warfare. But the argument was too subtle and not convincing enough for the public at large.

The EDC partisans, as time elapsed and the easing of the political situation continued, tried to base the case for German rearmament less on the Soviet threat than on the effects of its rejection upon Washington and Bonn. It was argued that the U.S. would not indefinitely maintain their troops in Europe if the Europeans refused to prepare and to participate in their own defense. The EDC, they added, has become the symbol of Franco-German reconciliation, the touchstone of European reconstruction. Its rejection would endanger the whole western coalition.

These arguments might have been sound (I believe they were).

But they had a major drawback: they presented German rearmament as the price France had to pay for the maintenance of the Atlantic Alliance and not as a free choice corresponding to her own view of her own interests.

The same unfortunate aura was created by the justifications used for specific clauses of the treaty. Theoretically, two arguments were possible, one positive and the other negative. The first would have shown that European Unity was a benefit in itself; that the transfer of sovereignty essential to this unity was desirable and not deplorable. The second stressed the dangers of a German rearmament and insisted that the only way to ward off this danger was to accept supranationality. On the whole, the EDC partisans concentrated more and more on this second argument.

"EDC or the *Wehrmacht*" was one of the slogans of the EDC partisans. But with this they coupled two other arguments that boomeranged on them. Germany, they said, is a claiming power and does not accept the present *status quo* in Europe. Today she claims reunification with the "Popular Democracy" of East Germany, and tomorrow she will claim back the Eastern territories beyond the Oder-Neisse. A claiming power cannot be accepted in the Atlantic Pact without changing its purely defensive character. Hence the need for constricting German ambitions within a European Army. But this argument for "containing" Germany was easily turned back on itself by EDC opponents as an argument against German rearmament in any form.

The use of the same argument for opposite ends occurred again regarding the risk of German-Russian collusion. Such collusion, often evoked in France by the name Rapallo, appeared to both EDC opponents and partisans as a major danger. Both parties suggested that only the Soviet Union was able to give Germany what she couldn't help wanting above everything: German unity and the recovery of the lost territories. What, argued the EDC partisans, could prevent the Federal Republic from going over to the other side, save a supranational European organisation that would definitely bind Germany to the Free World? An easier and safer course, replied the adversaries, was to deprive West Germany of its bargaining position by the absolute refusal of any kind of German rearmament.

As the debate proceeded, the EDC partisans almost inevitably lost ground. Giving back arms to a former enemy seemed the more unacceptable as the fear of Soviet aggression was diminishing. If German rearmament involved such dangers as to make necessary the precautions provided by the EDC and the transfer of military sovereignty by France, why could it not be simply and categorically refused, instead of adding one evil to another? Thus, the argument for EDC became slowly that of the lesser evil. Such an argument is always weak, because it puts those who use it on the defensive. The positive argument was that of European unity. But such unity as the EDC proposed was that of the Six; it would have led to the creation of a kind of European State. Rare were those, outside the group around Jean Monnet, who really desired the creation of such a United States of Europe.

Finally, in the controversy over the details of the treaty, the opponents prevailed easily over the supporters. The treaty was in fact defective, and the results could not be otherwise. We have pointed out the difficulties concerning its principles: the creation of a European military administration (equivalent to a European War Office), without a G.H.Q. and without a government above it. It was the simplest of tasks to enumerate circumstances in which the Constitution might not work: Who would decide on mobilization? Of the 15% of every national budget that would be spent outside the country, to whom would go the ultimate profit? In these terms EDC had meaning only if it could be considered as the first step towards a Federal Europe. But the EDC partisans did not dare, most of the time, to present it as such. They felt safe only in presenting it as a means of reducing the risks of German rearmament. On this ground, they were defeated by the coalescence of those who sought to avoid the risks by rejecting German rearmament altogether and those who wanted to *reduce* the risks by the means of classical guarantees.

From the proposal of the EDC project to the final vote in August 1954, there had been the threefold development we have analyzed above: the progressive reinforcement of the opposition to EDC both in the Parliament and in public opinion; the easing of the international situation (which seemed to weigh against the need for German rearmament); and the growing importance of EDC opponents in the governmental majority.

For the first of these trends, the votes of the different parliamentary commissions and the texts of their reports are testimony. The EDC project was submitted to the Foreign Affairs Commission on January 29, 1953. M. Jules Moch was appointed chairman on February 4. The Commission's report was drafted on May 13, 1953; it was studied in February and March 1954; the unfavorable vote occurred on June 5 (24 to 18). The National Defense Commission appointed General Koenig as chairman on February 4, 1954, studied the report from February to June and voted on June 18 (29 to 13). The votes in the Commissions on Justice and Legislation, on Overseas Territories and on Finances and Industrial Production were also unfavorable to the treaty.

After the failure of the Berlin Conference, EDC partisans could assert that German reunification was no more likely to occur during the Malenkov regime than it was during the Stalin era. But they had few other arguments to convince the undecided. They chose, in fact, to concentrate their efforts on the hesitants of the left, and mainly on the Socialist subgroup that was hostile to EDC. However, none of the Socialist "preliminaries" set by their leader, Guy Mollet, had been completely fulfilled by the Spring of 1954. The British Government had promised to maintain sufficient military forces on the continent (army as well as air-forces) and consented to the integration of an armored division; but it would not participate in the community. Those who could not conceive a Europe without British participation were not satisfied. Similarly, the engagements of President Eisenhower went as far as they could go; but they failed to satisfy the desires of many for American guarantees.

The Saar problem, finally, was far from being resolved. M. René Mayer had added the Saar Preliminary to the conditions of EDC ratification, partly because he attached exceptional importance to the problem, and partly because he needed the Gaullist votes. The Van Naters Plan constituted a basis for a Saar settlement, but was subject to innumerable disputes. France wanted the European status of the Saar to be maintained until the signature of the peace-treaty, and Germany hesitated to ratify an apparently temporary arrangement, but one which could last so long as to seem almost definitive. France wanted to keep, as long as possible, the advantages of economic union with the

Saar. Germany, even if she were to consent to this union, wanted the Saar to be opened more and more to German products on comparable terms with French products.

In the Socialist party, therefore, the EDC opponents had not been pacified. M. Jules Moch had subscribed to the initial idea of a European army, but with a very different conception of its organization. He had favored the formation of units (*combat-teams*) that could be integrated into a European system; but he opposed EDC as soon as it was agreed that the basic element would be strictly national. Moreover, M. Moch, who had been convinced in 1950 of the necessity for rearmament, had moved by 1954 toward a completely different view of East-West relations. The most decided adversaries of the German rearmament (M. Moch, Naegelen, Lejeune, Daniel Mayer) had not been converted to the EDC by guarantees offered, but were rather strengthened in their opposition because of the Franco-German fusion the treaty implied. To the extent to which hostility to German rearmament was due purely and simply to anti-German-ism, the EDC conception of rearmament seemed less acceptable than any other. This attitude was so strong among the anti-EDC Socialist group that the decision to enforce Party discipline in favor of EDC taken by the party majority at the Congress of Paris could not budge them. (It is impossible to expel half of a parliamentary group.) A similar reaction was even more pronounced among the Social Republicans and among the Moderates of the Right. Neither the opponents on the Right nor the Left could be won over.

Events in Indochina, in the spring of 1954, also played an important role against EDC. There had been some vague talk about an Indochinese "preliminary." M. Edgar Faure had insisted several times on the impossibility of entering a European Community as long as the élite of the French officers remained so far away and were being decimated. Other considerations were added: could France subscribe to German rearmament, opposing the Soviet Union, so long as Moscow had at its disposal such quick means of reprisal as increasing Chinese aid to the Viet-minh? The French expeditionary forces were, in a way, merely hostages. By the same token, if the end of the Indochinese war seemed to be a condition of a parliamentary vote on EDC, the Soviet Union had all the more reason to refuse to end the war.

At the Berlin Conference, M. Bidault, acting less from conviction than from a desire to satisfy the opposition, requested and obtained assurances that a Conference would meet to study the Indochinese and Korean problems. It was to take place at the end of April. When the Conference met on April 25 in Geneva, Dien Bien Phu was already doomed to fall; the fall of this stronghold threatened the expeditionary forces in the Tonkin Delta. The French military command could not guarantee the security of the Delta in case of a general attack by the Vietminh army. The negotiations for the granting of American military aid had failed. (The French government had only belatedly and reluctantly asked for this intervention, without being even unanimous.) The British government was violently opposed to such intervention. In Washington, some military (Admiral Radford) and political leaders (Dulles, Nixon) considered intervention desirable, but congressional leaders declared themselves unfavorable. President Eisenhower decided against it. At this point, one was obliged to wait and see whether M. Molotov and M. Chou En-lai would advise the Vietminh representatives to demand conditions no French government could ever accept or to limit their demands. The day before the decisive debate in the Assembly, M. Molotov delivered a violent speech against France that seemed to augur an intransigeant attitude. The Laniel cabinet fell and the Mendès-France cabinet was formed. On July 20, the Armistice was signed.

It was obvious that M. Molotov had granted M. Mendès-France the benefit of an armistice—naturally popular in France—in the hope that the French chief of government would reject EDC. This was indeed what happened. Did M. Mendès-France really want this result, or did he merely not oppose it? Interpretations are varied. The *facts* are known.

The Prime Minister stressed, in his inauguration speech, the necessity of finding a compromise that would rally a large majority in the Assembly. He entrusted two ministers, Generals Koenig and Bourgès-Maunoury, with the first attempt at a compromise. But this led only to the conclusion that there was no generally satisfactory remedy. After the Geneva armistice, M. Mendès-France took the documents into his own hands and proposed a series of amendments to the treaty. He submitted them for the approval of his ministers, three of whom promptly resigned

(General Koenig, M. Lemaire and M. Chaban-Delmas, the latter announcing to his friends that he would soon be back). He then took his own version of these proposed amendments to the Brussels Conference.

Could the modifications proposed by M. Mendès-France be accepted? In one sense, his request was almost exorbitant. Germany, Holland, and Belgium had already ratified the treaty, and the latter two had even modified their Constitutions to make them compatible with the treaty. If the amendments were not to be submitted to the Parliaments, what would be their values? The main modification was to give every country the right to lodge an appeal, during a probationary period, against decisions of the Commissariat that would affect their vital interests. The EDC partisans objected that, if the supranational power were affected by this change, the whole system would be compromised. They were right, from the symbolic or ideological point of view. But M. Mendès-France was trying, for the first time, to win over the opponents from the Right, who were even more opposed to the creation of a supranational power than to German rearmament. He had, therefore, to limit the surrender of sovereignty. Would the proposed right to appeal really work? Would vital interests ever be affected by a majority decision of the Commissariat? Nobody knew nor will they ever know. It was too late for a rational exposition of the operational meaning of the proposed changes. The battle had to be fought to the end.

Whatever the initial intentions of M. Mendès-France may have been, he had already given up, by the second day at Brussels, the idea of an agreement. He was offended by the hostility and distrust of his European colleagues. He resigned himself to taking official notice of failure. After a quick trip to London, where Sir Winston Churchill reprimanded him without promising anything, he decided to submit the project to the Assembly without waiting for a decision by his divided cabinet. He resigned himself to doing something he had earlier declared to be out of the question.

Was there any other way? Since the investiture of M. Pinay, no President of the Council had been able to avoid calling simultaneously upon both partisans and adversaries of EDC in the formation of his government. No President had been able to open a decisive debate because the EDC opponents refused a debate as long as they were not sure that its results would be negative. At the end of August, the only chance left to the EDC partisans was to defer the debate once more. The parliamentary discussions, the meaning of which is still questioned, resulted in the decisive vote being taken on a preliminary procedural motion. The vote on this "technicality" ruled out EDC definitely and completely. Thus, the National Assembly rejected the project born of French initiative, without granting it even the honor of a debate.

Some questions are still open at the conclusion of this survey that will never be clearly answered, but that nevertheless claim our attention.

The first concerns the role played by M. Mendès-France. Could he have obtained, if he had wanted to, the ratification of EDC? Would efforts, similar to those he displayed for the Accords of Paris, have made ratification possible? I am inclined to think not. Too many deputies had taken a position against the treaty in the spring of 1954, and they could no longer have changed their position even if they had had the desire to do so.

Further, it was almost impossible to ask M. Mendès-France to pledge himself to EDC since his government needed the support of its opponents. In 1951, the governmental majority included some deputies who voted finally against EDC. In 1954, the majority was composed of all the non-communist adversaries of EDC. From the day when the M.R.P. moved from the parliamentary majority into opposition ratification would have been a paradox. The change in the parliamentary majority had been a decisive cause of the non-ratification.

One might then wonder if the "Europeans" did not sacrifice their last chance by refusing to yield further to the demands of M. Mendès-France. Whatever the answer, one fact is clear: the failure at Brussels should have been considered as certain death for the EDC. But it was not acknowledged by the "Europeans" that thereafter M. Mendès-France represented, whatever his personal feelings might have been, the EDC opponents. For unless he had obtained a great success in Brussels, he had no reason whatever to compromise his government for a project of which he did not deeply approve. Both parties were blinded by ideological passions.

One might also wonder if it would have been possible to win over the Right opposition by making concessions on supranationality. I am personally inclined to believe so, but this opinion might be the consequence of attachment to my initial position. The difficulty seems to me to have been that for the theoreticians of Europe, the whole meaning of EDC was in its supranationality. They were more attached to this principle than to reality. On the other hand, the EDC opponents were more against the principle than against reality. The former dreamed about a European State of the Six growing out of EDC; the latter imagined this with horror. Hence the violence of the passions that erupted against M. Jean Monnet, the inspirer and the symbol of a Europe of the Six.

One might, finally, wonder if the EDC would have been ratified if proposed after the Accords of Paris, or if the Accords of Paris would not have been rejected if proposed before EDC. After all, less than 200 deputies voted against both EDC and the Accords of Paris. In 1951-2, the deputies were more hostile to Germany's entrance into the Atlantic Pact than to her participation in a defense community. Even in 1954 the majority of the deputies who were ready to vote for rearmament preferred EDC to the Accords of Paris. Yet the 100 deputies who were fiercely opposed to a supranational power prevailed over the 150 deputies who detested the idea of an autonomous German military administration which would participate in the Atlantic Pact.

What could have changed this situation? Had the EDC partisans said "There is another solution" and not "This is the only solution", the Assembly, free to choose between two solutions, might well have decided for the second. This observation is quite theoretical. It would have been difficult to present, simultaneously, two solutions. A minority, whose vote was an absolute necessity, had great power of harassment. The EDC partisans might have repaid their rejection of EDC by refusing the other solution. But this possibility was rather an illusion. The refusal would have endangered the Atlantic Pact, which both partisans and adversaries of the EDC were agreed on preserving.

Thus, the end of the story ironically contradicts its beginning; the National Assembly finished by preferring the solution proposed by the American government in 1950 over the French solution. The initial American proposition reflected principally the views of the *Pentagon*, i.e. the military, whereas the French project was seriously supported by those in the *State Department*, i.e. the diplomats. The French deputies finally preferred the *Pentagon* to the *State Department* solution, and this choice was approved by the European Left.

THE
FACTORS
AT
STAKE

2 : The Interplay of Interests and Passions

ANDRÉ PHILIP

The battle over EDC produced some strange encounters and queer bedfellows as a temporary stop gap for problems which are "chronic"—and still unsolved.

The opposition rallied around a purely negative program, persons hostile to EDC for absolutely different, even contradictory, reasons. The same platform was shared by militant communists, militarist generals, reactionary industrialists, small protectionist traders, and pacifist clergymen. They were utterly unable to define a common foreign or military policy; but they were agreed on an opposition which reflected both their interests and their passions. The USSR and the French Communist Party capitalized on this situation in their well-organized propaganda.

The Interests Involved

Arrayed against the EDC was a coalition of professional and economic interests which felt threatened by the project itself, as by its probable consequences on the road toward European integration.

(a) First, there were the militarists, particularly the older generation. While some younger officers considered favorably the idea of a unified army, within which innovations would be possible (such as promotion by merit), the ancient generals, at the summit of the hierarchy, knew that unification would mean either retirement or the end of advancement. Further, unification would necessitate a reappraisal of the military structure. For individuals used to the old system, this effort would be too much. Finally, a growing number of high-ranking French officers preferred the revival of a national German army—in the hands of fellow-officers for whom they had hostile but still fraternal feelings—to a unification that would result in the progressive erosion of their autonomy in the French national army.

(b) Second, the greater part of the French steel industry was hostile to EDC. We recall that the Schuman plan itself had originated in a report of the steel section of the UN's Economic Commission for Europe (E.C.E.), which had pointed out that, unless a public authority was created, the steel industry inevitably would revert to the old system of international cartels. During negotiations on the Schuman Plan, the French steel makers had been by-passed deliberately, for fear that they would be uncooperative. After the vote, some of them, particularly the younger ones, rallied around and cooperated honestly with the High Authority. But an important segment of the steel industry has tried to revive the old cartel and yearns for the time when it can escape the inconvenient rule of the High Authority. This segment of the steel industry financed the campaign against EDC, in the hope that its failure would be a blow to the authority of the C.E.C.A., which could be ultimately undermined.

(c) A special problem which the negotiators of the EDC treaty failed to foresee concerned the textile industry. The "15% rule," as M. Vernant has shown, created the risk that Germany or Italy would achieve a monopoly of textile production (uniforms, blankets, etc.) for the whole European army. This explains why France, whose textile industry is in difficult straits, worked so hard in opposition to EDC, and why until the very last moment (the Mendès-France proposals at the Brussels conference) amendments were presented for the purpose of protecting the interests of this industry.

The Passions Affected

A coalition of even the most powerful interests could not alone have produced such deep currents of feeling as became manifest. These interests were, in fact, reinforced by instinctive, sometimes subconscious, passions derived from basic elements in the personality formation of many Frenchmen.

(a) The strongest of these passions was, of course, *nationalism*, and in particular an anti-German variant—a string which is easy to vibrate by stimulating recall of recent sufferings and humiliations at German hands. The anti-EDC campaign evoked these feelings as well as pacifist and anti-militaristic sentiments. These normally contradictory feelings were convoked sometimes by division of labor between various spokesmen, but often by the same man in the same speech. The nationalistic appeal seems to have been more important in parliamentary circles than in public opinion as a whole, perhaps because Parliament would suffer heavy deprivations of power if EDC succeeded. The military budget would be prepared by the EDC Commissariat; the total budget as well as the contribution of each government would be decided by the EDC Council of Ministers. The global contribution of each country was to be approved by the national Parliament; but the European parliament would then vote the credits and decide the distribution of the total sum among the different military functions. This was certainly a transfer of national authority on a particularly sensitive matter. Moreover, though the leaders of European unification were almost all recruited among former chiefs of the "Résistance," the appeal to anti-German passions was employed by some politicians who, not having shown much heroism during the Vichy period, now tried to compensate by extreme nationalism and stern judgments about our allies. The complete intellectual void of President Herriot's speeches illustrated this state of mind. There was evoked the deeply rooted distrust of Germany at the very moment when, for the first time in its history, this nation was seeking genuine unity with the West. This coincided with a generally negative nationalism which, to assert its independence, rejected all projects proposed by others. It is clear that to some extent the Dien-Bien-Phu defeat was responsible for the rejection of EDC, linked as it was to the famous "agonizing reappraisal" of Mr. Dulles, a very clumsy maneuver which gave the impression of external pressure on French decision. Many felt that France, defeated by the Vietminh, could recover dignity by rebelling against the Americans. It was a mere act of psychological compensation, but it nevertheless played an important role at the time of the final decision in Parliament.

(b) The main passion which appears to have influenced public opinion was *fear*. The glorious era of imperialism when France could assert her power to rule inferior native populations was gone. But gone as well were the bases of that proud nationalism of Barrès, which boasted the cultural superiority of French national traditions and assumed their unique and irreplaceable character. We no longer have that sense of greatness expressed by de Gaulle, the readiness to sacrifice all Frenchmen necessary, for a great idea which conserves rights by obligations and a sense of duty. The nationalism which prevailed against EDC was a peevish and whimpering nationalism which affirmed France's inferiority and her incapacity to adapt to the modern world, by assuming that in a fair competition other countries inevitably would win because of their inherent technical superiority and organization. It feared to see EDC open the road to European unification, because certain French enterprises would have to modernize or founder. This argument recurred in so many shapes and forms as to require critical analysis.

To justify the high level of French prices and to explain French economic disadvantages, the heavy weight of social security and taxation was usually mentioned. This became, for many industries, the alibi which allowed them to avoid reconsidering their structure and the state of their technique. Four observations command our attention here:

(1) The comparison of the distribution of charges between two countries involves the analysis of costs. If costs are generally higher in one country, this shows that its currency is over-valued and that an adjustment is required to bring down costs. If this is not done, it is because cost differences *within* the country are greater than the differences between countries; hence it is worth keeping an over-valued currency as a means of pressure on inefficient enterprises. But this works only on condition that no other compensations are made to inefficiency through transfer taxes or export subsidies, which are equivalent to a general devaluation. The real problem of comparison is not between the total charge on industry, but between the distribution of these charges in any two countries. To clarify this problem, one should study each industry in twin categories; but we do not have at hand the essential

data for such a study. Hence, we merely outline some general considerations, which reveal the nature of the problem rather than its detailed aspects.

(2) The total of fiscal charges seems to be higher in France than in any other country. The studies made by the Nathan Commission showed that the percentage of gross national product paid in taxes reached 23% in France as against 25.5% in Germany and 29.6% in Great Britain. But this percentage varies according to the method of computation. If one considers the total of national and local taxes paid in 1952, one finds that the figure varies when based on net national product at factor prices or gross national product at market prices, from 41.1% to 31.4% in France, and from 39.7% to 32.6% in Great Britain. This illustrates the uncertainty of comparison between two countries.

But one thing is certain: distribution of the burden of taxation is not the same in France as in neighboring countries, e.g., in France 63.6% (as against 54.2% in Germany and 45% in Britain) comes from indirect taxes on consumption, whereas other countries rely more on direct taxes on income. Of course, it is difficult here again to produce absolute statements; but it appears to be a general rule that the progressive income-tax, laid upon high incomes, decreases both the demand for goods (mainly for luxury products) and rate of private investments. On the other hand, indirect taxes are included in the costs of consumption goods, and result in distortions of price which vary in degree according to the types of goods and services involved.

If indirect taxes are much heavier for all industries in one country as against another, the best way to correct it is by devaluation of the currency. The real problem is created by simultaneous differentials against a particular industry: e.g. in a country where, other industries being taxed 25%, the steel industry is taxed 30%; as compared with a country where, average taxation also being 25%, the steel industry is taxed only 20%. The balance among different industries would then be upset to such a degree that no monetary measures could correct it. However, such studies have not in fact been made; and arguments concerning the relative burden of fiscal charges are always in terms of comparison between the total tax burdens of different countries. On the point relevant to EDC there is no doubt: the totals of fiscal charges are roughly similar as between the countries involved; but France has much heavier indirect taxes which are added to prices and reduce France's capacity to compete internationally. While this condition persists it is useless to talk about a harmonization of fiscal charges, which France sought to make a preliminary condition for European unification: the other countries will not, in order to please France, create an inefficient and shamefully anti-democratic tax system in their own countries. France must reform her own tax structure, introducing gradually a system of direct taxation on income, with public declaration of income and effective control.

We have here a choice, which has always been evaded: if we refuse to tax individuals, we will necessarily tax products. The inadequacy of the French system necessarily results in consumption taxes which add greatly to prices and undermines France's competitive position in the European and world economy.

(3) A similar problem exists regarding social security—i.e. the social charges. Here, too, the tendency is to consider only those charges which are greater than in other countries and to forget those which are lower. In the French system, for instance, overtime is paid after fewer hours than in neighbor countries; the salary differential between men and women is also smaller; old age and retirement pension contributions seem to be higher; and supplementary payments for families are greater than elsewhere. On the other hand: the pay-scale of unmarried persons is lower; there is no unemployment insurance (which exists among almost all our neighbors); and, until very recently, neither the Government nor employers made payments for housing comparable to those made by most of our competitors.

The problem is, in reality, not the size of social charges, which are in any case difficult to evaluate. In some countries, like Germany, most of the social charges have been determined not by law, but by collective agreements that vary according to industry. In Great Britain and Scandinavia Social Security charges are heavy, but they are not added to prices (being regarded as a public service and financed by income taxes). It might be desirable for France to transform Social Security into a national service financed partly by direct taxes and partly by a tax on employers, based on the number of employees and not on the amount of salaries. In any case, it is false to consider social charges as additional factors of cost. They are simply a way of distributing among the workers the total wage bills. What must be compared, in reality, is the total cost accounted for by wages, and not the proportion according to which they are distributed among the working class.

On this basis: the direct costs of wages were, according to the Nathan Commission in October 1953, 138 francs per hour in France, 135 in Germany, 150 in Belgium, and 195 in Switzerland for manufacturing industries in general. A similar study made by M. Meroud (which has been published in the Bulletin de l'Association des Cadres industriels in the July 1954 issue), found the following average wages per hour distributed among industry as a whole: Italy 91.7 francs; Netherlands 94; Germany 124; France 131; Belgium 148; Britain 150; Switzerland 192. The total cost of wages per hour including all the social charges compared as follows: Netherlands 121.4 francs; Italy 147; Britain 164; Germany 170; France 186; Belgium 188.5; Switzerland 221.70. That is, with France at 100, the other countries were: Netherlands 65; Italy 79; Britain 88; Germany 91; Belgium 101; Switzerland 119. Thus, two countries only would have total wage costs higher than the French; and they are, curiously enough, small countries, great exporters, which have the benefit of only a very moderate tariff. Great Britain and Germany differ from France by only about 10%; the difference is greater with the Netherlands and Italy, but corresponds also to a difference in productivity, the other elements of costs being higher in these two countries.

Here again, we stress the relativity of such conclusions; in arguing about averages, one might conclude that to re-establish a balance with our main competitors, devaluation of the franc by about 10% would be necessary. But such an average does not square with reality; wage differences of 15% to 20% can be observed between one industry and another, and even within the same industry, between two enterprises in the same region.

If devaluation of the franc does not seem, at present, an adequate solution, the reason is that the difference between our average prices and average foreign prices is smaller than the differences of prices within our country between different industries; and, within the same industries, between different enterprises. There coexist in our country a minority of technically well-equipped enterprises with low costs and a mass of backward establishments which levy a heavy increase on market prices. It is necessary, if

France wants to survive, to eliminate some marginal enterprises, and to help those which can adapt by concentration and specialization, but we can no longer support the dictatorship of ignorance and routine.

This is the essential problem to face: there exists not one France, but two. If we draw a line from Rouen to Marseille, we have on the north-east of this line almost all the regions which are developing and progressing; to the south-west, over half of French territory, lie the towns and villages which are losing population, where production stagnates, and where there is a constant decline in the standard of living. If we move toward European unification and the creation of a common market with conventional concepts of economic Liberalism, then capital will naturally go where it is in demand and industries will settle in the already well-developed regions, where they will find manpower, transport, and access to raw materials. Thus, industrial concentration will only be aggravated in the Paris and Northern regions, where it has already passed the point of diminishing returns and has created living conditions conducive to social disturbances. The problem before France (and other European countries), is that of a controlled economy which is able to *encourage the creation of modern enterprises and progressive industries in the regions which are now underdeveloped.* It is not a matter of a return to the land, nor of the utopian revival of an industrial artisanat equipped with electricity. It is a question of creating, in the great regional centers (towns of 100,000 to 200,000 inhabitants), big, modern establishments with improved technique, likely to attract labor; to provide outlets for the sale of food products; and thus to become, for the whole surrounding country, a promoter of progress and modernization. The problem of balanced economic development for the underdeveloped regions is the essential problem of our country. The EDC debate helped us to become conscious of this, for it was mainly in the underdeveloped regions that the economic opposition to EDC had the most success.

I was impressed when, in July 1954, I drew up a map showing, by departments, the votes of the various federations at the Socialist congress. This map squared almost perfectly with the map of economic development in France; the rich departments gave a great majority to EDC. They had no fear of European unification, convinced not only that their industries could easily compete with foreign industries, but also that they would benefit from the reduction of costs that would result from widening their markets. On the other hand, the economically backward regions knew perfectly well that, if nothing special were done to protect them, European unification would increase the wealth of the rich regions, but would aggravate the poverty of the poor departments. They would be unable, without a complete overhaul of industry and new investment, to adapt to the new conditions created by a free European economy.

This fear played an important role in the struggle against EDC. We have seen that most of the arguments about fiscal and social charges had no real value, but *even false arguments can be the expression of a psychological reality of first importance*. We cannot ignore the phenomena revealed during the anti-EDC struggle. Europe cannot be created merely by opening a common market; this has to be accompanied by a coordinated policy of industrial rationalization, channeling of investments, and creation of modern enterprises in those regions which are still underdeveloped.

The interests and passions just analyzed were remarkably well utilized in the campaign fought by the USSR and by its Communist representatives in France. It is important here to analyze the fundamental psychological elements on which the USSR based her campaign. This again reveals those permanent, basic problems we must still face.

Let us recall, first, the fundamental facts of the problem. The USSR never really opposed German rearmament. As early as March 1948, she sent a note to the Allies, requesting the general withdrawal of all military forces from Germany, her neutralization, the creation of a national German army to enforce the military neutrality of Germany, and the opening of this army to former Nazi chiefs to allow them to rehabilitate themselves in the service of a new Germany called "democratic". *The USSR had always accepted German rearmament as long as it was national*. What she opposed was the unification of Europe in any aspect, including the military one. Her interest, indeed, consists in encouraging nationalism in every country. The clash of national interests permits her to fish more easily in troubled waters. But this essentially anti-European attitude has been cleverly presented in the form of a campaign for peace, denunciations of America as an aggressive power, and veiled threats as to what would happen if the Russian warnings were ignored.

(a) Russian propaganda, since the famous Stockholm declaration, assumed the aspect of a peace campaign. In France, it played simultaneously on the anti-militarism of the population and on its anti-German feelings. Remarkably well-organized by door-to-door pressure and through a series of intermediary organizations by signatures, declarations, and petitions to all elected representatives, the USSR presented the anti-EDC campaign as concerned mainly with German rearmament. It obscured what EDC was in reality: German rearmament *within the frame of European solidarity*. In this, they received the support of three different and influential sectors of present-day France:

(1) First, the deep anti-militarism of the French population as a whole, and mainly of the middle and peasant classes. An oft repeated argument was the following, "I am against armies; the French army exists already and I am obliged to put up with it; but do not ask me to give my approval to the creation of another army". Communist propaganda played on this anti-militarism, coupling it with appeals to nationalism and distrust for Germany.

(2) The campaign made its points mainly in the religious field, Protestant as well as Catholic. We face here a curious phenomenon which is very difficult to analyze. It concerns contemporary Christian "progressivism". The Church, during the whole XIXth century, had committed herself on the side of the powerful forces in the world; having let the working class escape from her influence, the Church today is in a state of repentance. She condemns her past, wants to make amends, and seeks by every means to increase her contact with the workers. Some of its members have gone so far as to proclaim a kind of Immaculate Conception of the labor class, as the sole virgin in a bordello of social sin. While the authentic labor militant speaks frankly to the worker, even resists labor as a class when it is led astray by passions or when it makes mistakes in the defense of its interests, the "progressive" Christian supports the working class, whatever it might do or say, because it is "disinherited." His feeling is that we have not the right to oppose labor, not even its mistakes, on account of the injustices and crimes committed towards it in the past. The "progressive" who *goes* to the people thus shows that he does not

belong to them, and, in fact, has no respect for them. His repentance, however lofty a feeling it may be, continues his connection
with the *bourgeoisie* which he vilifies, but a part of which he remains nevertheless. This kind of Christian masochism is animated
by the feeling that the gospel requires, above all, love for the
enemy. Consequently, the more real the enemy, the more he
opposes what we consider right and noble, the more he commits
crimes and abominations, then the more we have to love him, to
be indulgent with him, to seek not only a peaceful coexistence
but also negotiations in which we agree beforehand to surrender
everything. As to him who is so unfortunate as not to be an
enemy, but a friend who has the same beliefs, who has the same
values, and who can give us disinterested help, we can neglect
him, fight him and violently reproach even his slightest faults.
Since he is not an enemy, Christian feelings do not require that
we show charity or even justice to him.

Similar feelings have appeared among the intellectuals: con-
sciousness of privilege among those who have had educational
opportunities and feelings of humility towards the Proletarian,
conceived as a state of Nature, essentially good, acting according
to natural laws, whose reactions are always more valid than those
of people with recourse to reflection and to intellectual analysis.
Finally, the Christian "progressives" desire to be considered as
belonging to the "Left": this is accomplished by being opposed
to any army, and by considering dictatorship indulgently if it is
labelled "labor". These sectors helped the Soviet peace campaign
to delude an important part of the French public. It was echoed
by the Left which, traditionally, should have been attracted by
the defense of liberty and by the really pacific ideal of European
unification.

(b) At the same time the Communist campaign ceaselessly
attacked the Americans as potential aggressors in Eastern Europe,
an area which was sincerely devoted to peace. America was represented as the land of monopolies, of triumphant capitalism
seeking outlets for its exports and trying to establish economic
domination over the free countries. Here, too, insofar as the
propaganda took effect, it was because most of the French people
still think of the U.S. in terms of a half-century ago, and imagine
that American capitalism is European capitalism multiplied by
ten. They do not realize that, since Roosevelt's New Deal, the

United States has undergone an evolution which completely divorced it from the old-style capitalism and which, in fact, is oriented towards a new economic and social system. We cannot yet know if it will be toward socialism or a system of technocrat management, efficient from the technical point of view, but dangerous from the political. The XIXth century market, in which price was the objective and independent reality, has disappeared in the U.S. The pattern of the American economy today is set by the great "corporations." The Ford budget exceeds that of Belgium; those of DuPont or General Motors exceed the French budget. But they are not monopolies; rather they are the three or four major firms whose most violent competition is with each other. But they do not have to conform to prices which are set by the market; instead each has its own *price policy*, which it endeavors to impose on the market. During the last year 75% of total investment was made through re-investment of retained earnings. This shows that the relative influence of the banking system and the stock-market has declined. The power of Wall Street, or of such great banks as Morgan's, is no longer comparable to what it was before the Second World War. Indeed, most of the firms retain their earnings, and when reserves are accumulated, they are capitalized in the form of stock dividends which stock-holders generally sell in the stock-market. This results in the multiplication of the number of share-holders, which has reached several hundred thousand in some big corporations. It is, of course, impossible to assemble all of them at stockholders' meetings, so the boards of directors have acquired more and more independence. They now feel more responsibility towards the public interest because they identify the large number of share-holders with the public and the consumer. American industry is, in fact, dominated today by a few managers who have supreme control over the big corporations, and who *are the very image of the great civil servants and technicians of Soviet Russia,* in the measure that the latter participate in the actions of the Party. The only difference is that in Russia they are the sovereign masters, whereas in America they are opposed by two equally well-organized forces: the farmers in their various federations and cooperatives, and the workers in their unions. Labor's power is indeed so great today that collective bargaining agreements exist in all the great American industries, insuring high wages to the workers, and giving them guarantees of employment, seniority rights, and healthful conditions of employment. *America is no longer a capitalist regime; it is an intermediary system in which three powers counterbalance each other*—the managers, the workers, and the farmers, with the Government playing the role of coordinator, conciliator, and finally arbitrator among them. In this system, the fundamental forces in America are now favorable to the development of international exchanges and of a peaceful world settlement.

We have to admit, however, that following the Republican victory in the last elections and, in particular, following the discovery of espionage operations within high government circles, American public opinion has passed through a period of psychic disequilibrium, which found its expression in McCarthyism. In the struggle against EDC, McCarthyism was very valuable to Russian propaganda; his excesses, his violence of speech, gave the impression of an unbalanced being, full of hatred; they were utilized to denounce America as the country that would destroy liberty and threaten the peace of the world. Moreover, while Russia secretly rearms, and conducts atomic experiments in deserted regions of Siberia without giving any account of them, no experiments whatever may be made in America without an outbreak in the press which causes the uninformed to believe that the U.S. is preparing to use its bombs at any moment. American naivete has been an element in the success of Communist propaganda in France.

(c) Neither the peace campaign nor the denunciation of the U.S. as the potential aggressors should conceal the role played by the final threat. Poor Russia strives only for peace; she is encircled by evil America. If France associates with America by accepting German rearmament, she will then be responsible for the unavoidable consequences: the rupture of the Franco-Soviet Pact, the impossibility of negotiations, and maybe even the outbreak of a new world war. This general threat was accompanied by particular pressures and individual threats exerted by the Communist Party on those who, for opposing the "peace policy", would be victims marked for retaliation on the day when the invincible Russian troops would liberate France.

We see today how fruitless these threats were. In fact, it is only since France ratified the Accords of Paris that, for the first time, real negotiations began. But much of public opinion and many intellectuals, had been convinced that the defeat of EDC was the last chance for peace; they had agitated for a conference of Four, without regard for its meaning and its consequences. It is curious to see, when one has read the Yalta accounts and when one has seen the off-hand manner in which the "great" of this world handle the fate of smaller nations, how people can still become enthusiastic about the idea of a great power conference of Three, Four, or Five. A conference is arranged to obtain some specific gains in exchange for some specific sacrifices. But the opponents of EDC merely affirmed the necessity of negotiations *per se*. They did so to conceal what even the Communist party did not dare to declare openly, namely, that the only possible basis for such negotiations, before German rearmament, was an agreement bearing on the *neutralization of Germany*. Now, to neutralize Germany when Russia occupies half of Europe, and when defense on the Rhine is a tactical impossibility because of the lack of space to deploy an army, would have to mean in fact *the renunciation of any possibility of defending our own territory*.

I would like, in conclusion, to remark on another problem (also perennial) which became obvious during the EDC debate: *It is the artificial and unreal character of French political life*. In fact, the problem of German rearmament had been set by France in 1950, when we asked the U.S. to commit itself to the defense of Western Europe. The Americans then had to make a choice between the continental defense on the Elbe and peripheral defense. It was then, and as a condition of this choice, that the problem of German rearmament was set. The Americans warned us that if we did not accept German participation in the system of continental defense, they would be obliged to adopt the system of peripheral defense.

I remember the agonizing debate within the Executive Committee of the Socialist Party, which was followed by the proclamation, by all the Defense Ministers of the Western European countries meeting in Brussels, of the necessity for German participation in the defense of Europe. *From then on, France was pledged*. The government did not make up its mind overnight, but after a debate in which all the political parties participated. It was to forestall a *national* German rearmament that France had taken the initiative toward a European Defense Community. Here, too, the government had moved forward step by step, with debates and votes in Parliament at every stage. After that, the Parliament rejected the Treaty which the government had prepared on its authorization. Next, it came within an ace of rejecting also the Accords of Paris, after having granted a favorable majority to the responsible government. Neither the French Parliament nor French public opinion seems to have a sense of political responsibility; they do not want to recognize that when the final stage of negotiation is reached on ratification of a treaty negotiated under the constant surveillance of the Assembly, they are no longer free. They evade their obligations, refusing to perceive that when France has been pledged by its representatives, they no longer have the right to reverse their decision without destroying all confidence in our country abroad, and all respect for its institutions. This irresponsibility is due to grave aspects of French political life, which seems no longer to be guided by analysis of problems and search for their best solution. French politics seems to have become a quest for affirmation of absolute moral principles. After having lost their Christian faith, the French have transferred their religious faith to secular objects: *political life has become the center of their spiritual life*, the Party replacing the Church, and the vote replacing communion. During a British election, one goes to the ballot-box to elect a government. In France, the vote is a confession of faith. The test is to remain faithful to one's abstract values, not to influence the concrete consequences.

A repeated argument against EDC debate ran as follows: German rearmament may be inevitable; but a very bad solution forced on us by external pressure is preferable to a less bad one to which we freely adhere; if we reject the lesser evil, at least we retain a clear conscience and clean hands.

France will not recover and will not solve her problems as long as she does not eliminate from political life the predominance of moral-ideological absolutes. The EDC debate brought to light the unreality of French politics, the intellectual and moral irresponsibility of French public opinion. We must remember this, for it may well be the most serious problem we have to solve, the deepest transformation we have to introduce into our mentality.

3 : European Politics Faces French Economics

JACQUES VERNANT

Among the factors which culminated in the collapse of EDC, the political are most significant. Supporters and opponents of the treaty used mainly political arguments to impassion the debate. But other factors, economic or technical in nature, although less rousing to the public imagination, influenced the National Assembly and the elite (the *milieux dirigeants* whose views are reflected in Parliament) in ways that may have been decisive.

Two preliminary remarks seem noteworthy, before we analyze those economic and technical factors. First, EDC did not, in fact, come into being. Hence, the expression "economic causes of the EDC defeat" refers to conclusions drawn in advance by interested parties as to the probable consequences of the treaty for the general economic situation of France, and in particular for some sectors of economic activity. It is very difficult to know in what measure such inferences were drawn from objective economic observation or reasoning, and how much was due to subjective opinion. History would have enabled us to judge these predictions had the EDC come into being. As it is, we can only record, without estimating their correctness, the reasons put forth against the EDC treaty.

The second remark is that it is not possible to separate the treaty that was to institute a defense community from its political and economic setting. It is within its policy context that the economic clauses of the treaty must be judged, taking note both of what had preceded the treaty (the institution of a Coal and Steel Community) and what was supposed to follow (the creation of a European political community and of a common market).

In fact, the EDC treaty has been considered by well-informed Frenchmen as one essential element of a proposed general economic policy. Supporters and opponents both have insisted on this point. Supporters, noting the close connection between EDC and C.E.C.A., have pointed out that these two "functional" communities were the main columns of a European edifice that had to be rebuilt by a cautious integration policy. Adversaries of the treaty interpreted EDC (apart from its specifically military and political aspects) as a new step towards the creation of a common market for Europe, an advanced stage on the way opened by C.E.C.A. It is not surprising, then, that the real meaning of EDC was evaluated with respect to its antecedent step, the C.E.C.A., and with respect to its consequent step, a common European market.

The economic considerations that were ultimately to prevail against EDC had already been expressed, as M. Grosser shows with respect to the political themes, during the debate on the C.E.C.A. To sell ratification of that treaty, M. Pléven's government had "bought" an amendment, adopted by the Foreign Affairs Commission, which specified the obligations incurred by the government not toward the other signatories but toward the French National Assembly (an illustration of the "parliamentary dictatorship" that enrages critics of the present constitutional regime). This amendment, written into Article 2 of the government proposal, was submitted to the National Assembly on December 11, 1951 and was adopted before Article 1, concerning ratification of the treaty itself, had even been put to vote. Article 2 enumerated several measures that were aimed at giving the French industrial sectors most concerned (iron and steel) better conditions to compete with the other member nations of the C.E.C.A. These measures included:

(1) continuation of investments in the French coal and steel industries as prescribed in The Plan for modernization of equipment;

(2) negotiations with nations interested in canalizing the Moselle between Thionville and Coblentz. This canal was de-

signed to facilitate transport of coal and coke from the Ruhr to the Lorraine Basin in France (and to the Saar and Luxembourg Basins) as well as transport of steel products from Lorraine to the North Sea harbors. The consequent reduction of costs and prices to Lorraine steelmakers would improve their position and, consequently, that of all French metallurgy (*transformation des métaux*) in international competition;

(3) presentation, within four months, of an investment plan "designed to put the French coal and steel industries in a competitive position"; and a draft bill which would grant more favorable conditions on loans to the steel industries until the ratification of the treaty.

All these measures answered one purpose: to protect French coal mines and steel mills against the consequences which the common market was considered likely to produce. That this concern was shared by almost all the deputies is proved by the vote on Article 2, which was adopted by 501 votes against 114—i.e., by virtual unanimity of the National Assembly, with the exception of the Communists. But Article 1, on the contrary, which authorized the ratification of C.E.C.A., was adopted (on December 13) by only 377 votes to 233. Over 100 deputies who had voted for Article 2 refused to vote for Article 1, two days later, on the ground that the safeguards offered in Article 2 were not sufficient.

This background is relevant to the EDC debate because the national parties which had considered such safeguards necessary and unanimously voted them were to stress, three years later, that the government had not kept its promises. Indeed, while the investments in heavy industry provided for prior to the C.E.C.A. ratification had been realized, no additional efforts had been made by the government to put French industry in a better competitive condition. A difference of 10% still existed between the costs of French and German steel, and the stronger position of Germany could become dangerous during any possible French recession. The canalization of the Moselle, which M. Robert Schuman considered as "the test of the European spirit", could not be realized because of the opposition it encountered in Germany (and even in France).

The common market—last phase of the evolution in which C.E.C.A. was the initial phase and EDC was to be the intermediary phase—gave rise to resolute opposition among French industrial and agricultural producers. If reactions toward the economic clauses of EDC were rather varied, the opposition of French producers to the common market was unanimous. This creation had been proposed in the draft constitution for a European political community, drawn up by the constitutional Commission of the *ad hoc* Assembly in Strasbourg and adopted by the Assembly on March 10, 1953. The *ad hoc* Assembly was composed of delegates from the Council of Europe and from the consultative Assembly of the C.E.C.A. The Foreign Ministers of the six member nations had given it the mandate to draft the statute of a European political community, but the governments were in no way bound to accept their proposals. In fact, they were not accepted by the French government—not in Paris (May 12–13, 1953), nor in Baden-Baden (August 7–8), nor in Rome (September 22). French economic planners, however, considered as very important this proposal which, though non-governmental, expressed the views of an important number of parliamentarians from the six countries of "Small Europe" and was approved by the governments of some of these countries.

The opposition of French industry to the establishment of a common market, before France was ready for international competition, has been explained again and again. It is not my intention to come back to it. I only wish to cite the view expressed by Senator André Armengaud in a recent issue of *Politique Etrangère* [1]: French industrialists oppose a common market in the present situation because French industrial costs are much higher than those of foreign products. Factors which increase French costs include: prices of raw materials and labor (see Tables 1 and 2 below), taxes added to costs at the producer's level and to selling price at the consumer's level; costs of transport, up and down the line; financial charges; costs of merchandising (primarily distribution); costs of recovery of waste products for sale as eventual by-products. Thus, we obtain the table below, which was calculated by the temporary Committee for the organization of the EDC to show relative efficiency among the signatories, on the following assumptions: similar factories, producing at the same rate, the same products with the same output and the same plant, selling with equal distribution expenses, buying raw materials at

[1] "Europe, An Economic and Social Problem", *Politique Etrangère* (November–December 1954).

TABLE 1

Prices of raw materials in the principal industrial countries of the "free world", computed at official rates of exchange:

France = 100

	USA	GB	Germany	Italy	Belgium	France
Coal	42	72	67	144	97	100
Coke for metallurgy	80	66	62	165		100
Cast iron for founding	73	45	81	85	105	100
Steel (ingots)	81	81	95	137	81	100
Aluminum	77	67	87	104		100
Electrolytic copper	76	74	76	86	79	100
Lead	80	66	72	97	65	100
Zinc	61	66	70	97	113	100
Tin	81	79	80	90	79	100
Gas for touring	25	76	74	108	78	100
Rubber	99	106				100
Portland cement	134	89	108	110	64	100
Wool (Australia)	94		100	97	113	100
Cotton	82	91	92			100
Paper pulp for machine	103			112		100
Paper pulp, bisulfate	89		144	100	49	100
Calf skin (raw)	126		119	144		100
Cow skin (raw)	94	190	139	156		100

Source: I.N.S.E.E. Monthly Bulletin on the economic situation, situation of July 15, 1954 (Armengaud, quoted article p. 519)

TABLE 2

Salaries and additional charges (e.g., taxes on salary paid by the industries)
Average salary per hour, in manufacturing industries

MEN AND WOMEN

	France	Germany	Great Britain	Italy	Switzerland	Belgium	Holland
Jan. 52	131.1	124	150.1	91.7	191.6	148.4	94
Oct. 53	138	134.8	164	95	195	150	96.8

At the exchange rate: 1 DM = 83.3 FF; 1BF = 7FF; 1Fl = 92.1 FF; 1 lire = 0.56 FF; 1d = 4.07FF; 1SF = 86 FF

Source: Belgian Labor Review, Rassegna di Statistiche del Lavoro, Monthly Labor Gazette, revue belge *Industrie:* study made by Prof. Ritterhamm at Köln University, INSEE (Armengaud, p. 526)

the same prices, energy and transport at the same price. The theoretical selling price, fixed by the temporary Committee, would be applied to industrial products for purchase by the common authority of the nations participating in the Defense Community.

Theoretical selling-price (all taxes included) of a standard product in the different countries signatories to the treaty and in Great Britain

Item	France	Germany	Belgium	Holland	Italy	Great Britain
Salaries of workers	30	25.95	31.5	19.5	22.5	24.6
Salaries of staff and executives	5	4.38	5.49	3.39	3.56	4.59
Purchase during anterior phase	8.46	8.46	8.46	8.46	8.46	8.46
Amortization	9	7.13	8.04	5.46	6.24	6.40
Energy, transport	7.94	7.94	7.94	7.94	7.94	7.94
Benefits	3	2.38	2.68	1.99	2.08	2.13
Taxation on property		1.45	0.45	0.46	0.35	0.36
Export prices	83.65	76.18	85.41	63.14	67.30	71.06
Taxation on transaction	1	3.05	3.94	3.03	2.02	
Taxation on production	15.35					
Prices within the European community	100	79.23	89.35	66.17	69.32	71.06

See Armengaud, p. 536.

For an optimum price of 100 in France, the foreign prices are lower, *taxes included,* than French prices in the following proportion:

on internal markets:

in Germany	—20
in Belgium	—10
in Holland	—33
in Italy	—30
in Great Britain	—29

on foreign markets (or, on the assumption of a refund of indirect taxes on exportation):

Germany	— 9 (on French price norm of 100)
Belgium	+ 2
Holland	—25
Italy	—20
Great Britain	—15

See Armengaud, p. 537.

Of course, it should be mentioned that the project drafted by the *ad hoc* Assembly recommended a progressive realization of the common market as the "harmonization of the conditions of production" preceded by policies of reconversion and adjustment. During 1954, the Minister of Finance investigated the possibility of a fund for reconversion and adjustment, a fund which would be essential in the event tariff protection was eliminated (*libération des échanges*). But these precautionary measures increased instead of stilling the apprehension of French industrialists. Such was the climate in which the debate that was to decide the fate of EDC was being prepared in 1954.

Apart from the statistical comparison of costs and prices as between France and other countries, comparison between production trends in French and German industry seemed to justify French fears. Between 1950 (when the Schuman Plan was born) and 1954 (when the EDC was buried) a disquieting divergence between these two curves appeared: German production constantly increased in all fields, whereas French production was virtually stable. By 1954, as a result, economic integration with Germany was quite a different matter for France than it had been in 1950. Germany was no longer the equal partner she had been in 1950–51 when the C.E.C.A. treaty was ratified. Time had played a decisive role in creating a new climate for the decision which France took in August 1954: during the years since the C.E.C.A. was ratified and the EDC treaty initiated, the economic situation had changed so sharply that resistance to the economic clauses of the treaty was strengthened.

Before we analyze these economic clauses of the treaty, it is well to review briefly the comparative economic evolution of France and Germany between 1950–54, particularly in regard to industrial production, exports and investments. Table 3 shows, very strikingly, the differences in economic trends during these years:

TABLE 3

Indices of French and German production

(1950 = 100)

	1951		1952		1953		1954 1 term		2 term		3 term	
	Fr.	*Gr.*	*Fr.*	*Gr.*	*Fr.*	*Gr.*	*Fr.*	*Gr.*	*Fr.*	*Gr.*	*Fr.*	*Gr.*
Industrial production (general index)	109	119	108	128	109	139	116	143	123	154	110	154
Production of energy	111	115	117	124	117	132	129	142	121	138	115	141
Extraction of metals and metallurgy	115	121	122	134	111	129	115	133	120	146	112	153
Metals	111	133	115	150	114	154	110	165	120	184	107	177
Chemicals	113	120	107	123	114	145	126	156	135	170	124	170
Textiles	106	111	94	104	98	121	107	125	112	121	90	125
Home construction	107	117	112	131	110	160	96	93	116	177	115	207

Source: United Nations, Study on the European Economic Situation (Geneva, 1955).

(1) Whereas the general index of French industrial production remained almost the same from 1951 to 1953 (i.e., an increase of 9 per cent compared to 1950), the index rose 17 per cent during the same period in Germany (i.e., an increase of 39 per cent compared to 1950). For the third term of 1954, the indices are not comparable (because paid vacations are much longer in Germany than in France); but, if one considers the second term, the production increase compared to 1950 is 23 per cent for France and 54 per cent for Germany.

(2) In the field of energy output, the differences are less marked: the increase between the second term of 1954 and 1950 is, nevertheless, 21% for France and 38% for Germany; compared to 1951, the respective increases are 9% and 20%.

(3) For metallurgy, the movement of the two indices is nearly the same as for production in general: in the second term of 1954, compared to 1950 the increase was 20% for France and 46% for Germany; compared to 1952, the French index had declined 2% whereas the German had increased 12%.

(4) But it is in the metal industries (except construction) that Germany records the greatest increase; and here the disparity between the two indices is greatest: in the second term of 1954, respectively 120 and 180. The rate of growth of German industry

between 1950 and 1952 is remarkable (the order of increase is 50%, compared with 15% in France). In 1953, both indices remained constant. But in 1954, the German index resumed its climb, registering an increase of 30 units in the second term as compared with 1953, while the French index rose only about 6 units.

(5) The same trend appears in the chemical industries, but the disparity is less marked (respectively 35% and 70% increases compared to 1950) than in metals.

(6) In the textile industries (where the crisis is general), the German industry is more prosperous than the French (an increase of 12% in France and of 21% in Germany in comparison with 1950).

(7) In home construction, the indices of both countries have to be compared for the third term of 1954, since this field is most active during the summer months. The results are revealing: in each month Germany built twice as many lodgings as in 1950, whereas France increased its rate by only 15%.

The comparison of French and German foreign trade is also very significant. Table 4, which follows, shows the movement of the German trade balance since 1949: imports and exports are increasing simultaneously, but exports increase much faster, so that the 1948–51 deficit becomes a surplus from 1952 on. It was during April 1952, that Germany decided to free 77% of her foreign trade with the O.E.C.E. countries from restrictions (this figure was raised to 90% in July 1953). German industry was thus able to increase the volume of imports, to increase investments and to lower costs—all of which made a powerful incentive to economic development.

France, on the contrary, having already freed 76% of her O.E.C.E. trade in August 1951, was compelled to reverse this decision because of a growing deficit in her trade balance. In spite of this reversal, the French trade balance continued to run a deficit. The improvement noticeable since 1951 was due to the serious shrinking of imports through the reestablishment of the quota system (exports were also lower in 1953 than in 1951). The reduction of French imports, which the deterioration of her trade balance and her debts to the European Payments Union made necessary, aggravated the crisis that took place between end-1952 and end-1953.

TABLE 4

The Trade Balance of Western Germany

(in millions of $)

	Imports	Exports	Balance
1948	1,588	642	− 946
1949	2,237	1,123	−1,114
1950	2,704	1,981	− 723
1951	3,503	3,474	− 291
1952	3,854	4,037	+ 182
1953	8,810	4,422	+ 612

Source: *Der Aussenhandel der Bundesrepublik Deutschlands*

TABLE 5

Trade Balance of the Franc Area

(including freight and insurance)
(in millions of $)

	Imports	Exports	Deficit
1948	2,827.9	1,126.9	−1,701.0
1949	2,281.3	1,604.9	− 676.4
1950	2,124.5	1,905.0	− 219.5
1951	3,618.9	2,634.6	− 984.3
1952	2,968.0	2,172.8	− 795.2
1953	2,739.7	2,288.2	− 451.5

Source: Document published by the Ministry of Finance (Direction des finances extérieures) on the balance of payments of 1953.

Finally, the comparison between investment in Germany and in France from 1950 to 1954 increased the reluctance of French industrialists to accept any measure that could, even if only partially, bring about an integration of the two economies. In France, investment (computed in constant French francs) tended to fall from 1951 to 1953. The first quite perceptible increase occurs in 1954. Furthermore, public investment by metropolitan France, which had greatly diminished from 1949 to 1951 (from 61% to 41%), was stabilized at around 40% (former evaluations). This flagging of investment by the public sector, dictated by urgent financial and monetary considerations, was not without consequences for the total volume of investment realized.

In Germany, on the contrary, the increase is steady from 1950 to 1954: investment during this last year is more than double that in the earlier year (this, even though the rate of public investment tended rather to diminish).

The disparity is particularly striking in metallurgy. Investment in this industry has not varied much in France since 1951; in 1953, it was only 40% of the total realized (with the help of American aid) during the 1947–1950 period. In Germany, on the contrary, investments in iron-metallurgy increased more than 50% between 1951 and 1953. They represented, in 1953, 21% of the total sum of the investments made during the four years, 1947 to 1950.

The advance made by France in this sector during the immediate postwar years was more than caught up by Germany between 1951 and 1954. In the new look of German heavy industry, in 1954, France saw a justification of her fears that, under cover of supranational institutions, the reinforcement of existing national positions would result.

A final set of facts summarizes the disproportionate rates of growth. The total 1954 investment in German industry amounted to 30 milliards of marks, of which 22 were net investments and 8 amortization. The total 1954 investment in metropolitan France was 1500 millions of francs, of which but 500 were net investment. If one computes the currency exchange at 100 francs for 1 DM,

TABLE 6

Investment in the Franc Area
(in milliards of francs)

Years	Current francs	Constant francs (1949 value)	Proportion of public funds (% of total)
I. Former evaluations			
1949	1288	1288	61.0
1950	1436	1341	57.8
1951	1940	1405	41.2
1952	2175	1385	38.4
1953	2114	1360	40.0
II. New evaluations			
1952	2630	1675	31.8
1953	2581	1660	33.0
1954	2665	1741	32.3

1954 investment was four times greater in Germany than in France.

TABLE 7

Germany—Gross Investment

Civil year	Amount of investments in milliards of DM	Proportion of public funds (% of total)
1949–1950	14.81	23.3
1950–1951	18.00	29.5
1951–1952	22.54	26.6
1952–1953	24.60	23.2
1953–1954	27.75	21.6

Source: General report made by M. Charles Barangé on behalf of the Finance Commission for the financial bill for 1955, National Assembly, 1954 session, No. 9809, p. 234.

TABLE 8

Investment in Iron Metallurgy

	France (francs, add 000)	Germany (DM, add 000)
1947–1950	201,710	400
1951	72,000	600
1952	75,000	700
1953	78,000	950 *

Source: Commissariat Général du Plan, yearly report on the execution of the modernization and equipment plan of the French Union, 1954.

Conseil de la République. Information report for the Commission on application of the treaty of the Coal and Steel community, by Senators Armengaud and Coudé du Foresto. Doc. 171/CR/54.

* In 1954, the Federal Republic invested more than one milliard DM in iron metallurgy.

The economic clauses of the EDC treaty can be summed up as follows: it provided that the Commissariat of the Community would have the right to order armaments and supplies directly from the national industries of the member States. For this purpose, a budget consisting of contributions by the several States would be put at its disposal. In placing orders, the Commissariat would have to take into account the technical and economic potential of each country. It would also, before signing a purchase order, call for competitive bids to get the best offer.

These rules had to be applied, however, so as to avoid creating economic difficulties for any member. The Commissariat was obliged to maintain a certain proportion between the value of each country's contribution to the budget of the Community and the total value of orders placed by the Community in that country. The total value of orders could not be, as a general rule, more or less than 85% of the contribution made by any country to the common budget.

These clauses would have deprived the National Assembly of its control over the French military budget. They would also have put the French armament industries into unprotected competition with the industries of the other members of the Community. Since it is very difficult, theoretically and practically, to define clearly the term "armament", the system of free competition would have been applied in practice to the greater portion of industrial production, at least indirectly. Now, we have seen that French industry was, except for some particular sectors, far from prepared to bear the consequences of such a system. French industry is handicapped in international competition, even when limited to the Europe of Six, by financial and monetary conditions, by fiscal and social charges, and by her labor legislation. The common market would be acceptable only if the distribution of EDC orders were to take into account these handicaps and compensate for them.

For, French industry feared the consequences of the "15% rule"—whereby the Commissariat could spend 15% of the contribution made by any country to the EDC budget outside that country's territory. Since the manufacture of certain products was forbidden to Germany,[2] the application of this rule could help a certain number of French industries but it could also be prejudicial to others. Aeronautical production, for instance, was excluded by the EDC treaty from "strategically exposed areas". Consequently Germany, a strategically exposed territory, where

[2] This prohibition was established by an exchange of letters (dated May 27, 1952) between Chancellor Adenauer and the Governments of the co-signatories of the EDC treaty. The Chancellor agreed that "considering the present international tensions and the strategically exposed position of the territory of the Federal Republic" the products enumerated in Annex II of Article 107 of the treaty would not be manufactured on German territory. These products included, in addition to the A B C arms (atomic, biological and chemical), engines of long-range, guided missiles, mines, war-ships other than small defensive vessels, and military aircraft.

aeronautical production was in any case non-existent, would not re-build this industry from zero. Hence, if it did not get too far out of line with British and American bids, the French aeronautical industry could expect to receive important orders for the equip-ment of the European air forces. Naturally, this industry saw in EDC a chance finally to extricate itself from its difficult postwar situation—in which, for lack of a larger market, it could not reduce costs through mass production.

In the same way, the French electronics industry would have been encouraged, as production in this sector also was to be ex-cluded from the "strategically exposed areas"—i.e., Germany.

The advantages of this clause for two branches of French in-dustry would have been largely counterbalanced, however, by the effect of the 15% rule, whereby the gains for French aeronautical and electronics production would have to be registered as losses for other branches. It was feared, indeed, that the rule would have fatal consequences for other main sectors of French industry. The German steel industry, for example, would have had the lion's share of the orders; the textile industries of other countries, Italy for example, would have produced practically the total require-ments of the Community. French metallurgy and textile produc-tion would thus have been reduced to pauper status—with effects on all the French engineering trades, in which costs are much higher than in Germany. Consider: the French contribution to the budget of the Community was to have been 750 milliards a year (about the amount France had been spending on arma-ments during recent years). A loss of 15% on military purchasing would reduce the annual volume of sales by the French industry by about 100 milliards. This was the sum that could, at the discretion of the Commissariat, be spent to the benefit of foreign, to the detriment of French, industry. Some French industries (e.g. textiles) were already in a difficult situation. Since these in-dustries employ a considerable portion of the French labor force, it is clear why larger and larger segments of the French public were to become anxious over the potential threat posed to those in-dustries by the economic clauses of the EDC treaty.[3]

3 These considerations were presented by M. Max Brusset, rapporteur of the Finance Commission, and by Prime Minister M. Mendès-France to the National Assembly on August 29, 1954. They were emphasized by some of the proposals presented by the French delegation at the Brussels Conference in August, 1954.

Against the EDC treaty, partisans of *dirigisme* (government controls) and of *libéralisme* (free enterprise) formed, paradoxically, a common front. The partisans of *dirigisme* argued the impossibility of the shock tactic involved in exposing to uncontrolled competition an economy as weak and divided as that of France, without condemning it to chaos. They proposed that, in order to avoid such perturbations and operate effectively, the Commissariat should first harmonize the conditions of production in the six countries, mainly by supplying them with raw materials under similar conditions and by adjusting their taxation systems and social charges. In short, they proposed the extension of *dirigisme* to full-scale powers over the economic life of these countries. But the Liberals denounced the Commissariat as already a body of technocrats, unconcerned with national realities and interests, whose control over the national economies could only lead to a catastrophe.

Under these conditions, the EDC treaty seemed doomed to failure. Even if the treaty had been approved, in the 1954 climate, it could not have been applied. Thus, one may wonder if, all things considered, the vote of the National Assembly did not render a useful service to the cause of Europe by ending officially an affair that was already at a dead-end.

4 : Germany and France: A Confrontation

ALFRED GROSSER

"I believe I can say with confidence that French reluctance [on EDC] was the result of two main factors. On the one hand, the treaty contained, for a great number of deputies, too many supranational powers. Secondly, the non-participation of Great Britain caused fear that closer relations with Germany within a Community of Six might result in the further withdrawal of Britain".

In these terms, Mendès-France, presenting the Accords of Paris to the National Assembly on 7 October 1954, two months after the rejection of EDC, defined the opposition to EDC in the Parliament. If it is true that these factors were fundamental to the opinions of a great number of Socialist, Radical, and especially the Gaullist deputies, there was also a deeper cause of the EDC failure: the presence, within the proposed community, of a remilitarized Germany whose future evolution and frontiers were yet unsettled. Thus, if the Accords of Paris were ratified in December, it was despite the dissatisfaction caused by German participation among both partisans and adversaries of the Accords.

It is difficult to know how much of this attitude was emotional, and how much was rational. Was the hostility dictated by rational thinking or rather by an *a priori* sentiment of anti-Germanism? Were considerations of the present world situation or recollections of previous Franco-German relations uppermost? An analysis of this matter cannot be limited solely to the EDC affair. The evolution of French policy towards Germany since 1945 must be taken into account before we can understand French views of German rearmament.

French Policy Since 1945 [1]

Until 1947, French policy towards Germany was unambiguous. It was based on the principles of the famous directive JCS 1067 which guided American occupation in Germany. France wanted to destroy the Prussian, centralizing and military character of Germany, and to obtain "reparations for the heavy losses in human life and materials caused by the Hitlerian war". "Re-education", combined with an "isolation cure", would prepare the German nation to participate again, in a far-off future, in international life. In the meantime, Germany would be a mere pawn in international politics.

On February 5, 1947, a French memorandum was issued which opposed consultation of Germany about the future peace treaty. It recommended abiding by the economic principles defined by the other three occupying powers at Potsdam; that is to say, to limit the industrial development of Germany as much as possible. Speaking for the M.R.P. in recommending ratification of the Atlantic Pact, M. Georges Bidault expressed his pride in having obtained a limitation of German iron production. This was his only reference to Germany.

This policy became increasingly contradictory with another, initiated in 1946 and twice defined in July 1947. On July 11, the new directive JCS 1779 to the American Commander in Chief (as strict on denazification and demilitarization as JCS 1067 had been), stated also that "a prosperous and well-organized Europe requires the economic contribution of a productive and stable Germany". On July 12, representatives of 16 countries accepting American aid declared in Paris that "the German economy should be reintegrated within the European structure so as to contribute to the general increase in the standards of living".

M. Robert Schuman, who had become Minister of Foreign Affairs on July 17, 1948, favored the application of the new policy. He felt that to integrate Germany in a European Community would, politically and psychologically, render impossible any new

[1] Concerning this policy, consult *Documents Français relatifs à l'Allemagne* (août 1945–fevrier 1947) Paris, Imprimerie nationale 1947. 64 p.

German aggression. To achieve this, Western confidence would have to be granted to the democratically-elected leaders of post-war Germany. However, even M. Schuman needed two years to overcome the punitive attitude. From 1948 to 1950, although promoting the European Idea, French policy towards Germany remained purely negative. The only apparent aim was to retain, for the time at least, what France knew she would have to give up later. But the Anglo-Saxon partners had grown too accustomed to a certain amount of French obstruction, followed by resigned acceptance, to see anything unusual in her initial refusal of German rearmament. This was made by the French delegation at the New York Conference in September 1950. For the French, however, German rearmament was an entirely different matter from increasing German industrial potential or repealing occupation controls.

To appreciate adequately the scope of the difference, consider the relevant facts. On December 28, 1948, the Western occupying powers created the Military Office for Security, designed to prevent any military preparations in Germany. The occupation statute, on September 21, 1949, also insisted on disarmament and demilitarization. In the Petersberg Accord, concluded with the Allied High Commission on November 22, 1949, the Federal Government proclaimed its firm resolution (Article 3) to maintain the demilitarization of its territory and to prevent by all means the creation of any kind of military force. These engagements were to be voided when the Accords of Paris came into effect.

Most important, for the French, was the debate over ratification of the Atlantic Pact. M. René Mayer did not mention Germany; but M. Robert Schuman declared on July 25, 1949: "Germany does not yet have a peace treaty. She has no army and should not have any. She has no armaments and will not have any". And, refuting a claim published by Pierre Cot in Le Monde to the effect that "German rearmament is possible within the Pact", M. Schuman stated: "This is the greatest fallacy that has been made on the subject. This I declare as a representative of the French Government. The important fact is that German rearmament will not be possible without a great mistake or French complicity." (J.O. p. 5312)

But it is already clear that, while the idea of the Schuman plan can be rather easily defined in terms of the earlier Allied declarations, the idea of EDC, on the contrary, required a complete and sudden reversal of French policy towards Germany.

The Origins of the Saar Preliminary

The Saar affair played such an important role in the history of EDC that we should recall its main features. Since the Byrnes speech in Stuttgart on September 6, 1946, the Saar had been connected with the problem of reparations. Mr. Byrnes pointed out, in effect, that the U.S. would back French requests concerning the Saar economy if France would agree to modify her reparation-policy. But, in his "advisory" report to the National Assembly on behalf of the Finance Commission (December 21, 1954), M. André Liautey declared:

"All things considered, the human and material losses suffered by France, according to the Consultative Commission for Damages and Reparations, amount to 1,605,815,000 francs in 1938 values. This represents (when adjusted by the accepted coefficient of 25.3) the sum of 40,627,119,500,000 francs in 1953 values. Of this sum, how much did France get as compensation? A relatively low sum of 66,000 millions reparations from the Inter-allied Reparation Agency, and a sum of 51,876 millions in restitutions, making a total of 117,876 millions. . . . And we have yet to take into account that separation of the Saar from Germany, and the Saar union with France has been debited to France in the amount of $17,500,000 (1938) computed in current values" (*J.O.* p. 6677).

From 1950 on, the idea of an equilibrium within the C.E.C.A. was to be included in discussions of the Saar problem. The van Naters report in April 1954 cited the conclusions of the earlier report presented by M. Jacques Vendroux to the National Assembly: "France needs the Saar to maintain the balance of industrial forces within the C.E.C.A. With the Saar, France's part in the total resources of the C.E.C.A. is 32%, Germany's part, 45%; but they would be respectively 24% and 53% if the Saar belonged to Germany".

Other points stressed were familiar themes:

(a) France imports one third of her coal and one sixth of her coke from the Saar, along with other industrial products.

(b) The Saar contributes to French reserves in foreign currency a sum of more than 10 million francs a year.

(c) The Saar is an important market for French products, agricultural and others.

During the debate preceding his departure for the Big Three conference at Bermuda, M. Joseph Laniel declared (November 24, 1953):

". . . almost two years ago M. Robert Schuman declared in the Senate (on April 1, 1952, the day of the ratification of the Coal and Steel Community): 'We have two main requests: 1. The maintenance of economic union and of the conventions on which it is based: 2. The political autonomy of the Saar. These are the only things for which we are determined to secure agreement; the rest is a matter for study and negotiation.'

"Finally, addressing Sénateur Maroger, whose Council had just approved a motion to the same effect, M. Schuman concluded: 'I repeat here, before this Assembly, the engagements I contracted on behalf of the Government. Future governments will also be bound by this agreement concerning the Saar which we conclude tonight.'

"The government intends to be faithful to this agreement, ladies and gentlemen, for the interest of France and of Europe" (*J.O.* p. 5486).

M. Schuman had taken this stand in connection with ratification of the C.E.C.A.; it is as a preliminary condition to the EDC ratification that M. René Mayer, in his turn, defined a Saar settlement. The question arose: did this "preliminary" condition correspond to a genuine policy, or was it just a pretext to postpone the debate on the EDC? The answer is far from simple. We can make two comments without risk:

(a) The notion of a "preliminary" was a consequence of the conditions under which the Schuman Plan had been ratified. At that time, the National Assembly had merely stated its hopes concerning the canalization of the Moselle. Realizing, later, that its desires did not bind its C.E.C.A. partners, the National Assembly decided that, in the future, they would require such problems to be settled as a "preliminary condition" to ratification of a treaty.

(b) When the final EDC debate started on August 27, 1954, the Saar preliminary was far from settled. However, partisans as well as adversaries had proved by that time that the Saar question was secondary to the presence of Germany within EDC.

French Opinion and Germany

In 1945 the great majority of the French people condemned the Germans for the horrors done in their name, but did not seek revenge nor the outlawing of all Germans. They did want to see Germany rendered powerless, strictly controlled for a long time, and intelligently "re-educated". The policy of General de Gaulle and of M. Bidault satisfied most of the electorate.

However, even as the war ended, some Frenchmen believed it would be impossible to build the future on dislike and fear. Most of these came from the Resistance or out of German prisons and concentration camps. They did not believe in collective guilt. According to them, the majority of the German people was weak and undecided and had been deeply shattered by the complete collapse of their country. They were exposed to the influence of two opposed minorities: one preached extreme nationalism and hatred of their conquerors; the other sincerely wanted to participate in the creation of a new Germany. To refuse to help the latter would have meant strengthening the former. It was necessary to encourage the young, the faithful, the trade unionists and the anti-Nazi intellectuals who wanted to reform their country.

Thus a policy of cooperation with a democratic Germany was shaped by a small, but very active, group of Frenchmen. Unfortunately, however, the question of German rearmament was to divide them deeply. For some, rearmament spelled downfall for the promising new features in post-war Germany, and the reversion to traditional martial elements. These became the *anti-cédistes*. Others saw rearmament within EDC as a step toward the integration of Europe and the definitive democratization of Germany. Thus the partisans of a constructive policy toward Germany soon found themselves divided by EDC into two strongly opposed camps. This point was not understood outside France, and particularly not in Germany.

There had already been a division concerning the Schuman Plan among the "open-minded" Frenchmen. They did not agree on the idea of supranationality, nor on the conception of world policy underlying the C.E.C.A. The fact is that since 1947 the European Idea had had to bear the double mark of "constructive internationalism" and of an "anti-Communism" governed by fear.

The form and proportion of these feelings varied with each personality and with the evolution of the world situation.

For Frenchmen who had been partisans of a "punitive" policy before 1947, the problem became, as the Cold War bi-polarized the world, how to conciliate two dislikes. It was not easy to be, at the same time, anti-Communist and anti-German, or anti-Capitalist and anti-German. On the Communist side, the distinction had been established very early between a "good" and a "bad" Germany, geographically separated. To the East of the Elbe lived an industrious people who were rapidly recovering from their losses, which had been greater than those in any other country except Russia. A healthy and confident youth was getting ready to accomplish world-important feats [2] together with the Soviet youth. In the West, on the other hand, revengeful Nazi Germany was again coming to life.

The anti-Communist Germanophobes had greater difficulty in finding a clear-cut attitude. The Germans in the East were real Germans (i.e. Prussians), so there was no wonder that they so readily became Nazi-Communists; but they were also martyrs and victims of the Soviet tyranny. The Germans in the West could be firm allies in the struggle against Communism; but they were still Germans, and therefore enemies of France. The ideal solution for the problem of hitching German strength to Western defense would have been to use German mercenary troops—or, according to a German weekly paper, "German military forces superior to the Russian army, but inferior to the French army". Since it did neither of these, EDC divided the anti-German Frenchmen into two camps, just as it split those Frenchmen who had been hopeful of a renovation in Germany.

The Contacts Between Germany and the French Parties

Some aspects of the parliamentary debates on EDC can be understood only if one is aware of the close connections between the "internationalists". Without entering into the details of contacts between French parliamentarians and Germans—at the Council of Europe and elsewhere—we will outline four problems, the consequences of which have been important:

[2] Message from Stalin to Wilhelm Pieck on October 14, 1949.

M . R . P .   A N D   C . D . U .

There is not, strictly speaking an international Christian Democracy. This "New International" is not a union of parties but a loose network of militant supporters of the Catholic parties. In France those who play leading roles in the N.E.I. (Nouvelles Equipes Internationales) are not the national leaders of the M.R.P., but less influential party personalities who are "less likely to become ministers", such as Mme. Germaine Peyrolles or M. Robert Bichet.

Top M.R.P. leaders like Robert Schuman and P. H. Teitgen maintained their own direct relations with their opposite numbers in Germany—the leaders of the C.D.U. It was probably the close personal relations on this level which suggested that the whole M.R.P. was trustful on cooperation between France and Germany, and favorable to complete European integration. But M. Teitgen himself was to show, after the failure of EDC, that his own belief in a united Europe was mingled with considerable distrust toward Germany. So, too, M. Georges Bidault, President of the M.R.P. and Minister of Foreign Affairs before and after M. Schuman. When Chancellor Adenauer departed for Brussels in August 1954, he relied on the optimistic information M. Teitgen had given him about the pro-EDC attitude of the National Assembly, and did not realize the importance of the defeat that M. Bidault had inflicted upon the idea of European integration as early as 1953 at the Rome conference.

THE FRENCH RADICALS AND THE LIBERAL INTERNATIONAL

The "International" of liberal parties is another network of personal contacts and exchange of information. Here the difficulty has been French resentment that their German partners, namely the F.D.P., were too "Right". The pro-EDC group of the Radical Party comprised mainly those who had participated in the activities of the "International", e.g., M. René Mayer and Maurice Faure, General Secretary of the party. They considered the "International" as a means of promoting European integration and, as the "European-minded" members of the party, differed greatly from two other types of Radical personalities. Some, with M. Daladier, were more concerned about East-West relations than about European or Franco-German relations; others, with M. Mendès-France, were more preoccupied by the problems of the French Union and by international problems of the sort discussed at the Havana Conference.

This split the Radical party between those at home in a "European" atmosphere, language and climate, who were certain to be innovators; and those they considered as "backward", who, like M. Herriot, were attached to the past history, or, like M. Mendès-France, were insensitive to the affective force of the European idea. This cleavage, almost unnoticed at the time of the Schuman Plan, was to become evident with the issue of EDC.

THE SPLIT BETWEEN S.F.I.O. AND S.P.D.

The French section of the Socialist International had no close postwar relations with the Social Democratic Party of Germany. The French had complained about the "nationalism" of Dr. Schumacher, the Germans about the lack of labor influence in the S.F.I.O. The S.F.I.O. specialist for relations with Germany, M. Salomon Grumbach, a man with little influence in his party, was not replaced after his death. Disagreements between S.P.D. and S.F.I.O. on the European problem were both cause and consequence of this coldness. The two Socialist parties had disagreed consistently on the Council of Europe, the Schuman Plan, the EDC, and finally the Accords of Paris. Paradoxically, therefore, on all these problems the S.F.I.O. had found itself making common cause for Europe with the German C.D.U. (Christian Democratic Union), the Catholic party denounced by Socialists throughout Europe as part of the clerical "black international". The hostility of the S.P.D. toward EDC had no influence on the leadership of the S.F.I.O., which declared in favor of the treaty. In fact, those S.F.I.O. members who opposed EDC had reached their decision on grounds little influenced by confrontation with the German socialists.

THE FRENCH "BEVANITES" AND M. HEINEMANN

When M. Guy Mollet, Secretary General of the S.F.I.O., intervened in favor of the Accords of Paris on December 29, 1954, he was violently attacked by the Communists, who pointed to the disagreement between S.F.I.O. and S.P.D. His answer, not very convincing on the whole, was, as we see it, strong on one point.

M. Mollet told the Communist deputies: "You have tried many times to convince the S.P.D. to participate in joint action with you. Whereas other people, Frenchmen, have been willing, the German Social-Democrats have always refused" (*J.O.*, p. 6923).

These "other people" were either on the far Left or on the far Right of the French political chessboard: on the one hand, the nationalistic elements who were more anti-German than anti-Russian; on the other hand, the "Bevanites", who disagreed with the German Socialists in their conception of anti-Communism and of German reunification. These "Bevanites", who represented an appreciable part of French opinion, believed that German reunification should be a sort of synthesis between the Federal and the Democratic Republics, thus providing a test of "pacific coexistence".

The German Socialists, on the contrary, maintained that reunification should mean an extension of the Federal Republic toward the East. They considered the Pankow Government of East Germany as Quisling puppets, collaborating slavishly with the hated Soviet occupant.

The French "Bevanites" allied themselves with the group of Dr. Heinemann and of the clergyman Niemöller, without realizing that this group represented only a very small fraction of the German population.

The Ratification of the Schuman Plan

The debate of December 1951 in the National Assembly on the C.E.C.A. was well described by a comment of M. Pierre Schneiter: "The majority of the French people has been favorably impressed by the initiative of M. Robert Schuman in May 1950" (*J.O.*, p. 9010). None of the adversaries of ratification attacked the general principles of the project. The criticisms were addressed to specific clauses and not to its essential meaning, i.e. the constructive policy towards Germany. General Aumeran's acrimonious speech against Germany caused M. Robert Schuman to observe, without being contradicted: "I would like to tell General Aumeran, with all due respect, that I am happy for my country that he is the only, or almost the only, one in this Assembly, to recommend such a policy toward Germany and toward Europe" (*J.O.*, pp. 8881–82).

It is relevant that everybody seemed to admit that the C.E.C.A.

was, in principle, a step toward an economically coherent Europe; and that the treaty justified the hopes for social equality and for the abolition of nationalism. To grasp the differences regarding EDC, it is instructive to review the speeches made in favor of the C.E.C.A. by two persons who were later among the most passionate adversaries of EDC—M. André Denis, who gave vigorous support to C.E.C.A., was subsequently to be excluded from the M.R.P. for his opposition to German rearmament. M. Marcel Naegelen, the future Socialist candidate for the Presidency of the Republic in January 1954, was finally excluded from the S.F.I.O. for voting several times against both EDC and the Accords of Paris. Yet, on December 11, 1951, he had declared on behalf of the Socialist group in the Parliament:

"Ladies and Gentlemen, the Socialist group—which will vote in a few moments—will give its support, not to the policy of a government with which it does not always fully agree, but to the great European policy to which France is pledged [and therefore to the C.E.C.A.], for which she has and must keep the credit".

Objection was made. M. Pierre André asked for a postponement on the ground that risks were also implied in the C.E.C.A. scheme. Replied Naegelen: "We know it. We know that nothing great has ever been achieved in the world without risks" (*J.O.*, p. 9000).

Apart from the Communists and Progressives, the parties restricted their criticisms concerning Germany to two main points. One was legal: M. Gaston Palewski, for the R.P.F., observed that the French Constitution would be transgressed, since it permits a renunciation of sovereignty only in the case of reciprocity. The Federal Republic cannot renounce its full sovereignty, which is something it does not yet possess.

The argument was irrefutable. M. Schuman, in replying that Germany had regained her full economic sovereignty, forgot to mention the continued existence of the Ruhr Authority. He did not repeat his former assertion, that the scope of the Plan was political rather than economical. M. Palewski's point, underlining the poorly defined juristic status of Germany, was to reappear strongly in the EDC debates.

The other criticism concerned the fear of German supremacy in a Europe of the Six. This was the argument of the Right in the Assembly—e.g., of General Billotte, M. Diomede Catroux, M.

Alfred Krieger (with interests in Lorraine metallurgy). The latter said:

> "If Germany is again going to be an independent economic power, not within a European entity which alone would enclose and stem her new power, she will reestablish the coal and steel "Verbund-betriebe" which would guarantee her predominance. I personally have many relations with Germany; I also have friends there. I believe that Germany has a sincere desire to construct a new Europe and to bring an end to the outdated Franco-German antagonism. But, hear me well, one should never tempt the devil" (*J.O.*, p. 8912).

The idea that a strong political organization of Europe was needed to avoid the dangers of the pool, had been introduced by M. Jacques Soustelle. In spite of his reservations about Germany, and his subsequent leadership of opposition to EDC and the Accords of Paris, he affirmed:

> "We found it difficult to understand the violent emotion manifested by some of our colleagues when M. Aumeran recalled some recent historical facts (anti-German facts). Wisdom, however, obliges us to sit down to discussions with Germany, our neighbor for ever.
> "On the other hand, and this is the fundamental difference in orientation that separates us from our colleagues, we believe, with all our faith, in the realization of the European Confederation, the main condition of prosperity and peace on the Continent. Such a Confederation must naturally include Germany. It implies, of course, the creation of common political powers, democratic in their origin as well as in their responsibilities before the confederated nations" (*J.O.*, p. 8882).

The great majority of the Assembly, whatever its fears of the German future might have been, accepted the declaration of M. Alfred Coste-Fleuret: "Germany is in full growth, but this is a growth which has never stopped. It is precisely at the moment when we could conceive some fears about this development, that the Schuman Plan intervenes opportunely to stabilize the situation and to take from the German State, as it does from the French, the disposition over her heavy industry for war-purposes" (*J.O.*, p. 8862).

We now recall that M. Schuman had asserted that the C.E.C.A.

had no relation whatsoever with a project of a European Army. And when Loustaunau-Lacau, rapporteur of the National Defense Commission, put forth the opposite idea, President René Pléven had replied: "He talks exactly like a Communist" (*J.O.*, p. 8873).

German Rearmament and The Fight for EDC

Without recounting the details of EDC history, we note that its underlying strategy was this: in order to make the unpopular German rearmament acceptable to French public opinion, it was wrapped in and covered by the popularity of the European idea as expressed in the Schuman Plan (C.E.C.A.). This circumvented also the Order of the Day of October 26, 1950, which permitted German rearmament only by counter-project and stated: "They will not permit the creation of a German Army and German Staff of Officers".[3]

Some EDC partisans set forth arguments similar to those used for the C.E.C.A. In his speech of August 29, 1954, M. Coste-Fleuret declared: "We know that the two sources of power of modern Germany in recent times, are the Ruhr arsenal (to neutralize it we have constructed the C.E.C.A.) and the national German army, which we also want to neutralize by integrating German soldiers into the discipline of a supra-national army. German growth is a fact, but the question is to control its direction" (*J.O.*, p. 4451).

In the December 1953 debate, M. Legaret had expounded similar views:

> "The European idea, which is partly realized by the Defense Community, seems to be able to offer Germany, for the first time, a new mystique that can animate her spirit and the enthusiasm of her youth just as it did ours.
>
> "For the first time since the French Revolution, a great idea is offered to the nations that is neither hatred nor war. It is for those who have launched the idea, to help it develop in Germany. Otherwise we shall have missed the occasion to reshape the German will . . . instead of sustaining it as has been three times the case" (*J.O.*, p. 5472).

[3] See p. 524 of the special issue of *Chronique de politique étrangère* (Brussels: Institut de Relations Internationales, Sept.–Nov. 1952), p. 356. This issue contains all the essential texts concerning the first period of EDC.

The opponents of EDC stressed four main themes:

(a) *The "traditional" German danger:* On this affective argument was based the Communist propaganda campaign against EDC. Without saying so directly, this suggests that it is against France that the "congenital" German aggressiveness will turn. M. Pierre Lebon, Gaullist, declared on August 28: "Germany invaded us in 1792, in 1814, in 1815, in 1870, in 1914 and in 1940. I have only gone back to 1792, but the problem is much older" (*J.O.*, p. 4444).

(b) *The "new" German danger:* a rearmed Western Germany is apt to lead the West into war against the East to gain its reunification and to recover the territories beyond the Oder-Neisse.

(c) *French Union vs. German Europe:* The overseas obligations of France are so great as to permit the Federal Republic, while France is engaged elsewhere (even after the Indochina war ends), to establish its military supremacy on the continent.

(d) *Democracy:* To rearm Germany is to act against the German democracy.

It is essential to distinguish (a) from (d), although some politicians like M. Herriot employed argument (d) late in the debate to conceal a systematic anti-Germanism. M. Jules Moch, who realized that French opposition to EDC was presented in Germany as the direct consequence of Germanophobia, declared in his parliamentary report:

"Germany first. Will she be hurt or induced to new adventures if we refuse her army divisions? Yes, doubtless she will be hurt if our opposition is only the will of the conquerors determined to tread down their enemy, and if we revive certain policies of the inter-war period. But if, on the contrary, we explain clearly to our neighbours that our aim is still disarmament; that we do not want to deviate from this aim by rearming them as long as the present disarmament negotiations are seriously carried on; and that we plan to bring ourselves, as well as the other nations, back to controlled and reduced armaments that could assure the internal order and international obligations of every country; if, at the same time, we restore to Germany her full sovereignty in other fields and propose to settle the problem of military occupation and of her reunification—why, then, would the Germans at large not rally themselves to a policy of reason and peace? Maybe this is not the present policy of the Bonn government. But its domestic policy is not our affair. And I imagine that it is not to strengthen a political fraction in Germany that we are asked to ratify the Treaty of Paris" (*J.O.*, p. 4386).

Similarly, during the ratification debate on the Accords of Paris, M. Daladier declared:

"Against this rearmament, 6 millions of German workers, members of non-Communist labor unions, with a Social Democrat as president and a Christian Democrat as vice-president, rise up in protest.

"What can France answer to these German workers, to these real democrats of Federal Germany?

"Their opposition joins with that of a great part of German youth. We have seen recently the numerous protests of their parents, who have pointed out that the German Constitution sanctions, in Article 6, the conscience clause. This shows the degree of peacefulness to which German minds had come after the breakdown. It is self-evident that, if the Accords are voted, the conscience clause will not survive very long in the German Constitution.

"Much has been said about a French-German understanding. I prefer this term to 'reconciliation'. We have done nothing to Germany and the contrary only is true. A loyal understanding has been talked about. I personally favor it, and, as much as anyone else here, I understand the huge advantage of a loyal understanding with Germany.

"But, would it not be better to have this loyal understanding with the youth, with the labor unions, with the German Socialist party and the democratic forces, rather than with the Ruhr magnates or with the politicians, some of whom have been on the American list of war criminals? This is the question I am submitting to you" (*J.O.*, p. 6763).

M. Herriot adopted the same thesis the next day, December 23:

"There is another Germany that is trying to free herself, to enter the way of liberty. These are the young generation, the syndicalists and the socialists. These are also—and I affirm it without partisan motives [M. Herriot is the patriarch of anti-clericalism] but rather because it is an historical element in the German Constitution—the Protestant churches and their congregations, who are in complete opposition to the other opinion.

"Speaking as a Frenchman and a Republican, I think it inadmissible and paradoxical that France should support the reactionary elements of Germany against this other Germany that is trying to free herself and to follow the lessons of French history, this other Germany that has always helped freedom where she could, even when freedom was only dawning and beginning its efforts" (*J.O.*, p. 6810).

But, by the time of the Accords of Paris, the situation was no longer the same in Germany. The failure of EDC had separated the idea of rearmament from the European idea. This produced a change in the French debate, namely, the adoption by Former EDC partisans, on the day after their defeat, of arguments that had been used against EDC. On August 28, 1954, M. Max Lejeune, Socialist president of the National Defense Commission, declared: "The German soldier, who has always considered himself the bearer of the conscience of the German nation, will soon resume those traditional tendencies which we know, increasingly in fact as the staff of the German army, integrated or not, comes, ten years after the war, out of Hitler's Wehrmacht" (*J.O.*, p. 4399).

On August 31, M. Paul Reynaud, complaining about the rejection of EDC, now used almost the same terms to argue against the Accords of Paris:

"Yes, ladies and gentlemen, the Wehrmacht has marched down the Champs Elysées and through all the French towns. It is the Wehrmacht which the German democrats have been telling us about at the Strasbourg Assembly for years. Do not allow the great military staff of Germany to be restored, since it would control the German government—for the history of the pressure of the German military forces is too well known, too bloody . . .

"You know that they contain in the greatest degree, the dynamism of the German nation. It is a nation that is never static, always in movement, always unsettled. The proponents of a 'hale and hearty' war, the militarists, the former Nazis will take the lead in the new independent Wehrmacht" (*J.O.*, p. 4478).

On December 22, M. Jean Le Bail, Socialist deputy and EDC partisan, attempted to defend the Accords of Paris by saying: "I remain, for my part, faithful to the old Socialist tradition, to the tradition of Jaurès who was confident of the German democracy". M. Alfred Coste-Fleuret cut in with "the German democracy, yes; the German military staff, no" (*J.O.*, p. 6754).

Conclusion

In the same speech, M. Le Bail had declared:

> "We know that nationalistic and chauvinistic currents have a tendency to develop much more quickly in Germany than anywhere else. The present generation, which has seen the war and suffered from it, will be replaced by less cautious generations, that could become, if we do not keep watch, equally dangerous . . .
>
> "Let us not repeat the same errors on German problems that we made in the period between the wars. We did not trust the German Weimar democracy, which, with difficulties and amidst a general indifference, was trying to find its way. However, at the same time that we refused her our confidence, we left her free to act at her own will.
>
> "We kept making errors, and at the end of this long succession of mistakes there was Hitler and the war.
>
> "To profit from the lessons of history does not imply remembering and cursing out of impotence. Being faithful to the teaching of history means, on the contrary, remembering and sparing future generations those unfortunate experiences we have known" (J.O., p. 6745).

The tragedy of EDC—for Franco-German relations—was that the issue became completely confused. EDC put into the same camp those who continued "to curse because of their impotence" and those others who believed that rearmament presented genuine dangers, both for the internal evolution of Germany and for the harmonious development of relations between the two countries. The drama reached the point where it required courage to assert, as did M. Mendès-France on December 23, 1954: "France has suffered greatly during the last hundred years because of Germany, a traditional Germany from which the German nation must break. The German people also suffered from Nazism and there is no doubt about the attachment of its youth to values which are common to us" (J.O., p. 6813).

THE
PRESS
AND THE
PUBLIC

5 : The Evolution of French Opinion *

JEAN STOETZEL

The uncertainties and divisions of French opinion on EDC derived from complex factors. By joining France and Germany within one military system, EDC involved traditional French feelings toward the Germans: Would the system satisfy French security claims upon the neighbor she had faced on the battlefield three times in a century? Would it lead to a union that could reconcile internal rivalries? Would the bipolar appraisal of the new historic situation, opposing two antagonistic blocs between which the German space could not be left empty, correspond to French views on the particular situation of their country?

In other words: Would the risks run by France be reduced by EDC? Would EDC be a sufficient safeguard or would it aggravate some dangers? And finally was the threat so urgent that serious inconveniences had to be accepted in order to avert it? All these questions were set before the national conscience, and the public did not ignore them. Public attitudes from the war's end to the rejection of EDC show, despite frequent assertions to the contrary, a remarkable stability. Several attitudes are clearly stated,

* The main sources of this study are *Sondages,* French review of public opinion Paris, 20, rue d'Aumale, which regularly publishes the result of the polls made by the *Institut Français d'opinion publique.* It also takes into account unpublished surveys done by the Institute between 1952 and 1954 for other institutions. The latter have been willing to authorize the publication of these data, for which the author of the present article is very thankful.

among which some may seem to us contradictory; but public anxiety results precisely from that complex psychological situation, in which ultimate aims encounter pressing necessities, but in which no *present* need is obvious enough to silence the deep feelings that are rooted in the collective conscience. Various pressures are exerted in opposite senses and impassion the debate. An objective analysis takes all the elements, and their main components, into account.

Feelings towards Germany and the Germans

The allies entered into the war in 1939 to destroy the military power of Germany. They proclaimed unconditional surrender as their war aim and fought until it was obtained. The postwar fate imposed on Germany reflected the allied determination to prevent the renewal of aggression. At the end of the war, to the extent that these matters are known to us, agreement seemed to be reached on this point among the nations which had united against Hitlerism.

For the French, no doubt was possible. To be convinced, one has merely to look through the results of opinion polls made in September 1944 and in 1945. The harshest treatment for Germany, any solution leaving her in a state of inferiority, was approved by the great majority: there were those who hesitated, but almost no dissenters. Prolonged military occupation, transfer of the most harmful elements of population, dismemberment annexation of the Saar to France, lasting allied control of German industry, international trusteeship of the Ruhr, pastoralization of Germany according to the Morgenthau Plan—any measure seemed acceptable as long as it was radical and severe.

British and American attitudes were no weaker than the French. In September 1944, the British declared themselves favorable to partition, and large majorities approved complete reparations, prolonged occupation, and total disarmament. In the United States public opinion also supported, in January 1944, a harsher peace treaty than Versailles.

Nevertheless, a certain anxiety revealed itself in French opinion. The French remembered well the fate of the Versailles treaty. They were convinced, immediately after the suspension of hostilities (June 1945), that the Russians intended to treat the Germans very harshly, but they were less sure of English severity, and they believed that the Americans would ultimately incline towards indulgence.

After all, they could not forget the sufferings endured on the battle-fields, in their own territory, during the two great wars. They still bore the physical scars: 1 out of 5 were wounded or had their health impaired; 1 out of 4 lost a close relation; 1 out of 3 had their homes destroyed, plundered or damaged. Many had suffered several of these evils. Such was the account made about ten years after the suspension of hostilities and such were the fundamental data of French feelings toward the Germans.

Questioned in October 1950 about their preferences for nine different nations, the French placed the English and then the Americans at top places in their sympathies; but the Germans came last, in a position of clear enmity—and, it should be pointed out, after the Russians. The recollections of evil had not been wiped out. The results obtained by I.F.O.P. correspond to those found by the *Institut national d'études démographiques*, in January 1951, in a wholly different context. On questions concerning immigration quotas, the Germans were again the last place; the people that the French cared least to have as immigrants.

Time did not change these affective reactions. A survey in July 1954, when partisans and adversaries of EDC were facing each other, showed clearly their persistence. The French conceded to the Germans many qualities such as orderliness, discipline, industriousness, and energy; but the list of shortcomings was longer: cruelty, lack of humanity, superiority complex, militarism, passive obedience, will to power. And the virtues even aggravate the defects, by bestowing on the defects the German attribute of systematic strictness. Moreover, the Germans are regarded as deeply fond of war; and the atrocities committed in both wars are regarded as facts, not in the least exaggerated. If circumstances were again to permit it, concentration camps and extermination would reappear. It is difficult to condemn a whole nation, and it may well be that there are "good" Germans—according to a variously accepted rationalization in France. But the belief that the trans-Rhine mentality has changed since the war cannot be accepted without proof, and the majority do not accept it.

Compared with this perennial distrust in the French attitude, Anglo-Saxon attitudes underwent a certain reversal. The harsh postwar feelings toward Germany were succeeded by feelings of sympathy in England, the U.S., and Canada. The countries which neighbor on Germany, and which suffered invasion—France in particular—did not undergo such a change, as was revealed by an international poll in December 1946.

December 1946	*feelings of* sympathy	antipathy toward the Germans
	%	%
France	3	56
Netherlands	29	53
Norway	21	44
Great Britain	42	36
Canada	41	28
United States	45	28

During 1946, too, there was a marked change in Anglo-Saxon policy towards Germany. The Americans seemed decided, henceforth, to forget the past; the fear of Germany vanished before another fear; they decided to revive—under their control, of course —the very military apparatus they previously had had to fight.

The French were very attentive to the momentous speech delivered in Stuttgart, on September 6, 1946, by Secretary of State Byrnes. He there expressed the idea that a central German government might now be necessary to open the way to a democratic Germany. He hinted that the eastern frontier with Poland could not really be considered as definitive. The Saar could eventually come back to France, *if* the French would accept a diminution of their reparation claims. And he added: "The population of the Ruhr and the Rhineland wish to remain united with the rest of Germany, and the U.S. is not against this desire." This last declaration opposed the French governmental position and also the wish expressed on various occasions by the majority of the French public for the separation of the Ruhr from the rest of Germany. The speech of Mr. Byrnes met with the disapproval of the Frenchmen who heard it.

A new factor had been introduced into the world political arena, the opposition between East and West. The German problem now became but an element in this larger framework. Would the French abandon all other considerations because of this new conception? Would they forget, in particular, the danger that a re-unified Germany would present to peace and to their own security?

France in the East-West Contest

According to the French, two powers were trying to dominate the world: the USSR in the first place, but also the United States:

	February *1946*	*July* *1947*	*January* *1953*
There is one nation which tries to dominate the world	68%	79%	78%
It is:			
the USSR	26	36	22
the United States	25	29	15
the USSR and the U.S.	12	13	30

At first glance, France was not directly concerned in this rivalry, as she was in the French-German conflict; and one could understand the temptation which since 1946 neutrality constantly presented to the French. In 1954 this temptation was still strong.

October 1954	%
France should be at the present time	
in the Western camp	37
in the Eastern camp	2
in neither of the camps	39
no opinion	22
	100

In case of a war between the U.S. and USSR, France should be:	
on the side of the U.S.	22
on the side of the USSR	2
neutral	53
no opinion	23
	100

But the temptation, while expressing a deep-rooted desire, was not accepted after reflection. The French knew that they could not remain neutral and that they must be involved in any conflict. Moreover, the majority considered that a conflict would be also a French affair, and they understood why the French government had already chosen for the West.

Even in their hesitation to commit themselves, one can perceive sympathy for the West. As the tables reveal, sympathy is much more often on the American side than on the Soviet side. That is why, when the question was raised in 1949, they were in favor of the signature of the Atlantic Pact; and why they considered, four years later, in spite of strong reservations, that it was good for France to participate in it.

French policy—and the public knows it very well—is based on evaluation of the postwar situation and on the place France occupies in the vast conflict which divides the antagonistic bloc. It would be an easier choice, made without hesitations, if the dangers came exclusively from one side. But this is not the case. While the greatest war danger does come from the USSR, the U.S. also might start a conflict at any moment if they felt that their present chances might be lost in the future. Would France then have to be involved in a preventive war she did not desire, without having been attacked?

The danger of war comes rather from:	September 1951	May 1953
the USSR	44%	38%
the United States	13	16
the USSR and the United States	14	6

Public opinion thus considered that responsibility was to some extent shared between U.S. and the USSR and that the latter was not alone to be blamed:

September 1952	%
In this conflict	
The USSR is most to blame	39
The U.S. is most to blame	11
The USSR and the U.S. are to blame	35

Since the risk of a general conflagration did not seem immediate to them, the French did not reject the idea that Germany also could endanger peace, to a lesser but not negligible degree:

July 1954
Countries which are a threat to peace

USSR	56%
United States	36
Germany	10

The French were not in the state of hostility that they attributed to the Russians and the Americans. In any case they did not perceive one sole enemy, but several:

	International Enmities		
June 1953	*France*	*United States*	*USSR*
have no enemy	33%	9%	10%
have one or several enemies	43	72	69
the USSR	17	61	—
Germany	16	1	1
the U.S.	5	—	56
July 1954			
have one or several enemies	59		
namely		—	—
the USSR	27	—	—
Germany	22	—	—
the U.S.	10	—	—

Thus the situation of France appears to be particularly complex. The public feels itself a part, in a limited degree, of the conflict which surrounds it. Its sympathies go spontaneously to one of the camps, but without any aggressive ideas and concerned exclusively about defense. There is concern about being committed to action for purposes which do not seem very clear. The threat from the East does not appear so blinding as to obliterate the dangers run in the recent past from Germany; and these dangers still exist. Committing itself to the West, the public fears, may increase the risks.

European Unification

European unification, in conciliating national antagonisms, could be a means of insuring self-defense by the creation of military forces equal to those of the U.S. or of the USSR. This was a perspective welcomed by the French and, at the beginning, they even took the lead in the movement.

A united Europe was desirable, and opinion on this point never wavered since the end of the war, whatever the course of events. According to an international survey, in September 1947, most Frenchmen considered the "United States of Europe" a good idea.

Continued hostility towards Germany was evident, in that French opinion did not welcome Germany into a united Europe as much as did the respondents in other countries. Among French respondents 8 out of 10 included France, Belgium, Switzerland, Great Britain in the European construction; but only 6 out of 10 included Germany, which took last place on a list of 26 countries. Only two got fewer votes, but these countries were regarded as not quite European: Turkey and the USSR. (Nevertheless, almost half the French respondents would have welcomed the USSR within a United Europe.)

In the period after this international survey, European ideas progressed and European institutions were created: the Council of Europe and the European Assembly in Strasbourg convened members of parliaments of the various European countries, including West Germany. Two years later, when the first project for economic cooperation had materialized in the Coal and Steel Community, public opinion was still favorable to European unification. The public agreed on French participation in a European government, even when aware that such a government might be led into decisions unfavorable to France. Among the arguments predisposing people toward such a government, the one which gained widespread acceptance was the theme "unity is strength". The other themes were rather economic or military, but they all counterbalanced the disadvantages—of which the major one was the loss of sovereignty.

At the time of the EDC rejection, in September 1954, there was still the same favorable attitude toward European unification in general, but the same uncertainty when the form proposed for such unification resembled a common government with supranational powers of decision. There was a great difference between good will on essential purpose (a kind of declaration of intentions) and readiness to overcome specific obstacles, such as the loss of sovereignty which this purpose implied. But neither was unification regarded as some remote utopia. Almost half of the respondents under 65 years old predicted that they would see its creation during their lifetime; reservations on the "here and now" only proved the genuine difficulties involved. French opinion was confronted with a new dilemma: how to avoid alienating national sovereignty while contributing to the creation of a new sovereignty for Europe.

The creation of the C.E.C.A. had been a test case for this dilemma, for its High Authority was to be sovereign and to take its decisions independently of the participating governments. When the idea was launched as the Schuman Plan in 1950, at which point the public was not yet fully informed, it was favorably received. Attitudes toward this specific plan were derived from attitudes toward European unification in general; very few approved one while disapproving the other.

When the Schuman Plan was better known in 1952, in particular when the public became aware that West Germany was participating, the plan was still widely accepted. It was seen as bearing economic advantages for France and for all participant countries; it was also seen as a first step towards the United States of Europe, hence as a case of "unity makes strength". Opposition was divided into three equal groups: the isolationists, who did not perceive France's interest in participation in such a community; the pacifists (or neutralists) who feared that adhesion to an imperialistic bloc might lead to war; and finally, those who were frankly opposed to Germany. The fears which underlay these attitudes, and in particular the distrust for Germany, were to be found again in the opposition to EDC. But the C.E.C.A. covered a field in which such apprehension could more easily be overcome. Nevertheless a poll on C.E.C.A. made in July 1954, at the height of the EDC debate, revealed the existence of a divided opinion:

January 1954

The C.E.C.A. makes the economic power of Germany

more dangerous	20%
less dangerous	17
does not change anything	15
no opinion	22
do not know the C.E.C.A.	26
	100

But it was felt that the C.E.C.A. would serve the interests of all European countries as much as, or more than, those of Germany. Hence, while the particular features of the C.E.C.A. were not widely known, the Plan was generally understood and approved:

July 1954

Attitudes toward the European Coal and Steel Community

favorable	22%
rather favorable	20
rather against	6
against	8
no opinion	44
	100

Thus, on the level of economic cooperation and even at the cost of a certain limitation of sovereignty, French reservations were not irreducible. The majority even admitted possible extension of such supranational Communities to other fields besides coal and steel.

German Rearmament

The attitudes toward military cooperation were completely different. Even if prompted by international events to accept the *idea* of German rearmament, the French conscience refused to face the practical and concrete consequences of such acceptance.

The empty space created in Europe by the destruction of the German military apparatus seemed to some very dangerous in the face of Soviet power. German rearmament appeared to the Anglo-Saxons as the only means of warding off this danger. French opinion remained, however, deliberately hostile: 51% voted in October 1950 against the inclusion of German units in the European army as against 21% who rallied to the proposition. The reason was very simple: the rearmament of Germany and the existence of German troops, even in a European army, threaten France's security. This defensive reflex, which we have already emphasized, here came into full play:

German rearmament	October 1950 %	April 1951 %
would augment France's security	20	18
would diminish	45	34
would have no influence	16	17
no opinion	19	31
	100	100

The existence of German troops	May 1953 %
constitutes a danger for France	57
does not	25
no opinion	18
	100

The existence of German troops within the Western army:	June 1953 %
endangers the security of France	37
does not	28
no opinion	35
	100

Distrust was very strong. The French felt that, in case of war, Germany might change camps or rally to the stronger one according to circumstances. Of the above respondents 45% would not trust Germany at all, and 33% would trust her only up to a certain point.

These feelings in the national conscience did orient the conduct of several French governments. As it was impossible to misunderstand the intentions of their allies within the Atlantic pact, French leaders conceived their plans in such a way as to quiet popular fears. Thus EDC was, in principle, designed to prevent the revival of an independent Wehrmacht by integrating German troops within a European army. The boldest of these plans, instituting the EDC, long remained in suspense, for want of a government ready to present it to Parliament for ratification.

Public opinion seemed at first very doubtful, but a slight majority rallied to the idea of a European army, considering it as a lesser evil:

Regarding a European army:	September 1951 %	September 1952 %	May 1953 %	June 1953 %
For	42	48	46	43
Against	26	30	22	23
No opinion	32	22	32	34
	100	100	100	100

The partisans stressed the necessity of forming a single bloc to fight communism and to insure the common security; they also favored EDC as an important step towards the unification of Europe. The adversaries, on the contrary, feared aggravation of the risks of war and stressed the perennial distrust of Germany. The hesitants spoke of the technical and practical difficulties of such an enterprise. But one also saw distrust toward Germany in such expressions as: "All this would be very well, if there were no Germans"; or "Without the Germans, it would be all right, but I am always worried about the Germans".

The choice was not clear-cut between the two different solutions for insuring the defense of Europe: the traditional solution of national armies or the new solution of a European army.

The best defense of Western Europe	September 1952 %	May 1953 %	June 1953 %
National armies	23	20	20
European army	32	39	29
Both	15	15	18
No opinion	30	26	33

Opinion on the European army was thus about the same as on the unification of Europe: so long as one remained on the level of general principles there was a dominant tendency (if not a majority) in France toward approval. Difficulties began and reservations appeared on the level of specific proposals: were the safeguards sufficient? Would not Germany revive her general staff and lead Europe into a new conflict over her lost territory? Would not France run the risk of seeing her vital interests sacrificed to those of Germany, in supporting the costs of a European policy, by having to default on her responsibilities in the French Union?

No additional clause put in to alleviate French fears about the Saar could ever appear unnecessary in any concrete agreement. Finally, the non-participation of Great Britain in the European system was also a subject for anxiety. The French army, of course, could not by its own strength prevent an invasion in case of Soviet aggression. It might be able to do so in the future with the help of allied armies, but at present even this was far from sure. Hence, no military arrangement currently feasible could ward off the greatest danger: i.e., an invasion of French territory. Thus emerged a special hypothesis on the military treaty; while its rejection might or not endanger the security of the country, its acceptance clearly did not insure it. If the threat were really urgent, the collective conscience might be mobilized, its attention might be focussed on the Soviet danger, and these doubts might disappear. But such was not the case. The danger was not focussed on a single adversary and the solution was thus not well-defined. Hence, for most Frenchmen, one conviction fatal to EDC remained strong: German rearmament, under any form, was a danger for France.

German Rearmament	July 1954
Is a danger under any form	56%
It depends on the form	24
No danger	5
No opinion	15
	100

The persistence of French distrust toward Germany, at the very moment when EDC was up for ratification, gave rise to violent apprehensions. Opinion was divided even on the chances of a general *understanding* with Germany. While a majority of Frenchmen were favorable to a German-French rapprochement, they accepted this with reservations and primarily with respect to pacific (not military) cooperation. Sociological analysis shows these favorable attitudes on German-French rapprochement to derive rather from a rational effort of comprehension than from instinctive reflexes. This effort was made more by men than by women; by employees, civil servants, managers and professional people rather than by workers and peasants; and, generally speaking, by those with a higher intellectual level. It was less frequent among former prisoners and deportees, as well as among older people.

It was felt that one could not bypass other stages on the way toward military cooperation. Understanding had to be realized first on the economic level, then on the cultural level, to encourage public acceptance on other levels:

July 1954
Fields in which Franco-German cooperation can be achieved (listed in order of facility)

	1st	2nd	3rd	4th	5th & 6th	No opinion	Total
Economic	38%	15%	10%	4%	2%	31%	100
Cultural	14	15	13	12	13	33	100
Technical	8	19	17	12	11	33	100
Political	6	10	7	10	29	38	100
Military	5	4	4	6	40	41	100
Financial	2	6	13	20	21	38	100

On the whole, the French public remained very divided on the specific question of German military participation in the defense of Western Europe. Responses on this question revealed the same attitudes and viewpoints as on the EDC project:

October 1954
Military participation of Germany in European defense

very favorable	7%
rather favorable	28
rather against	24
very much against	13
no opinion	28
	100

The European Defense Community

These are the fundamental data which explain public attitudes toward EDC. Moreover, the project was little known among the public for a long time, as is shown by a survey made in May 1953:

—21% had never heard anything about the project;
—52% did not know if the National Assembly had already ratified the treaty (and 8% wrongly believed it had been ratified);

— 6% wrongly believed that Germany did not participate,
and a third did not know whether she did;

—13% wrongly believed that Great Britain did participate
and 38% did not know whether she did.

It is clear that opinions formed on the basis of such scanty information about the essential features of EDC were likely to change once the actual provisions of the treaty were more widely publicized. Certainly fewer errors of prediction about EDC would have been made if the early lack of information among the public had been properly evaluated. This became clear at the period when the EDC finally entered the field of the collective conscience. This was during the summer of 1954, with the installation of M. Mendès-France, who pledged himself to submit the treaty to Parliament. Thereafter, at every hand, the problem was publicly discussed and the political parties fixed their positions. Several were divided and could not even maintain voting discipline among their deputies. The press echoed these difficulties daily. The leaders pressed their points of view, the journalists argued all the pros and cons, and finally, the public came to know the main lines of the treaty.

The dénouement is well-known: M. Mendès-France tried to obtain from France's partners guarantees in the form of additional protocols. But the Brussels Conference, which met for this purpose, failed. Parliament expressed its will by rejecting the treaty.

Two successive surveys make it possible to describe public opinion at critical junctures: in July (just after the installation of Mendès-France); and from August 19 to September 8 (before and after the Brussels Conference, and after the vote of the National Assembly.) The currents of opinion had crystallized and, between the two surveys, there was but a slight recession in the favorable attitudes towards EDC. While the official game was played out on the national and international levels, the French public retained their articulated views, with no apparent reaction to official developments.

Public opinion was the image of Parliamentary opinion at this particular moment. No current, pro or con, had the complete adherence of the public. Perplexity was great, and a third of the public abstained. But the other two thirds were equally divided for and against the treaty. On each side an important nucleus was more decidedly for or against. As it was easier to accept than to refuse, people who had no firmly settled opinion, seemed likely to rally to EDC.

Attitudes toward EDC	July 1954 %		August 19 & September 8, 1954 %	
definitely for	19		15	
slightly for	17		17	
Total for		36		32
slightly against	11		12	
definitely against	20		21	
Total against		31		33
No opinion		33		35
TOTAL		100		100

The absence of a favorable majority appeared to be the most important fact. And this was not the result of external pressure, or of opposing ideologies and foreign propaganda, but of a conflict between rational attitudes and affective impulses which divided the national conscience. Analysis of the various ideological stratifications within the electorate make this clear.

THE INFLUENCE OF IDEOLOGIES

It would be possible to prove that the division of public opinion was not homogenous according to sociological categories: that women were more hesitant than men; that the different generations did not have similar reactions; and mainly that various milieux reacted differently. But such analysis would, at bottom, only reflect the unequal distribution of ideological affiliations within the different sociological groups. For variation of opinion depended strictly on political attitudes in general.

The more settled the attitude of a party, the more strictly did its voters adhere to this attitude. This was the case with the Communist voters on the hostile side; and with the M.R.P. voters on the favorable side. Nevertheless, even within these two parties, there were some abstentions and a slight minority of opponents to the official position of the party.

Elsewhere, abstentions were very numerous, and a favorable majority appeared only among the Moderate party voters. Among the Socialists, R.G.R., Radicals, and U.D.S.R. the division of opinion was very clear. In short, public opinion showed no majority, either for or against EDC.

Attitudes toward EDC (according to expressed political preferences): August 19–September 8, 1954

	Communists	Socialists	R.P.F. (U.R.A.S.)	R.G.R.	Moderates	M.R.P.
	%	%	%	%	%	%
definitely for	3	15	22	19	25	30
slightly for	3	20	16	25	25	30
Total for	6	35	38	44	50	60
slightly against	9	15	11	16	12	7
definitely against	69	23	25	17	12	4
Total against	78	38	36	33	24	11
No opinion	16	27	26	23	26	29
TOTAL	100	100	100	100	100	100

One might try to evaluate the effect of communist propaganda against EDC on public opinion, and to speculate what the result would have been without this propaganda. This is of course purely theoretical, but it seems obvious that communist propaganda would have had no results, or results of little significance, if it had not been sown on ground ready to receive it. This propaganda emphasized feelings of distrust towards Germany, which were as deeply rooted in the national conscience in 1954 as they had been in the immediate postwar period.

Additional evidence is given by the voters' conception of the enemies of France. The Communists were almost the only ones to believe that the U.S. was France's enemy and that the USSR was not. The further one goes from Left to Right on the political spectrum, the more the USSR was considered an enemy; but an equal proportion in all parties considered Germany the enemy of their country:

June 1953 France's Enemy (according to expressed political preferences)

	Whole sample	Communists	Socialists	R.G.R.	M.R.P.	Moderates	R.P.F.
	%	%	%	%	%	%	%
USSR	17	5	16	23	23	21	32
Germany	16	14	14	20	17	14	19
U.S.A.	5	16	3	2	2	2	5

French diplomacy was very active after the rejection of EDC by the Parliament. A conference of Western European countries met in London; Canada and the U.S. were also represented. The result was the Accords of Paris, signed by the ministers of the six countries previously involved in EDC, with the addition of Great Britain. The Accords of Paris were approved at the end of December 1954 by the National Assembly, and in March by the Senate.

We do not yet have at our disposal studies which permit us to estimate the reactions of the French public towards the Accords of Paris. But we may assume that, to the extent that they were favorable, British and American guarantees to the new form of European association (W.E.U.) were certainly connected with this favorable reaction.

In any case, at the end of October 1954, the public preferred these new decisions to the former EDC. It had the feeling that this was not merely a simple military alliance, but a step towards European unification, to which it remained devoted. In this sense, the London Conference represented progress in the public mind.

General consideration of postwar French public opinion toward European defense gives the impression of stability and constancy. The opinions collected are parallel, if not identical, for almost ten years. French attititudes towards the EDC can best be understood in this context. These attitudes were not simple, and the public was sometimes uncertain that its own interests wholly coincided with the objectives of its allies. It had, often, the impression of being handled only as one anonymous element, just like Germany for instance, in a vast scheme of these allies. That is why it never approved without reservations American policy towards France.

Rightly or wrongly, French opinion could not think of German rearmament without manifesting the most violent fears. There was no majority at any time in favor of German rearmament, and the defeat of EDC is inscribed in the collective conscience, still hypersensitive after the three wars. The instinct for preservation remained strong on the eve of decision, the seriousness of which it could not ignore.

The apparent paradox is that this same public opinion declared itself favorable to the unification of Europe. It could not cut Germany out of the world map, and it admitted, without enthusiasm but with a cool mind, that Germany had to participate in a unified Europe. For France such a Europe automatically included

Great Britain (even if the latter, however, did not care to commit herself too deeply to the continent). Moreover, European unification involving Franco-German cooperation could only be realized in successive stages. The French public supported efforts toward economic integration. But it refused priority to military integration as a first objective, since this would not necessarily imply an acceptable European policy. French public opinion had, indeed, no aggressive ideas whatsoever; its hesitations arose from the imposed obligation to connect her own self-defense to a cause that was not necessarily her own. The common defense of Europe, in which France and Germany were to be the mainstays, could indeed threaten her very existence. The scheme seemed to settle her fate on the basis of an uncertain bet.

Considering the present state of world power relationships, the French know that they cannot assure their own defense. But, though conscious of the threat of Soviet power, they are not blinded by this threat; and they fear, above everything else, involvement in a military system which might imperil their peace and their independence.

The EDC defeat does not mean anything other than a refusal to impair this independence. It is not a negation of the "European idea", which is usually considered by Frenchmen in a different perspective. The stability of French public opinion during the last ten years shows how many needs, with which it is difficult to contend, are involved in the matter.

APPENDIX TO CHAPTER 5

Results of surveys cited in the text

(chronological order)

British and American opinions on the fate of post-war Germany.

Great Britain (September 1944)

Germany should be compelled to pay war damages she caused to the other nations: 88% for and 6% against

Would approve a plan for dismembering Germany: 56% would approve and 23% would disapprove.

Germany should be forbidden to have armaments and an army for a certain time: 93%, but 4% do not think it necessary. The time span selected is as follows:

	%
4 years at least	3
5 to 9 years	7
10 to 19 years	14
20 to 29 years	19
30 years and more	22
always	31

Great Britain (September 1945)

Feelings towards the German people:

	%
hostile	53 (among which hatred 21% and disgust 14%)
indifferent	11
sympathetic	25

Satisfied with the way Germany is treated today—55% and 25% dissatisfied.

United States (January 1944)

Should the peace treaty with Germany be harsher or easier than the Versailles peace?

	%
harsher	76
less harsh	8
don't know	16
	100

United States (September 1944)

A harsh treaty with Germany would better insure peace in Europe say 80% but 2% are for a moderate treaty.

June 1945

Do you think that the English, the Americans and the Russians intend to treat the German people very harshly?

	English %	Americans %	Russians %
in a very harsh way	48	9	87
not harsh enough	39	82	8
not decided	13	9	5
	100	100	100

September 1946

Of those who heard M. Byrnes' speech in Stuttgart (61%): 8% approved, 41% disapproved, 12% undecided.

December 1946   International Survey

Will Germany become a peaceful and democratic nation, or a warlike nation, which will start a new war?

	peaceful and democratic %	warlike %	undecided %
Netherlands	14	63	23
Canada	20	58	22
United States	22	58	20
Great Britain	23	43	36
Czechoslovakia	2	81	17

In France, think that Germany will become a democratic nation:

10% will become a pacific nation as against 63%
18% as against 55%
56% will try to start a new war as again 16%

March 1946: The Atlantic Pact

	%	among informed persons %
France should sign the Atlantic Pact	39	51
France should not sign	18	23
undecided	20	26
didn't hear anything about the Pact	23	—
	100	100

August 1950
In case of a war, on which side would your sympathy be?

	%
on the American side	52
on the Soviet side	13
undecided	35
	100

September 1952   *European unification*
Are you partisan of the efforts made for European unification?

	%
partisan	55
not partisan	16
undecided	29
	100

Should France, in your opinion, participate in a European government?

	%
yes	59
no	18
no opinion	23
	100

Such a government could be led into taking unfavorable decisions for a country, in particular for France. In such conditions, do you think that France should participate?

	%
yes	44
no	8
no opinion	48
	100

Motives of favorable attitudes toward European unification

	%
unity makes strength	14
better cooperation of Europe	11
widening of the market	8
economic interest of France	7
more strength in case of an aggression	7

Motives of hostile attitudes toward European unification:

	%
loss of liberty	27
subject of conflict resulting from disagreements between the participants	5
deplorable economic consequences for France	4

Attitudes towards the Schuman Plan

	%
Partisans of the Schuman Plan	46
Adversaries	12
Undecided	14
Didn't hear anything about the plan	28
	100

After explanations had been made of the nature and objectives of the Schuman Plan:

	%
declare themselves partisan	60
declare themselves adversaries	17
undecided	23
	100

Motives behind the favorable attitudes

	%
economic advantage for France	17
economic advantage for all the participating countries	11
first step towards the United States of Europe	11
unity makes strength	9

Motives behind the hostile attitudes

	%
France has no proper interest in participating in such a plan	5
fear participation in an imperialistic bloc leading to war	5
because Germany participates	5

The U.S. and USSR rivalry and war risks

	%
conflict (U.S. & USSR) is also our affair	56
it is not our affair	25
undecided	19
	100

	%
The French government has already sided with the West	67
The French government did not take a position	5
undecided	28
	100

If, in one year there might be a conflict, could the European armies and the U.S. forces prevent France from being invaded?

	%
Yes	22
No	45
No opinion	35
	100

June 1953   *European unification and war risks*

In case of war, could French forces prevent the invasion of French territory?

	%
yes	2
no	82
no opinion	16
	100

Could they prevent it with the help of allied forces?

	%
yes	43
no	16
no opinion	23
	100

Is it a good or a bad thing for France to participate in the Atlantic pact?

	%
a good thing	38
a bad thing	16
no opinion	46
	100

Besides the military question, are you for or against the idea of a union of Western European countries?

	June 1953 %	May 1953 %
for	65	70
against	13	10
no opinion	22	20
	100	100

Do you think it necessary for France to have an army, or isn't it important?

	%
absolutely necessary	56
quite important	21
not important	11
useless	7
no opinion	5
	100

January 1954   *Attitudes towards the European Coal and Steel Community*

Does the C.E.C.A. seem to you to serve the interests of all the European countries, or mainly the interests of one particular country; and of which country, in this case?

	%
the interest of all European countries	40
the interest of Germany	7.5
the interest of the U.S.	2.5
the interest of other countries	1.5
no opinion	22.5
do not know the C.E.C.A.	26
	100.

In your opinion, would it be a good idea to extend the powers of the C.E.C.A. to other fields than coal and steel; and in which fields for instance?

	%
good idea	33
bad idea	12
no opinion	29
do not know the C.E.C.A.	26
	100

An extension to the agricultural sector was mentioned most often by the public (16%).

July 1954   *Attitudes towards Germany and the Germans*

Through the 1914–1918 or 1939–1945 war:

	%	%
Have suffered damage		49*
have lost near-parents (father, mother, brother, sister, son, daughter, husband, wife, fiancé)	24	
had their home destroyed, plundered, or seriously damaged	29	
had been wounded themselves, or their health impaired	19	
Have suffered no damage		51
		100

* Some persons suffered several kinds of damage.

Do you think you have the right to pass judgments on Germany or on the Germans?

	%
yes	56
no	27
undecided	17
	100

What are, according to you, the good points and defects of the Germans?

good points	%
orderliness and discipline	36
industrious	36
energetic	17

defects	
cruelty, lack of humanity	37
sense of superiority	21
militarism	20
blind obedience	14
will power	10

Do the German people deeply love war?

yes	51
no	29
no opinion	20
	100

The atrocities committed by the Germans during the two last wars: are they true, minimized or exaggerated?

	1914–1918 war %	*1939–1945* war %
minimized	2	6
true	66	85
exaggerated	12	4
no opinion	20	5
	100	100

Could the concentration and extermination camps be created again?

	%
yes	61
no	9
no opinion	30
	100

Might France and Germany understand each other ultimately?

	%
yes	29
no	32
no opinion	39
	100

Would it be better for France for Germany to remain divided or for her to be reunified?

	%
divided	45
reunified	23
no opinion	32
	100

Do you accept the differentiation between a "good" and a "bad" German?

	%
accept it	62
do not accept it	28
no opinion	10
	100

Is the German mentality different today than during Hitler's time?

	%
yes	31
no	36
no opinion	33
	100

Do you have confidence in the signature of a treaty between France and Germany?

	%
confidence	24
no confidence	43
no opinion	33
	100

Would you have more or less confidence in a treaty signed with Germany than with England?

	%
more confidence in a treaty with England	44
the same	29
less confidence	7
no opinion	20
	100

July 1954   *Attitudes towards the French-German rapprochement in various sociological categories*

	For %	Against %
Total	54	23
Sex		
Men	62	22
Women	47	24
Age		
from 18 to 24 years	60	14
25 to 34	56	23
35 to 44	52	26
45 to 54	59	23
55 to 64	53	26
65 and above	50	25
Have gone to Germany as		
prisoners, deported	54	29
fighters	65	23
tourists, business men	75	14
Profession		
farmers	43	27
workers	49	28
employees, civil servants	64	17
cadres, industrials, liberal professions	70	17

Cultural level

primary	46	28
high primary	63	20
technical	63	17
secondary	73	15
superior	81	9

October 1954   After the EDC rejection

Is the London Conference, according to you, a mere military alliance or a step towards the unification of Western Europe?

%

mere military alliance	17
step towards the unification of Europe	52
no opinion	31
	100

(If it is rather a step towards the unification of Europe), do you think that the London conference goes further or less far toward European unification than the former EDC, or is it the same?

%

in London: it goes further	23
in London: it goes less far	10
the same	8
no opinion	11
	52

If a choice were possible, what would you prefer: the decisions of the London conference or the former EDC?

%

the London decisions	35
the former EDC	8
no opinion	57
	100

Were you, in general, for or against the attempts of unification of Western Europe?

%

for	62
against	9
no opinion	29
	100

6 : A Tableau of the French Press

JEAN JOSÉ MARCHAND

It is difficult to measure the direct effect of the press on political opinion. Two Paris dailies, *le Figaro* and *Combat*, conducted an inquiry to learn the views of their readers on EDC. In each case, a large minority of those consulted showed themselves hostile to the position of the newspaper they were reading every morning. What can be measured is the way in which the press tries to impose different points of view on the public. There are in France today 94 daily papers, a number of weeklies, and some monthly papers. We have undertaken to analyze closely their activity regarding EDC and the results are presented herein.

The Paris Dailies

The Paris dailies number thirteen. Eight appear in the morning. The following table gives the circulation (in thousands) of these papers on the important dates of the discussions about EDC.

Specialists on journalistic matters in France state that a paper is not a "good investment" unless its sale exceeds 175,000 copies (below this number, there is no profit on the advertising fees which would permit it to exist). Therefore, among the morning papers, only three are "good investments": *L'Aurore, Le Figaro, Le Parisien libéré*.

With the evening papers the situation is somewhat different: to *France-Soir* should be added *Le Monde* which has no photo-

	October 1950	February 1952	May 1952	November 1953	April 1954	August 1954
Aurore (AM) *	333	332	334	420	432	455
Combat (AM)	77	66	63	61	61	58
Croix (PM)	164	164	160	151	151	157
Figaro (AM)	424	453	434	458	468	476
France-Soir (PM)	670	810	742	990	1050	991
Franc-Tireur (AM)	183	141	143	125	129	119
Humanité (AM)	220	200	170	173	171	154
Information (PM)	20	36	32	32	34	47
Libération (AM)	130	126	124	129	127	125
Monde (AM)	163	151	150	155	160	165
Parisien libéré (AM)	485	517	510	675	652	654
Paris-Presse-L'Intransigeant (PM)	337	205	190	177	161	143
Populaire (AM)	32	30	28	25	25	25

* AM means morning paper, PM evening paper.

engraving expenses, and *La Croix* whose clientele is mostly composed of regular subscribers (country priests and provincial people of influence), which fact allows it some financial security. Therefore, we should note the very important fact that the other *seven* of the daily papers exist only by virtue of political rather than commercial initiative. (*L'Humanité* and *Le Populaire* send out Sunday editions whose circulation greatly exceeds that on weekdays. This, however, does not balance the budgets of these two dailies, which are full of appeals to their readers for donations.) Five Paris dailies have seen their subscriptions drop: *Combat, Franc-Tireur, l'Humanité, Paris-Presse-L'Intransigeant, le Populaire.* Three are about stationary: *La Croix, Libération, le Monde.* Five have swelled their circulation: *L'Aurore, le Figaro, France-Soir, L'Information,* and *Le Parisien libéré.*

METHODS OF STUDY OF THE PARIS DAILY PAPERS

For our study of press activity, we chose the six special periods when what might be called "information needs" put EDC in the foreground.

(1) the French proposal of EDC in October 1950;
(2) the Parliamentary debate on foreign policy in February 1952;
(3) the signing of the treaty in May 1952;
(4) the second parliamentary debate on foreign policy in November 1953;

(5)   Marshall Juin's recall from command after his public stand against EDC on April 1, 1954, followed by incidents during a ceremony at the Arc de Triomphe (M. Pléven, National Defense Minister, was slapped in the face and M. Laniel, President of the Council, was kicked in the leg);

(6)   the last month, August 1954: the search for a compromise, the failure of the Brussels conference, and the final debate ending with the "guillotining" of the EDC.

The morning papers are placed first, in alphabetical order, and then the evening papers in the same order. When a newspaper does not have any admitted leanings, we have characterized it with the customary reservations.

L'Aurore: This newspaper would like to be the spokesman for the "small businessman". From the time the EDC was proposed, Robert Bony (pseudonym of the Director, Robert Lazurick) asked that a politically united Europe be created before trying to give it an army. Later he accepted EDC on one condition, that Germany not have the right to produce its own munitions. As time went on, there were additional reservations: France risked cutting herself off from the French Union, and Germany had territorial claims in the East which the French had no reason to support (February 18, 1952). *L'Aurore* remained strongly pro-American; it was later to attack violently the alleged Fechteler Report when it was published by *Le Monde.* (This attack was based on an apocryphal report, supposedly expressing the opinion of the Pentagon, which recommended an evacuation of Europe by the Americans in case of a sudden attack from the East). On May 24, 1952, the paper seemed to join the pro-EDC group on condition that certain guarantees be made to France. On November 17, 1953, Bony-Lazurick enumerated them: a) French economic control of the Saar; b) the participation of Great Britain; c) watchful inspection of German rearmament; d) election of a House of Nations (as in the Bidault plan) which would control the EDC army. Two days later, the noted writer Jules Romains took a clear stand for the European army—whose defeat, according to him, would set off independent German rearmament.

But the next morning, General Weygand opposed this stand on the political level (restriction of French sovereignty) and on the military level (inefficiency). He called for a "federation" with limited aims (standardization of arms, for instance). From then on, *L'Aurore* allowed its readers to choose between the two points of view.

One of its contributors, Henry Bénazet, published openly "anti-EDC" articles and from the time of the Juin affair, the silences of this newspaper about "supranationalism" were quite marked. On April 6, 1954, it printed a page devoted to General Bradley's arguments and on the opposite page the arguments of the Parliamentary Socialists who had just published a pamphlet opposing the pro-EDC position of their Party's executive committee. On July 2, 1954, it published a striking article by Edouard Herriot against the treaty: it is the end of our sovereignty; such an army is a bad thing; reunited Germany will not be bound by the actions of the Bonn government, and Russia will attract it more than the West. On July 13th, it approved the protocols proposed at Brussels; from then on, the paper insisted only on the necessity of not giving up the Atlantic Alliance and not allowing Communist votes to be determining factors.

Thus the position of *L'Aurore* cannot be defined by a formula: it seemed to lean toward an "alternative solution" (*solution de réchange*). The EDC seems to have shocked the basic nationalism of its readers; but these same readers feared "playing into Communist hands". Hence profound uncertainty in this matter.

Combat: It is difficult to define the color of this newspaper. From 1944 to 1946 it was the spokesman for the intelligentsia with "democratic" leanings (the intelligentsia with anti-democratic leanings being out of action, owing to collaboration with the occupation and the postwar disapproval surrounding Right-Wing ideologies). After two changes of staff, it kept its intellectual complexion as the unofficial organ of "Left Wing Moralists" without any very clearly defined line. It was commonly assumed to live on subsidies from its director, a Tunisian businessman, M. Smadja.

Beginning on October 30, 1950, the editorial writer stated that "our country must be the link between the two antagonists" (U.S. and U.S.S.R.). *Combat's* opposition to EDC kept growing as time went on. It became one of the rare newspapers which tried to use the Fechteler report as an argument against the European army.

On May 26, 1952, an article signed by Marcel Gimont denounced "American pressure" and "insufficient guarantees". The next day, Jean Fabiani wrote "The European army is nothing more or less than the *Wehrmacht* . . . Hitler's Europe without Hitler." Two days later, Marcel Gimont concluded: "The United States is handing France over to Germany". In 1953, *Combat* published a great number of articles against the EDC, signed by Senator Michel Debré (Gaullist), by editorial writer Jean Fabiani, and by General Niessel. The latter took principally the military point of view. Michel Debré insisted on: injured patriotism; the rebirth of the *Wehrmacht*; French weakening in North Africa where the Americans are based. Jean Fabiani generally used more vivid arguments: the Six-Nation Europe is an artificial monster; the French army is going to be replaced by a supra-national coalition directed by an American general staff; this is a crusade preached in Washington; there is no majority in the French Parlement in favor of such a crusade; its directors are cosmopolitan technocrats; it will be a European SS corps. *Combat* took Marshal Juin's side against the government. On April 5th, it published a questionnaire on EDC:

(1)   Under present conditions would you feel like allowing Parlement complete freedom to make binding agreements for France?

(2)   Are you in favor of a referendum (national and official) on this problem? Do you feel at least a partial rearmament of Germany is necessary?

(3)   If you feel this rearmament necessary, do you think the EDC limits the danger of it?

(4)   Do you think, no matter how much the unification of Europe is needed, that France should set aside its sovereignty to the extent of giving up control of its army command?

(5)   Toward what solution should the government's efforts be pledged?

A double page is devoted to the arguments, "pro" and "con": the attitude of Great Britain; the formation of French military units; the relations between Europe and the French Union; the control of German rearmament; the real intentions of the U.S.S.R.; the constitutionality of the treaties; the economic consequences; the exact degree of military efficiency; the alternative solutions.

The results appeared in the issue of July 12th: 1035 answers of various shades of opinion, quite a number of which were favorable to the EDC. During this time, numerous occasional contributors, like Professor Bernard Lavergne, who attacked "Vatican Europe", continued the campaign against the treaty. J. Schneider, a Councilor of the French Union, proposed negotiating the simultaneous withdrawal of the Americans and the Soviets to their own frontiers; Jacques Soustelle, Gaullist leader, asked for negotiations with the East; and lastly, from Albert Bayet to General de Gaulle, and even in the statement signed by General Weygand, the German danger and the protection of the French army were the things most discussed, especially in the final weeks between the Brussels conference and the rejection of EDC.

Let it be noted, in any case, that this anti-Germanism was not based on the same grounds by all writers: some wanted to negotiate with the East; others simply wanted to protect the national army.

Le Figaro: This newspaper is the great spokesman of the "Moderates". At first it was very reserved, fearing that a "great idea" was serving to conceal French hedging on the necessity of a German contribution to the defense of the West. (The same view of EDC was attributed by many observers to Pentagon leaders in 1950.) From 1952 on, its editorial staff became completely pro-EDC. Raymond Aron, especially, campaigned against any neutralization of Germany which would create a military vacuum in the center of Europe. François Mauriac, in 1952, "does not see any other alternative" to the policy of the EDC, since Germany otherwise would have possibilities for playing off the Soviets against the free world. While André Siegfried and Jean Schlumberger were raising their voices against those who admit defeat before they start in any economic rivalry with Germany, Clarence Streit recommended a direct federation of the NATO countries with the United States and Canada. Raymond Aron predicted, on November 20, 1953, that to rearm Germany would force the Soviet Union to propose general negotiations. With all of these contributors, common anxiety about Communism seemed to determine their adherence to the EDC. On the question of German rearmament, *Figaro* answered that the alternative solutions would be more favorable to the Germans in the long run.

At the moment of the Brussels negotiations, there was vacillation. However, on August 17, 1954, Raymond Aron, after moderate criticism of the treaty (he implied loss of sovereignty and complicated relations with the French Union) advised the ratification in order to barter in the future with the U.S.S.R. Whereupon there appeared also: an article by Professor René Courtin, president of the Movement for European Union; a petition of 192 teachers in favor of the EDC; and especially a striking article by Robert Schuman (August 19th) against the protocols proposed in Brussels by the head of the government, Mendès-France. The day before the rejection vote, Raymond Aron showed that Churchill had the alternative solution in his pocket but would not present it until Europe was on the edge of the abyss so that England's good offices would seem more valuable to the United States. This position made it possible to foresee *Figaro's* rallying to any alternative solution of "Atlantic" inspiration. As a matter of fact, in spite of varying shades of opinion as between strong partisans of EDC (like its director Brisson) and moderate supporters (like its columnist Aron), *Figaro* never once failed to put Atlantic solidarity above every other consideration.

Franc-Tireur: The Independent Socialist *Franc-Tireur* followed a policy very close to that of the Socialist executive committee. Their general thesis: the European army is useful if it is a step forward toward unification of the continent and a European government. But on February 12, 1952 the editorial writer, Charles Ronsac, objected that there had been no solution of the problem of the German military caste nor of that of the lost Eastern territories. He came out in favor of a four-power conference. In 1953, *Franc-Tireur* rallied to the European Army because those opposing it were also hostile to the political community (Nationalists and Communists). It called Marshal Juin to task for his stand. At the time of the Brussels conference, the editorial line was uncertain. The paper published an open letter by André Philip which was entirely hostile to the proposed Mendès-France compromise. During the debate, *Franc-Tireur* demanded the opening of negotiations. After the vote of rejection, it attacked the "bewildering abstention of the government" in this matter and complained that the 99 Communist votes had decided the result. This newspaper devoted to this problem only the articles by Charles Ronsac and the open letter by André Philip. This indicates that it was more opposed to the enemies of EDC than in favor of the treaty itself.

L'Humanité: Though it is the French Communist Party organ, *L'Humanité* did not, for all that, center its campaign around the class struggle but around the theme of German danger, to which it tied indissolubly the "struggle for peace". On November 26, 1950 the paper stated: "We are ready to agree with everybody in order to oppose the German rearmament". Thereafter, not a day went by without two or three columns, and sometimes more, devoted to this problem with large headlines and constant appeals to the fighting wing of the party. Delegations, including always non-Communist members, were sent to Parlement, and the statements of each deputy were immediately recorded. They appealed to former prisoners of war, to a mother whose two children were burned in the church at Oradour, to the anti-EDC appeal of Deputy Heuillard who died about this time (a "victim of his deportation") etc. On November 2, 1953, the struggle against German rearmament was explained in the four following arguments:

(1) The EDC is the vengeful Wehrmacht which would take back Kaliningrad (Königsberg), Alsace and Lorraine;

(2) French military service would be under the control of foreigners, especially Nazis;

(3) The Bonn government would start things, just as South Korea provoked North Korea;

(4) The EDC prepares the way for the supremacy of German trusts over those of France.

On November 19, Laurent Casanova, member of the Central Committee, explained the necessity of "national and peaceful unity" with the group led by Pierre André (Lorraine deputy) who was defending the interest of the French middle class against the German middle class. On the same basis General Malleret-Joinville approved Marshal Juin; and on April 8, 1954, General de Gaulle's press conference was printed with laudatory remarks. On

April 10, 1954, however, there appeared at last a Marxist-type argument: "The EDC will work toward enriching the trusts. It will justify deplacement of workers. It is a strong fortress against nationalization. The campaign against the European army is to be waged jointly with that against the 'damned war' (in Indo-China)."

During the last month, atrocity photos from the last war were published. Statements were made by very different personalities. *L'Humanité* reprinted an article by the Gaullist spokesman Jacques Soustelle: "German rearmament, with or without EDC, is WAR—put off for a while but still near". "Harass the deputies," Pierre André recommended. Even the petition of 14 very influential people (normally hate-symbols in *L'Humanité*), signed by Marshal Weygand, was reprinted and publicized. On August 25, 1954, *L'Humanité* recapitulated all the usable arguments: "France is abandoning its own national responsibilities for the good of the (European) community"; "Germany predominates in the EDC (33% of the votes, as opposed to 24% for France)"; "the EDC is under the orders of the American army command"; "our army is chopped into two stumps"; "we shall not be able to determine the number of troops we can send overseas"; "our soldiers will be obliged to wear the European uniform"; "there will no longer be any French military secrets hidden from the Hitler generals"; "the constitution has been emptied of its substance, since it is the Council which will fix the military budget for each state and will distribute the ranks"; "the Germans will be bivouacked on French national soil"; "our industry is being handed over to foreign competitors"; "we should not be able to make any international agreements in contradiction to the treaty"; "we shall no longer have any judiciary unity, since infractions committed by the European forces will no longer depend on French courts"; "there are secret protocols."

L'Humanité is the newspaper which gave the most space to EDC, but always called it "German rearmament". This newspaper did not have to evolve in the direction of the traditional Nationalists and the Gaullists; from the beginning it had stood on their ground.

Libération: The Progressive (crypto-Communist) newspaper *Libération* followed very exactly the campaign of *l'Humanité*, but its attack was less vigorous and there was no daily dosage on the subject. The danger of German rearmament (except for a few rare allusions to economics) was the main argument developed without letup.

Le Parisien Libéré: The most important French morning daily, *Le Parisien Libéré*, has no political color. It did not take any set line except by giving much space to General de Gaulle's press conferences, for which this newspaper showed great respect on every occasion. Careful reading of the commentaries on foreign policy do not reveal any leanings. There is one critical opinion on February 18, 1952 (signed by Robert de Saint-Jean): "The French have too much tendency to collect papers which are a mockery of reality. German rearmament is an inescapable reality, no matter what treaties surround it."

Le Populaire: The organ of the S.F.I.O. is more a guidance bulletin for Socialist Militants of the Paris region rather than a genuine newspaper. Reserved at first, accepting the European army only "with a heavy heart", this paper finally declared itself (on October 30, 1950) against the "pedants of neutrality". (This was a reference to Maurice Duverger and the journalists of *le Monde*). But its attitude remained careful. In 1952, Guy Mollet, general secretary of the S.F.I.O., favored EDC in order to prevent an independent German army. In May, the Party took a stand and *le Populaire* defined its attitude, which did not vary thereafter, as pro-EDC, with the following restrictions; a) negotiations of the four powers; b) no national German army; c) American guarantees; d) special agreement with Great Britain.

Sometimes there was a feeling of party unrest. Though only the stand of the Party's Executive Committee can normally be expressed in *le Populaire* because of the 1944 directive prohibiting organized factions, the debates at meetings where different motions were opposed were published in their entirety, with all the arguments. Distrust of Germany and a tendency to look toward Great Britain (or at least the Labour Party) rather than the United States are often shown in this paper.

La Croix: This evening paper, official organ of French Catholicism, stayed absolutely neutral until 1953. On November 20, 1953

Father Emile Gabel, its director, openly took sides: it is necessary to "get around the evil" (of German rearmament); we should not therefore "torpedo a great idea and perhaps our only hope". The Academician, Robert d'Harcourt, wrote articles favoring the treaty. However, in August 1954, an article by Joseph Folliet opened a debate in which the participants were Jacques Soustelle, General Béthouart, Jules Romains, Pierre Le Brun, Alfred Coste-Floret, René Capitant, Gaston Tessier, General de Monsabert, Maurice Byé, Georges Vedel, Francois Perroux, Robert d'Harcourt, Alfred Grosser. The morning after the rejection vote, Father Gabel declared that he was rather pro-EDC. On the whole, while remaining very careful and reserving the right for its readers to have an opposing view, la Croix appeared favorable to the treaty.

France-Soir: This is the most important evening paper, with the largest daily circulation. Until 1952, along with the rest of the French press, this paper had certain reservations to make about German rearmament. From 1953 on, it decided to stand for absolute neutrality.

L'Information: This is a very peculiar case. *L'Information* is the only daily paper with a limited circulation which grew in size and circulation during the period which we are studying. It changed its format and added more pages; at the same time, there was a gradual development in its stand on the EDC. (Some connection between these two facts has been perceived by various Paris observers.)

In 1950, it published open letters with opposite views by Deputy Gérard Jouve (anti-EDC) and Paul Reynaud (pro-EDC). But the newspaper shortly thereafter became a vigorous opponent of the treaty. It appealed right and left, to all political figures except the Communists (who were developing very different arguments): e.g. opening its pages to Palewski (Gaullist), Naegelen and Daniel Mayer (Socialists), Daladier, Plaisant and Bastid (Radicals), etc. Thus (on May 17, 1952) M. Jules Moch declared that Chancellor Adenauer was not representative and that there should be negotiations with the Russians. In 1953, *l'Information* changed to a 14-page paper, made more emphatic attacks and published all petitions against the EDC. Its director, André Bollack, wrote: "If the EDC is a straitjacket for Germany, look after it yourselves, Anglo-Americans" (October 31, 1953). Its guest writers wrote: "The treaty means the end of the French nation" (Philippe Barrés, Gaullist deputy); "the end of the French Union" (Capitant, Gaullist leader); an opportunity for Germany to start war in the East (various writers).

On November 18, 1953, M. Lanet (U.D.S.R. deputy) gave other reasons for his opposition: the EDC is an economic problem; we shall be beaten by other nations in contract bids for armaments and textiles. (See the chapter by Jacques Vernant, in this volume, for exposition of this point.)

But in May 1954, *l'Information* changed again. Two facts determined its attitude: the iron and steel interests obtained from the government the necessary credits to stand up to German competition without any loss; and M. Laniel was replaced by M. Mendès-France, whose exact intentions were not well known. On August 14, 1954, *l'Information* rallied to the idea of a compromise EDC. On the 24th, M. Paul Reynaud was interviewed again as were other pro-EDC persons of note. On September 1st, this paper proposed "reconciliation and redress".

Le Monde: At first, *le Monde*, the evening paper read by political and parliamentary groups, took a stand which was labeled "neutralist". On October 26, 1950, the first reaction of this paper's directors can be summed up in the following sentence by Jacques Fauvet: "For many people, (the future army) means a sort of neutrality which does not dare say its name. Thus it is that, while there are no neutralists anywhere, there is neutralism everywhere." The direction taken by the treaty negotiations did not satisfy *le Monde*. In 1952, it laid special emphasis on the absence of England from the EDC; on the "German wish" to recover territories in the East; on French obligations in Indo-China. On February 16 its columnist Maurice Duverger proposed, for example, linking the question of rearmament with that of German unification; only if the unity of a neutralized Germany were not brought about would a European army be formed. In May, *le Monde* published the so-called "Fechteler Report" whose contents tended to persuade French public opinion that the Americans did not believe in the efficacy of a European army, their strategy foreseeing a mass withdrawal in case of war. This incident brought about the resignation of the editorial writer, Rémy Roure, who moved over to the pro-EDC *Figaro* (which broke many lances with *le Monde*). "To sign is not the same as to ratify": this is the line which *le Monde* took the day after the signing of the treaty.

From 1953 on, there is a notable increase in the number of open letters by various people of note: two out of three among these are unfavorable to EDC. On the other hand, *le Monde* allowed M. Jean Monnet to answer the hostile statement by General de Gaulle. For M. Monnet and the partisans of the treaty, the General's policy of "a great alliance" would end in the reconstruction of an independent German army. The opponents of EDC answered with a barrage: the problem of the Saar has not been settled; the treaty is not constitutional; the French Union should come before the European Union; we do not have the strength to fight Germany on the economic level; this army is ineffectual in a military sense; the Soviets have not aggressive intentions; only West Germany is signed up.

Defining the stand of this newspaper even more clearly, Maurice Duverger wrote (on November 18, 1953) that within the EDC there was a new popular front—which would give soldiers to Germany while depriving the French army of its independence. Germany would withdraw from the European community as soon as it was armed and would try to reconquer its unity by force. EDC is the war for Leipzig and Koenigsberg. (The clear echo evoked was: "Why die for Danzig?") At the least, he concluded, it would be a means of recruiting soldiers to maintain order and to check the Communist party; hence, a "police for Europe." Moderating this extremist position, *le Monde's* editorial writer André Fontaine, while not hostile to the Bidault Plan (for a European Parlement with two Houses), demanded at once a referendum on the European army.

On April 18th, Sirius (pen-name of *le Monde's* editor, Hubert Beuve-Méry) asked that the *status quo* be maintained. During the entire month of April, the ratio of "open letters" was ten unfavorable to the EDC for every single one favoring it; the latter, moreover, were mainly defensive. (One author, M. Legaret, merely complained that certain *anticédistes* were treating their opponents as "collabos"—the colloquial pejorative for collaborators with the Germans). The anti-EDC action of *le Monde* did not let up until August 15th. One editorial writer, "seeking for the lesser evil", asked the U.S.S.R. to give guarantees of peace. On August 18th, Sirius wrote that since everybody was against German rearmament, there should be a final negotiation; on the 24th his editorial called for "careful control of Germany".

Paris-Presse-L'Intransigeant: This "general information" evening paper is considered somewhat colored by Center-Right Wing opinions. At first very cautious, *Paris-Presse-l'Intransigeant* contented itself with presenting opposing deputies in its open letter columns: Robert Lecourt (M.R.P.) believed that independent French rearmament is beyond our means and pronounced himself "pro-EDC"; Loustaunau-Lacau (Peasant Party) declared that he did not want to die for Koenigsberg. (See the echo of this theme by Duverger in *le Monde* above).

In May 1952, this paper seemed to take sides. A long article by Jean Jacques Servan-Schreiber (director of *l'Express* and close colleague of Mendès-France) said: "the EDC is an act of courage and great politics", for to "want to break up German strength is a dream like neutrality." He concluded: "Our sole chance of remaining free is in the union of all forces in Europe."

In 1953, the editorials stood out against nationalism, the enemy of a United Europe. *Paris-Presse l'Intransigeant* was, indeed, one of the rare papers to criticize Marshal Juin for having rebelled against the government. During the final month, the editor specifically attacked the Communists. On August 28th, he thus summarized the impending vote on EDC: the choice proposed to Europe is integration or disintegration. However, these statements were never visible in the headlines; *Paris-Presse l'Intransigeant* was in favor of EDC, but discreetly.

Daily Newspapers in the Provinces

We have counted 81 daily papers in the provinces, *not including* those of Corsica, Africa, and the bilingual newspapers in Alsace whose editorials are sometimes in German. This number would be increased if we were to count as an additional newspaper each edition which bears a different title (For example, *Le Lorrain* is the Moselle edition of *l'Est Républicain*). We have coupled these "double" newspapers together in our comments.

CIRCULATION AND INFLUENCE

The circulation of a paper does not necessarily measure influence in the provinces any more than it does in Paris. We must, however, emphasize one important point: No daily paper appearing outside of Paris has national influence, such as the *Manchester Guardian* has in England.

The table below gives the average circulation (in thousands) of newspapers which published more than 50,000 copies a day during the three years important for this debate: 1952, 1953, 1954. The political attitudes noted here are based on the personal evaluation of this writer.

Newspaper	Region	Political Attitude	Circulation (add 000) 1952	1953	1954
Allobroges	Grenoble	Communist	88	81	72
L'Alsace	Mulhouse	Center	85	84	87
Courrier de l'Est	Angers	Moderate	88	89	90
Dauphiné Libéré	Grenoble	Center	225	230	243
Dépèche	Saint-Etienne	M.R.P.	60	57	58
Dépèche du Midi	Toulouse	Radical	217	232	238
Dernières Nouvelles	Strasbourg	Moderate	128	124	131
Echo-Liberté	Lyon	Moderate	60	61	60
Est-Républicain	Nancy	Moderate	204	202	211
Liberté	Lille	Communist	65	74	77
Liberté du Massif Central	Clermont	Moderate	56	61	61
Marseillaise	Marseilles	Communist	86	107	105
Le Méridional-la France	Marseilles	Moderate	120	114	102
Midi-libre	Montpellier	Center Left Wing	140	141	151
Montagne	Clermont	Center Left Wing	115	116	120
Nice-Matin	Nice	Center	127	125	132
Nord-Matin	Lille	Socialist	159	159	167
Nouvelle République	Bordeaux	Socialist & Radical	98	98	101
Nouvelle-République	Tours	Center	225	221	226
Ouest-France	Rennes	M.R.P.	444	460	482
Paris-Normandie	Rouen	Center Left Wing	137	146	146

Newspaper	Region	Political Attitude	Circulation (add 000)		
			1952	1953	1954
Progrès de Lyon	Lyons	Center	305	308	319
Provençal	Marseilles	Socialist & Radical	224	222	219
Républicain lorrain	Nancy	Moderate	152	152	158
République du centre	Orléans	Radical	58	57	60
Résistance de l'Ouest	Nantes	Moderate	77	79	80
Sud-Ouest	Bordeaux	Moderate	300	285	200
Télégramme	Brest	Center	101	102	106
Tribune	Saint-Etienne	Moderate	63	62	68
Union	Rheims	Union	126	129	137
Voix du Nord	Lille	Moderate & with Gaullist leanings	296	309	310

It should be noted that the average sales of the large regional dailies remain very constant.

Method of Study of the Provincial Dailies: We chose, as a "test week" of EDC attitudes, the week which began right after the Brussels conference and ended with the vote of rejection in the National Assembly. During this period, all those who had taken sides made a last effort, giving the arguments which seemed to them most pertinent.*

The Place of EDC in the Provincial Press: To judge the place given to EDC by the provincial press problem, one must distinguish two different aspects:

a) *Information:* there was wide and detailed coverage during the last week. It is exceptional in the French provincial press that any single problem should, as did EDC, take up most of the columns of the front page *for eight days in a row.*

b) *Commentary:* On this point the provincial press cannot compare with the Paris press. As we shall see below, editorials on EDC had disappeared in many of the newspapers which had decided to remain neutral; in a majority of the other papers, the problem was given only limited editorial space.

* We should like to thank M. Jacques Kayser for his information, advice and newspaper collections which were especially useful to us at this point.

GENERAL CHARACTERISTICS OF PROVINCIAL PRESS ATTITUDES

A certain number of facts emerge from the general analysis of the provincial press: 30 provincial dailies took no position at all on EDC (eight of these being in the class exceeding 50,000 daily circulation). Of the 15 dailies explicitly opposed to EDC, 12 were Communist papers and 3 were Gaullist papers. In addition there were 6 dailies, of various political persuasion, which were opposed to EDC in the sense that they insisted upon the advantages of some substitute solution (*les solutions de rechange*). On the other side, 18 dailies explicitly supported EDC (of these 7 in the class of 50,000 daily circulation) and 9 were discreetly favorable—i.e., they printed mainly pro-EDC letters, but without editorial commentary. On both sides of the issue were three dailies which regularly printed roughly equivalent amounts of material pro and con. (See the appendix to this article for the details of the foregoing summary.)

Our study suggests these conclusions:

(1) On the whole the provincial press took a much less decided stand than the Paris press. Most of the newspapers seemed afraid of losing some of their readers if they ventured to speak too frankly on this question.

(2) However, the specific weight of "anti-EDC" newspapers, among the non-Communist ones, was much less than the weight of the "pro-EDC" newspapers.

(3) Nevertheless, the general statements developed in the provincial press were more or less defensive answers to "anti-EDC" arguments. The haunting fear of Germany kept cropping up in all the articles either for or against the EDC. Only now and then a rare newspaper emphasized the fact that the EDC was a *defensive* army in the minds of its proponents. No one upheld its military value. Reading the majority of provincial articles favoring the EDC, *one might think that the EDC had been invented to patrol Germany.*

To summarize the matter: even though the provincial press did not take a stand in this debate except very cautiously, and even though most papers observed a benevolent neutrality about the treaty, the mass of press content was dominated by the question of German rearmament, for historical reasons which are easily understandable. And this was the battleground chosen by the opponents of EDC.

Political, Labor and Management Weeklies

The political weeklies are only a very small part of the French weekly press. They are feeble compared to *Paris-Match* and *Radar* which have, respectively, a circulation of about a million and 600,000. Among the genuinely political weeklies, *Le Bulletin de Paris* has a circulation of about 35,000 and *France-Observateur* only barely exceeds this number. (The two categories compare about the way that *Life* and *Look* compare with *The Nation* and *New Republic* in the U.S.A.)

However, the political weeklies are said to have a widespread influence among members of parliament, while the political influence of the big picture weeklies is regarded as nil. The figures given below are, moreover, the number of copies printed and not the number sold. It is difficult to know the latter. We therefore give the following table (figures in thousands) with many reservations.

		Copies Printed (add 000)	
Weekly	*Political Attitude*	*1953*	*1954*
Aspects de la France	Monarchist (Maurras type)	30	28
Aux Ecoutes	Center	67	66
Bulletin de Paris	Moderate (Center-Right)	31	35
Carrefour	Moderate (Somewhat Gaullist)	75	63
France-Observateur	Neutralist	30	48
Express	"Left" (Mendès-France)	64	122
Rassemblement	Gaullist	30	25
Réforme	Protestant	20	22
Rivarol	Neo-Fascist	45	44
Témoignage chrétien	Left-Wing (Catholic)	74	71

We did not find any special attention to the EDC treaty in the weeklies devoted to the theater, art or literature; in the sports weeklies; or in the feminine weeklies. *L'Humanité-Dimanche* and *Le Populaire-Dimanche*, which mirror exactly the attitudes of those two daily newspapers already analyzed, are omitted here. *La Vie Catholique* (with M.R.P. leanings) remained neutral on the subject of the EDC. Soundings taken in various issues of

Paris-Match, France-Dimanche, Radar, Points de Vue, Noir et Blanc, and the other picture magazines showed that these weeklies help positions in general only vaguely "pro-Atlantic". It remains therefore to consider the weeklies listed in our table. Their respective positions may be characterized as follows:

Aspects de la France: Traditional nationalist position—"Eternal Germany", French sovereignty, protection of the Army.

Aux Ecoutes: "Against the German EDC"; for an alternative solution.

Bulletin de Paris: Against the EDC because: a) it touches our sovereignty; b) the French will be crushed by it economically and financially; c) it would be ineffectual. This weekly came out for General Weygand's alternative solution (issue of January 22, 1954): creation of an armaments bureau and a bureau of combined forces under the direction of NATO and of a council of the defense ministers, including those of England, Denmark and Norway.

Carrefour: Mostly against the EDC, but for a United Europe; the paper restated the Gaullist arguments for an alternative solution.

France-Observateur: Opposed to EDC. We should negotiate with the Russians; the guarantees are not realistic; there is danger in a moral order upheld by German troops.

L'Express: "The editorial staff of *l'Express* is divided on this affair" (August 28, 1954). It took no stand.

Le Rassemblement: Against the EDC. It would mean giving an army to Germany which has none and which is claiming Eastern territories; it would mean increasing unemployment in France to "equalize" employment elsewhere in Europe ("la péréquation des chomages"); it would mean the end of French sovereignty; the plan leaves Great Britain out. On January 4, 1952, this paper made an alternative proposal: a European federation with an elected assembly.

Réforme: Semi-official weekly of French Protestantism. Rather for than against the EDC: for the sake of the ideal of a United States of Europe.

Rivarol: For the EDC; necessity of a United Europe to resist communism.

Témoignage chrétien: Against the EDC: it means German rearmament and the control of French politics by the Pentagon. We should first construct a politically united Europe.

THE WEEKLIES OF THE LABOR GROUPS

The following list gives the most important weeklies with their political attitudes and affiliations:

Weekly	Politics	Printing	re EDC
Vie Ouvrière	Communist	260,000	against
Le Peuple	C.G.T. (Communist)	125,000	against
Syndicalisme	C.F.T.C. (Christian)	56,000	undecided
Force Ouvrière	C.G.T.F.O. (Socialist)	20,000	more or less for
Monde Ouvrier	Left Wing Christians	20,000	more or less against

These last three may be classified under the rubric "labor union neutrality". Moreover, the influence of all these papers, as compared with that of the political weeklies analyzed above, is rather weak.

THE MANAGEMENT BULLETINS

Officially, management did not take a stand. On April 15, 1954, M. Georges Villiers, president of the Conseil National du Patronat Français (National Association of French Employers) wrote in the business weekly *Entreprise:*

"I was very much astonished to read, in your March 1st number, a news item according to which 'a group of studies made by the directors of the National Association of French Employers on the problems posed by the EDC treaty' had come to the conclusion that the 'ratification of this treaty is politically indispensable'.

"I should be very grateful to you to contradict this news item which has no basis whatsoever. Indeed, even though the National Association of French Employers had the opportunity of presenting to the government their observations about the economic provisions of the plan, this organization never took any stand on the plan itself, considering that the problems of ratification were of a political nature and fell outside its sphere".

This withholding of any official statement (considered by partisans of EDC as the sign of secret opposition) was respected, as far as we know, by almost all the management journals. However, one very important exception should be noted. In its supplement of March-April 1953, *Le Bulletin des Industries Mécaniques*, reprinted an address by its president, M. Alfred Métral. He was violently opposed to the treaty and his arguments were not uniquely economic ones. Eleven reasons of a political nature are stated first: 1) the EDC would be the army of a non-existent state; 2) it would cut off overseas territories; 3) the members of the high command are not responsible to any body politic; 4) the Six-Minister Council is without authority; 5) the assembly of the C.E.C.A. (Coal and Steel Community) has no connection with defense; 6) France would no longer control the rules for the advancement of its officers; 7) France could no longer fix the size of the armed forces which we send overseas; 8) Saint-Cyr (the French West Point) would no longer exist; 9) our high command would be absorbed by the EDC; 10) our territorial military organization would be subordinated; 11) we would have no more judiciary power.

M. Métral then came to his economic arguments: not only does the Commissariat control the arms program, but it also watches the markets and assigns its orders to the most advantageous bids. French defense markets would therefore run the risk of slipping away from French industry. Even if, according to article 101, 85% of the participation costs of each state must be purchased in that state, the treaty does not specify the proportion to be purchased from different branches of agriculture and industry. (Thus all the potatoes necessary for EDC could be bought from France and not a single mechanical unit). Article 107, which forbids exportation without authorization, was also much criticized by M. Métral. In short: M. Métral feared that French industry would lose its markets. It would seem that this outburst was followed by the

C.N.P.F. (National Association of French Employers) taking all its federations in hand, since the latter subsequently abstained from taking any stand publicly, at least in their official capacity.

General Conclusion

Analysis of the French press as a whole leads us to the following conclusion: EDC was very little criticized on military grounds (its own terms), or on economic grounds, or as an instrument of European unification. Little by little, the opponents of the plan so handled the question that it seemed to center about a criticism of German rearmament. With the exception of a few Socialist papers, the partisans of EDC followed its adversaries along this line of debate.

One is forced to conclude that public opinion was not made aware of much besides this aspect of the question. Supporting in good faith, but against the weight of evidence, the idea that the rejection of EDC was the rejection of German rearmament, certain propagandists presented us with "pure confusion" of the two issues. Public opinion little by little obliterated the wide variety of opinions which separated General Weygand and Marshal Juin (an alternative solution with German divisions), General de Gaulle (the priority of negotiating with the East), and the Neutralists (neutralization of East and West Germany). Whence the amazing sequence of *quid pro quos* and paradoxes of September 1954 which are reviewed elsewhere in this volume.

Provincial Dailies Which Remained Absolutely Neutral

Thirty provincial daily papers took no position at all on the EDC. Eight of these sold over 50,000 copies daily: *La Dépèche du midi* (Radical); *Le Méridional-la-France* of Marseilles (Moderate); *la Montagne* of Clermont-Ferrand (Radical); *Nice-Matin* (Center); *La Nouvelle République* of Tours (Moderate); *Le Républicain Lorrain* (Moderate); *La Tribune* of Saint Etienne (Moderate); *Le Télégramme* of Brest.

The 22 others are: *La Charente Libre; Centre-Eclair; La Croix du Nord et du Pas de Calais; l'Eclair méridional* of Montpellier; *L'Espoir* of Saint-Etienne; *Est-Eclair* of Troyes; *Le Haut-Marnais républicain; Le Havre Libre; Le Havre; La Haute Marne libérée; L'Indépendant de l'Aube; L'Indépendant* of Perpignan; *Le Journal du Centre; Libération-Champagne; La Liberté de l'Est; La Liberté* (Clermont); *Les Nouvelles de Bretagne et du Maine; La Presse de la Manche; La République de Toulon et du Var; Rouergue républicain; L'Yonne républicaine.* It is difficult to sense the exact shadings of political opinion in many of these papers, but all of them are either Moderate or Radical (labels which correspond to the tendencies of the political parties so named).

Provincial Dailies Opposed to EDC

First of all, the twelve Communist papers (*Les Allobroges, L'Echo du Centre* coupled with *la Marseillaise du Berry; La Liberté* of Lille, *La Marseillaise* of Marseilles; *Le petit-Var-Marseillaise; La République-le Patriote* (Saint-Etienne); *Le Patriote* (Nice); *Le Patriote* (Toulouse); *Le Patriote* (Lyons); *Ouest-Matin* (Rennes); *Les Nouvelles* (Bordeaux). This list does not include *l'Humanité d'Alsace et de Lorraine*, which appears in German and in French. These papers took over the arguments of *l'Humanité* sometimes expressing them more moderately (*Allobroges, Ouest-Matin*). The other anti-EDC papers are *Le Courrier* and *La Liberté* of Limoges, which adhere strictly to the Gaullist line; also *le Libre Poitou*, and *Nord-Littoral* (Calais), papers of the Center-Left Wing and partisans of Mendès-France policies.

Provincial Dailies Favorable to EDC

Eighteen provincial daily papers took a stand for the EDC. Of these, seven sold more than 50,000 copies daily: *L'Alsace* (Moderate); *Le*

Courrier de l'Ouest (Moderate); la Dépêche-la Liberté of Saint-Etienne (with M.R.P. leanings); Nord-Matin (Socialist); Le Provencal (Socialist and Radical); la Résistance de l'Ouest (Moderate).

The eleven others are: *Basque-Eclair* of Bayonne, coupled with *Eclair-Pyrénées* of Tarbes (Moderate); *Le Bien Public* of Dijon (Moderate); *Le Journal du Pas de Calais* (Moderate); *Nord Eclair* (M.R.P.); *Le Populaire du Centre* of Limoges (Socialist); *Le Populaire de l'Ouest* of Nantes (Radical); *La République de Franche-Comté* (Moderate); *la Quatrième République* of Pau (Center Left).

Provincial Dailies Moderately Opposed

We have classified under this heading six newspapers which did not attack the EDC openly. They simply insisted on the disadvantages of it or on the advantages of an alternative solution. These papers are: *Le Berri Républicain* (Center Left); *Le Courrier Picard* (Socialist of the type of M. Max Lejeune, minority Socialist); *Le Maine libre* (Moderate and Gaullist); and three newspapers whose circulation exceeds 50,000 copies daily: *Paris-Normandie* (Center Left); *La Nouvelle République du Sud-Ouest*, of Bordeaux (Radical and Socialist); and *La Voix du Nord* (Moderate and somewhat Gaullist).

Provincial Dailies Moderately Favorable

Nine newspapers never did any active campaigning for the EDC at any time, but they published open letters which were generally in favor of it and commentaries without hostility to the EDC. These papers are: *L'Ardennais* (Center) and eight others whose circulation exceeds 50,000 copies daily: *Le Dauphiné libéré* (Center); *Les Dernières Nouvelles d'Alsace* (Moderate); *L'Echo Liberté* of Lyons (Moderate); *Ouest-France* of Rennes (M.R.P.); *Le Progrès de Lyon* (Center); and *Sud-Ouest* of Bordeaux (Moderate).

Provincial Dailies Deliberately Eclectic on EDC

Only three newspapers published contradictory articles: *La Bourgogne Républicaine* (Socialist), and two others whose circulation exceeds 50,000 copies daily; *Midi-Libre* of Montpellier (Center Left); and *L'Union* of Rheims, organ of the Marne Liberation Committee.

THE
PARLIAMENTARY
GAME

7 : Birth and Death of a Treaty

(from Pléven Plan to vote of August 30, 1954)

JACQUES FAUVET

The EDC was conceived in the fear of Germany and in the hope of Europe. It was, from the moment it appeared on the Parliamentary scene, doomed to failure. Ill-cared for by its promoters and little loved by its foster-parents, it collapsed under the combined attacks of its adversaries from the Left and Right. Its death only helped to emphasize the mistakes which had been committed by its supporters and the gap left by its disappearance.

Chronology is important. The "Pléven Plan" was launched before the National Assembly on October 20, 1950; the Treaty of Paris was signed on May 25, 1952; it was repudiated on August 30, 1954.

Two Decisive Events

During these three stages, two events occurred in French domestic politics. Both had a decisive influence on the fate of the project and on the course of foreign policy.

(1) Between 1950 and 1952, general elections took place (June 17, 1951). The popular vote showed both an absolute and a relative decline in the two parties most favorable to the "European Idea": the M.R.P. and the S.F.I.O. At the same time, more than 100 Gaullists, declared opponents of an integrated army, entered the Assembly.

As a consequence, the project of European integration, which was started under a favorable parliament, had to be continued under a less favorable or hostile legislature. While the new Assembly that was ultimately to reject the EDC in 1954 voted on December 11, 1951 for the C.E.C.A. (European Coal and Steel Community or Schuman Plan), 240 deputies were already against the plan. These included 97 Communists and 116 R.P.F. (Gaullists). The Socialists who no longer participated in the government, but who still voted with the majority, voted for the Plan with one dissenting voice. On the question of the economic integration of Europe, the Socialist party was not divided.

From this time on, a change is visible. The evidence appears three months later. On February 19, 1952, eve of the Lisbon Conference, the National Assembly agreed on the principle of a European army (but with reservations and conditions) only by 327 votes to 287. This time, 20 Socialists and 10 Radicals voted against it, a sign that should have warned the supporters of the project.

(2) Between 1952 and 1953, the Socialists went over to the opposition and the Gaullists entered the government coalition. This double movement was effected in successive stages, each marked by a deterioration in the governmental and parliamentary situation relative to the European idea.

In March 1952, when M. Pinay (Modéré) was invested as Prime Minister of the first conservative government that France has known since 1935, the Socialists definitely left the majority and went over to the opposition. Their withdrawal, however, was counterbalanced by the entrance of a part of the RPF within the government, which made it possible for M. Pinay to take office.

The consequences were immediate. The dissident Gaullists, as a condition of joining the government, required M. Robert Schuman to leave the Quai d'Orsay. Concentrating on the person of M. Schuman, they were already attacking a whole policy. But the M.R.P. agreed to participate in the government only on the condition that the Foreign Minister remain in power. M. Pinay accepted the M.R.P. view. But the attack on Schuman should have warned the "Europeans."

In January 1953, the entire group of Gaullist deputies joined the government majority, and five months later entered the government itself. M. Robert Schuman left the Quai d'Orsay. The M.R.P. installed as his successor M. Georges Bidault, who was

considered then as a very cool supporter of the Treaty of Paris.
In January M. René Mayer came to power, and in June M.
Laniel, but the ambiguity of the government's position toward
EDC continued. The Socialists, "European" or not, violently at-
tacked these two governments and particularly the second. M.
Laniel fell on June 12, 1954, when the Treaty of Paris had not yet
been presented for parliamentary vote.

From October 20, 1950 to June 12, 1954 France thus passed
from a Pléven government including M. Guy Mollet, Robert
Schuman and René Mayer (the most ardent supporters of the
EDC) to a Laniel government in which only M. Pléven remained
—but with M. Bidault at the Quai d'Orsay. During this crucial
period for the future of the treaty, the government included at
first the Socialists, while the Gaullists and the Communists were
in the opposition; then the Gaullists against the Socialists and the
Communists.

The consequences of this evolution and of the reversal of the
governmental and parliamentary situation will be analyzed in the
following pages.

The Painful Birth of the Treaty
(from February to December 1952)

Before the Lisbon Conference: The Communists and the Gaullists had from the start fought any form of European integration,
whether economic, military, or political. It must be remembered
that without the electoral law of alliances (*apparentement*), these
two great parties would have obtained an absolute majority at the
1951 elections. They could not have governed together, of course.
But their joint opposition would have prevented the formation of
any government favorable to European integration. The C.E.C.A.
would have been rejected and the EDC would never have been
born at all.

The Communist and the Gaullist representations had been
artificially reduced by the electoral law, less to save the "European" policy than to protect the parliamentary system. But, as a
result, this 1951 legislature began with a "European" majority,
including the Socialists, which did ratify the C.E.C.A.

It was only on the eve of the Lisbon Conference designed to
work out a European army plan, that the first serious divisions

appeared in the National Assembly. The Gaullist and Communist opposition expressed itself violently. Even the majority parties of "Europeans" also showed, for the first time, their internal divisions. M. Daladier among the Radicals, MM. Daniel Mayer and Jules Moch among the Socialists, MM. Pierre André, Loustaunau-Lacau and General Aumeran among the Moderates, M. André Monteil among the M.R.P., etc., spoke against the European army. We will meet them again, three years later, when they will have many followers. But even in 1951, as a result of their action, the majority was already deeply shaken.

The Socialist party refused to accept the first "order of the day" on the European Army plan presented by the government. Threatened with a vote of no confidence, the Government presented a new order of the day which included a reference to British participation. However, 20 Socialists still voted against the text, even when various other conditions were added—e.g., distribution of expenses taking into account French sacrifices in Indochina; guarantees from the U.S. and from Great Britain against the violation of the treaty; integration at the lowest level possible; submitting the European army to a supranational political power. . . .

These conditions were very important, for they enabled adversaries to claim three months later, at the signature of the treaty, and three and a half years later, during the debate, that the essential "preliminaries" had not been fulfilled.

In February 1952, the parliamentary situation that was finally to destroy the treaty was taking shape. It included:

—the Communists and their allied *Progressistes* (101), hostile to any kind of rearmament of Western Germany.

—the Gaullists (116), most of them favorable to a certain kind of German rearmament, but unanimously hostile to a policy of integration and of supranationality limited to the six nations of continental Europe.

—some Socialists (20), Radicals (10) and M.R.P. (6), at the time a minority, adversaries of German rearmament prior to negotiation with the Soviet Union.

—some Nationalists from the Right, Independents and Peasants (20 to 30) hostile both to Germany and to European integration.

We will find all these deputies among those who rejected EDC in 1954. Their number will be augmented, as we will see later, by many Socialists and Radicals who join them for reasons of domestic and of foreign policy.

The Signature of the Treaty: Meanwhile, schisms became more apparent at the Congress of the Socialist party, in the Radical party and in the M.R.P. during the month of May, at the very moment when the treaty was going to be signed.

On May 23, at the Radical Congress, M. Herriot joined M. Daladier. He lodged an appeal to the Americans: "Don't lead us into the same mistakes which you drew us into between the two wars"; and he declared himself favorable to a conversation with the East. The official motion of the Congress does not mention the EDC treaty, but merely asks that "France not be committed to a policy that could endanger her peace and her security for the benefit of the strength of Germany".

On the same day, at the Socialist Congress, after MM. Naegelen, Jules Moch, Daniel Mayer, Leenhardt and Edouard Depreux had condemned the treaty, it was defended by MM. Jaquet, Le Bail, Félix Gouin, André Philip, Guy Mollet who summed up the debate by the formula: "no refusal, no acceptance". "A refusal", he said, "would be the most beautiful victory the Russians can hope for". Acceptance may not, however, be considered, "because there are guarantees we have to obtain".

Even the M.R.P. Congress expressed the wish, on May 25, that the treaty "be ratified only if it includes the guarantees demanded by the National Assembly, namely, an effective guarantee from the U.S. and from Great Britain, in case of a German secession [from EDC]". The M.R.P. also declared itself in favor of "pacific coexistence" between East and West, and endorsed "parallel negotiations" with the U.S.S.R. as absolutely necessary for lasting peace. (Thus the M.R.P. tried to incorporate the effective slogans of the EDC adversaries.)

It took the adoption of all these conditions before the Council of Ministers allowed M. Robert Schuman to sign the treaty, a decision which required several meetings of the Council. Busy with economic questions, the cabinet seemed to have discovered the treaty only when they *had* to authorize its signature. It then became clear that the Ministers had given too much leeway to the experts; the text of the treaty had been kept secret too long. When they finally examined the project, they were startled. Four days before the signature, one Minister declared that his colleagues and he were "stricken with deep anxiety". The government decided to sign only on condition of the Anglo-American guarantee. The long and mournful process of the "preliminary conditions" was starting.

M. Robert Schuman was then in Bonn to sign the contractual agreements on the reestablishment of German sovereignty. MM. Dean Acheson and Eden were also present. The French Minister intervened and notified the Council of Ministers in Paris, through the intermediacy of M. Maurice Schumann, that he had obtained satisfaction: the Anglo-American guarantee would be added to the treaty. *The French Government decided then to authorize the signature but not the deposition of the treaty in Parliament for ratification.* This distinction is essential. It was the ultimate cause of the failure of the treaty.

The Council of Ministers decided, at the same time, to make ratification depend on a more general agreement among the Allies on a so-called "extension of solidarity". As she was getting more deeply involved in Europe, France now required that her responsibilities in Asia and in Africa be taken into greater account.

In short, to sign was not the same as to ratify. The official communiqué pointed that out in the declaration of May 23, 1952 at 12 noon: "The Council of Ministers has specified the conditions to which it intends to subordinate France's signature as well as the deposition before Parliament for ratification". M. Robert Schuman confirmed this a few days after the signature by declaring that no date could be fixed for ratification. If the conditions of signature were fulfilled, those of ratification were still far from met.

Here, too, we must recall chronology. Signed in May 1952 by the Pinay government, the treaty of Paris was submitted to the National Assembly under the René Mayer government in January 1953. Nothing further happened between July 1953 and June 1954, during the whole period of the Laniel government. The Assembly debate took place only after the Brussels Conference in 1954, under the Mendès-France government, and the treaty was rejected in August. Two long periods of time thus were lost in vain, since nothing was undertaken, neither parliamentary procedures nor new negotiations. The first lasted eight months under the Pinay government, the second almost a year under the Laniel government. How and why?

One can assert *that in 1952 and even in 1953, the treaty would have been ratified if it had been submitted to the Assembly.* At this time, indeed, only the Communists were really fighting the battle against ratification. The fatal schisms had hardly appeared among the Socialists and were barely discernible among the Radicals. The Gaullists, most of them in the opposition, did not influence the majority. And, finally, neither Marshal Juin nor General Weygand [1] had yet declared himself against the treaty. On whom falls, then, the responsibility of the first eight months' delay? The historian will be able to give a better answer than the chronicler.

The official reason was given at the end of September 1952— three months after the signature—by M. Robert Schuman himself. When asked if the government would soon submit the treaty, he replied: "There is nothing dramatic in this delay, which is due to the necessity to prepare a detailed memorandum and to have it accepted by the government".

Was this document, which attracted nobody's attention, the reason for the delay? It can be doubted. One could take it seriously only by forgetting the conditions laid down three months earlier by the Council of Ministers: "the extension of solidarity". Since then, M. Schuman had had a conversation with M. Eden. There was even a question of resuming negotiations with the Six. A conversation *had* been initiated with Chancellor Adenauer on the Saar—another preliminary condition that was to become *sine qua non* in 1953. But nothing had resulted from these talks.

Were internal factors of some special importance? The hostility of M. Vincent Auriol, who was then President of the Republic, had been taken into consideration. But the Chief of State has not the power to prevent the deposition of a treaty before Parliament. In reality, the hostility of M. Auriol only compounded the hostility of General de Gaulle,[2] MM. Herriot and Daladier, all of whom manifested their opposition during the fall of 1952.

[1] The first manifestation of hostility came during the month of October 1952; "the creation of an European army such as is conceived, dismembers the French army and leads to political surrenders of great seriousness." (*Revue des deux Mondes*).

[2] General de Gaulle declared to the press on June 5, 1952: "Pell mell with the two vanquished nations, Germany and Italy, France has to give man-power, arms and money to a stateless melting pot. This humiliation is imposed on her in the name of equality of rights, so that Germany can be considered as

The truth is that already the EDC partisans were afraid that some dozens of votes would be lacking in the Assembly. Their mistake was to believe that the situation would improve if they put the debate off indefinitely, when in fact time was working more and more against the treaty. The opposition was strengthening by uniting; the schisms within "European" ranks were increasing.

After the Signature: The crisis within the R.P.F. was a consequence of the signature of the Treaty of Paris. Until then, the "dissidents" had not been excluded and had not resigned from the Gaullist group. In June, they wrote to General de Gaulle who answered: "It is partly with the help of the vote of confidence you have granted—even if the reasons were different—that the ministers in power could conclude the recent agreements concerning Germany, the so-called 'European' army and the annihilation of the French army . . ."

This exchange of viewpoints is important. The dissident Gaullists had supported the government on internal policy, but had remained *opponents* of its foreign policy. After their resignation from the R.P.F. on July 1, they intervened several times through M. Pinay, and one wondered if he was going to abandon the E.D.C. On October 6, he asked the U.S. Ambassador to withdraw a note concerning American aid, since the President of the Council considered its tone unacceptable. The dissident Gaullists praised this firm attitude.

The M.R.P. began to be anxious about the true intentions of M. Pinay. Some days later, at the Congress of the Radical party, MM. Herriot and Daladier renewed their attack against EDC. M. Edgar Faure then declared that France cannot ratify the treaty before a solution was found on Indochina: "We cannot bring into an organization, in which we shall not be the masters, an army burdened with such a heavy load." Even M. René Mayer, who defended the treaty, admitted that "some of its points can be criticized".

These declarations were already sensational. But the surprise was even greater when M. Pinay, the President of the Council, was said to have declared, "I cannot disavow the Radical lead-

---

not rearmed while rebuilding her military strength. France is, of all the great nations which have their own army today, the only nation which is to lose hers".

ers . . ." (dispatch A.F.P. October 19). This statement provoked much excitement in Paris. Some hours later, it was formally denied. But it was too late.

The following day, the President of the M.R.P., M. Teitgen, after a conversation with M. Robert Schuman, declared: "The present situation cannot last. Either the President of the Council and the government are wholly solid with MM. Pléven and Schuman (they will have to declare it in all cases where there could be confusion, and their acts have to follow accordingly), or the government is divided on foreign policy, and will have to face the consequences immediately". For the M.R.P., the Radical Congress was the "drop of water which makes the vase overflow". The M.R.P. decided to ask for the deposition of the treaty, which is to be the touchstone of the "government's fidelity to the policy and the men who have supported it up to that time".

Two days later, the question was raised in the Council of Ministers. In spite of opposition by most of the Radical ministers [3] the Council decided to submit the treaty for ratification after an "exposé of motives" was composed. It was then November 22. Two months later, the government fell, but the project had still not been deposed.

"We have signed a treaty, and we shall remain faithful to it; we will defend it before Parliament", had declared M. Pinay. But he was in a situation *in which all his successors found themselves.*

M. Pinay had been installed only as a result of the dissidence of 27 R.P.F. deputies on matters of internal policy. But these deputies had given up none of their hostility toward the European army. They had parted with General de Gaulle, but they meant to stick to his foreign policy. As they wrote him, they still agreed on the national aims of the Rassemblement. This process was later to be renewed on the occasion of the ministerial crisis. Then the orthodox Gaullists, and not merely the dissidents, were to participate in the governmental majority. They were to back its internal policy, but sabotage its foreign policy. This will soon be described.

[3] The Radical ministers accused M. Pinay of having yielded to an M.R.P. "ultimatum."

From January to November 1953: Prolonged Illness

Thus, in 18 months, only one positive step had been accomplished: the project was officially deposed in the Assembly. This opened the way to parliamentary procedures. But the two important commissions hastened to choose chairmen who were hostile to the treaty.

The Foreign Affairs Commission elected M. Jules Moch by 21 votes, against 16 for an Independent, and 5 for a Communist. A majority of the commission seemed clearly against the treaty since a Socialist hostile to the treaty had been nominated without the help of the Communists. Moreover, he was elected by 5 of the 8 Socialists, 8 orthodox and dissident Gaullists, 2 Moderates, 1 Radical (M. Daladier), and 1 M.R.P. (M. Denis, who was soon excluded from his party).

The National Defense Commission entrusted its presidency to General Koenig, another opponent of the treaty. General Koenig was to become, 18 months later, a minister under M. Mendès-France. He was to resign on the eve of the Brussels Conference, in protest against the attempt to amend the treaty so as to make it acceptable.

Meanwhile, two governments came and went. The first, from January to May 1953, was presided over by a partisan of the treaty, M. René Mayer. The second, from June 1953 to June 1954, was presided over by M. Laniel, who was neither a partisan nor an opponent. During both these governments, M. Bidault was Foreign Minister; he was considered, rightly or wrongly, as a less warm partisan of EDC than was M. Robert Schuman. It is a fact that he admitted, on several occasions, that he would never have signed such a treaty. But, having inherited it, he considered it his duty to amend and defend the treaty. He regarded the European military community *as a lesser but necessary evil;* the somewhat complex technique of the treaty discouraged him; the general philosophy which inspired its promoters seemed to him an ideal, but an unrealistic one.

In any case, M. Bidault soon proved that he was rather hostile to the project for *a political community of Europe.* The idea receded further and further at every conference. But, the creation of an effective political authority intended to control democratically the military community, and in particular the Germans, had been an important French "preliminary" condition for ratification.

M. Bidault was a man of distinctly nationalist temper as compared with M. Schuman. He was inclined to distrust Germany, a country he neither knew nor valued as much as his predecessor; he had little confidence in a supranational Europe. He insisted that it is necessary "to build Europe without destroying France". (The Gaullists and Nationalists had accused EDC of threatening to break up the integrity of France and the French Union.)

This nationalist perspective of M. Bidault was obvious during the Indochinese and North African affairs; it led him also, to be wary of the "Holy Roman and Germanic Empire" (in the phrase of EDC opponents). Bidault is a "Gallican", jealous of the independence of his country and of his church. But this belongs more to psychology, even to psychoanalysis, than to politics.

We make such a long detour around the personality of M. Bidault because he remained in power from the deposition to the failure of the treaty, during the Mayer and Laniel governments. These two men and their Foreign Minister were responsible for the delay, hence, to a certain extent, for the failure of the treaty. In fact, they made only one mistake: they had come to power in an equivocal situation. Since the adversaries of the treaty had contributed to the formation of these two governments, they remained the masters of their life and death. Events were to prove this.

THE R.P.F. AND M. RENÉ MAYER

Called in after the fall of M. Pinay, M. René Mayer came up against the Gaullist R.P.F. Their votes were absolutely necessary, since Mayer could not count, as Pinay had, on the Socialists or on the Moderates (especially the Peasant party which never forgave him the exchange of 5,000-franc notes in 1947). He began by declaring that he would not ask for a vote of confidence when the Assembly voted on the treaty. But this was not enough. The Gaullists required "the promise that negotiations will be opened on the initiative of the French government among the co-signatories of the EDC treaty in order to amend a certain number of provisions so as to protect the unity of the national army and the integrity of the French Union."

When the Assembly was invited, the following day, to declare itself on the investiture of M. Mayer, he merely declared: "negotiations will have to be opened in order to organize, to complete, to specify, and to elucidate certain clauses of the treaty in additional protocols, and also in order to prepare a closer association of Great Britain with the Community." This was still not sufficient. The R.P.F. threatened to refuse its votes. To obtain them, M. Mayer agreed to declare later that "these protocols have to allow the maintenance of the unity and integrity of our army and of the French Union; they have also to admit, as a preliminary condition to the ratification, an agreement on the Saar problem." The integrity of the treaty signed eight months earlier was now threatened.

The treaty has "lead in its wings," M. Schuman declared, and tendered his resignation because he no longer had the confidence of the majority for the continuation of his policy. The truth, however, is that he had neither refused to reopen negotiations on the treaty, nor had he succeeded in deposing the project in the Assembly. When M. Bidault replaced M. Schuman two days later, the R.P.F. expressed its satisfaction. The ambiguity began in earnest.

The Catholic M.R.P. now asked for deposition "without delay." The Gaullist R.P.F., on the contrary, wanted the treaty shelved. During the whole ensuing period of the Mayer and Laniel governments, there was to be a constant duel on this priority between the M.R.P. and the non-communist adversaries of EDC (mainly the R.P.F.). The latter finally won.

M. Mayer tried, as did later M. Laniel, to keep a balance between M.R.P. and R.P.F. *Note:* on the very day when they seemed too favorable to the M.R.P., both were overthrown by the R.P.F., without the "European" Socialists (who went more and more over to the opposition) coming to their rescue.

On March 1, M. Mayer declared himself favorable to ratification. He asked the Assembly to decide "at the right moment," i.e., when the protocols then under discussion had been signed.

At the end of March 1953, these protocols were signed by the six participant nations. April went by, with country and Parliament intensely concerned by the Indochinese affair. In May, Germany ratified the EDC. Now, the die was cast: Would France follow this example? The required protocols had been signed.

Even the R.P.F. felt the pressure. On May 24, M. Mayer was overthrown: 71 among the 83 Gaullist deputies voted against him.

The Gaullists, weak as they were, succeeded, by undermining the government they had helped to create, in gaining the time that was to destroy the EDC.

M. LANIEL AND THE M.R.P.

The May crisis was soon dominated by foreign policy questions, as the January crisis had been.

A partisan of EDC, M. Paul Reynaud tried to form a new government but obtained only 34 of 81 R.P.F. votes—this despite his proposal to strengthen the Executive power, a proposition which should have pleased the Gaullists, as it was a part of their program. Nevertheless, he was defeated.

M. Mendès-France—this was his first and unsuccessful attempt —proposed to postpone the EDC debate until the fall. But this made the M.R.P. worry about the "continuity of France's foreign policy." M. Mendès-France then proposed a social program which should have suited the M.R.P. But he too was defeated: only 52 of the 89 M.R.P. voted for him. Another 13 votes would have been enough to elect him, but these were not to be found.

Called in next, M. Bidault pronounced a sentence that should have resounded pleasantly in the ears of the R.P.F.: "We have to build Europe without destroying France, I mean, in any case, without destroying France." But then he announced that his government staked its existence on the EDC treaty. He was defeated: 64 of the 81 R.P.F. voted for him, and he lacked only 1 vote.

M. André Marie then tried his luck. Weariness came into play. The R.P.F. took the occasion to suggest that "some questions of foreign policy on which we are divided be purely and simply reserved." But the M.R.P. did not agree. It accused M. André Marie of favoring "immobilisme in European problems." The Radical leader obtained even less votes than M. Reynaud and was defeated: only 12 M.R.P. and 42 R.P.F. voted for him.

It should be noted that if the Socialists, who were at that time mainly favorable to the treaty, had voted for either MM. Reynaud or Bidault (who were both "Europeans"), each would have been invested.

Finally, M. Laniel. France was now without a government for

over one month. The weary Assembly accepted a candidate who, in his own words, had presented himself with "modesty." He insured the continuity of French foreign policy, so the M.R.P. was satisfied. But everybody wondered that the R.P.F. did not try to obtain more details from the candidate. The reason became clear on the following day, when, for the first time since the 1951 elections, the R.P.F. entered into the government. Being within the fortress, the R.P.F. did not have to besiege it, nor to impose conditions on the candidate. They had arranged to continue the fight against EDC from within. This was June 27. Until November 17, nothing further was heard about Europe nor about EDC. The Parliament took its vacation from July 24 to October 6. Attention was turned toward other events: the Italian and German elections, the project for the Bermuda conference, the aggravation of the North African, and particularly Moroccan, situation, the Indochinese war. Domestic interests were concentrated on social problems, on financial difficulties and on the presidential election that was to take place at the end of December.

The political parties gave interim attention to EDC, only to learn that they were more and more divided on this problem.

Hostility increased among the Socialists. At the July Congress, the motion which approved "the principle of a unified European army" was accepted by only 1979 votes against 1189 and 228 abstentions. The Congress referred to an extraordinary council the problem of deciding what was to be the attitude of the party during the ratification debate.

Even the U.D.S.R., the party of M. Pléven, father of EDC, was confused. MM. Bonnefous and Lanet fought against the project and MM. Claudius Petit and Legaret defended it.

In September, there was a serious alarm in the government. It was necessary to give directives about the proposed European political community to the French delegates to the Rome conference. The R.P.F. minister opposed the M.R.P. minister, M. Teitgen. The first refused to accept the supranational character of the community; the latter did not yield and required the political community to be at least above the existing communities (EDC and C.E.C.A.). Several meetings took place without any result. No agreement was possible. Hence the government could give only general directives to the head of the French delegation, M. Fouques Duparc. Once more, the Gaullists and the Popular Re-

publicans had opposed and neutralized each other. The President
did not arbitrate. The Minister of Overseas France, M. Jacquinot
(an Independent), protested in a letter to M. Laniel against the
French delegation's position on the relations of Overseas France
with the community. The Rome conference practically buried the
project for a European political community.

THE DEBATE OF NOVEMBER 17, 1953

It was in these conditions that a great debate on European policy
began, on November 17, in the National Assembly. It was the
first debate since February 1952 and the last before the defeat of
the treaty. It was also an interesting one: the various groups announced to each other their points of view.

The Communists condemned the treaty and declared themselves ready to join those who wanted above all "to avert the
deadly danger of a reconstitution of the German army." They
approved the proposal of the Soviet Union to give an army to a
reunified Germany, on condition that it would not participate in
any coalition.

The Gaullists were more than ever intransigeant, since the General had renewed his absolute opposition to the treaty on the very
eve of the debate. The *nationalistic* slogans were multiplied:
"Europe would be constructed on the corpse of France," "The
French Union would be delivered into the hands of Germany and
Italy." Other slogans were pacific: "Is EDC not the creation of a
frightened Europe against the Soviet Union?" "A rearmed Germany would be tempted to recover the Eastern territories."

The Radicals were divided. M. René Mayer recalled the conditions he had set: Saar agreement and additional protocols. One
of his arguments struck the Assembly: if France feels too weak
before Germany to carry on an integration policy, how could she
feel strong enough to practice an isolation policy? And, at the end,
it would be not only dangerous but criminal to refuse a foreign
policy without having any substitute for it.

M. Daladier pointed out that neither the Saar problem nor the
problem of British participation had been resolved. He maintained
that it was impossible to impose on the Soviet Union a solution of
the German problem, and that a future Europe could only be
born in a negotiated peace.

Among the Moderates, some, like M. Guérin de Beaumont,

stressed the consequences of the rejection of the treaty; others, like M. J. Vigier, asserted that its failure would bring about the "reversal of alliances." But General Aumeran, M. Pierre André and M. Loustaunau-Lacau untiringly stood against any kind of German rearmament.

So that among the divided groups as well as in the two camps, it was less a dialogue than two separate monologues. This was obvious until the very end. Partisans and adversaries of the treaty stood up against each other. They did not speak the same language, nor of the same things. It is striking to note that the "Europeans" were less conscious of the treaty itself than of its meaning at large, or the conditions of ratification and the consequences of rejection.

This was also the attitude of the Socialists during the debate. Only partisans of the treaty were accorded the right (by the party's decision on discipline) to speak on the floor of the Assembly; adversaries had not even the right to speak in public. But to invoke party discipline was in this case a tactical mistake, for the parliamentary delegation was deeply divided in fact. The opponents remained silent, but did not change their opinion. Silence was merely obedience; so that great illusions were formed as to the inner composition of this party. Eight months later, its leaders saw how greatly mistaken they were about the seriousness of the discrepancy.

Meanwhile, M. Jaquet asserted that an isolated Germany would have to be more feared than an integrated one. M. Gouin felt that Europe should unite if she wanted to remain a power between the United States and the Soviet world. M. LeBail pointed out that Soviet policy would not change as long as Europe remained weak. "And why should the Soviet policy change when some French politicians intend to ask the USSR for a guarantee against Germany?"

Finally, M. Guy Mollet recalled the two conditions set by his party: *"the effective association of Great Britain and a supranational authority, with limited, but effective power."* In August 1954, the Socialist adversaries maintained, not without grounds, that these two conditions had not been fulfilled.

All the spokesmen of the M.R.P. were favorable, but they expressed the opinion of the quasi-totality of the members of their party. The official thesis of the party was expounded by M.

Alfred Coste-Floret: "German militarism can only be neutralized if it is integrated within the discipline of a non-national army. Germany alone cannot be neutralized; she should not be allowed to participate in N.A.T.O."

M. Coste-Floret considered, on the other hand, that the European status of the Saar should not be a preliminary condition to the ratification of EDC, since "the status quo satisfied France." M. Robert Schuman observed then that the debate was not oriented to the conclusion of an agreement on the Saar statute, but only to a German-French understanding on the main points of this statute.

To the question: "Would the rearmament of Germany not aggravate relations with the East?", the former Foreign Minister answered with another question: "It is already three years since the EDC was proposed. What has the Soviet Union done since then to quiet the anxiety of the West?" and further: "The Parliament has the right to refuse ratification but not the right to shirk its duty."

At the conclusion of the debate, M. Bidault was supposed to make a great speech. But, being overtired, the minister had a fainting attack. The effect was unfortunate and an ill omen. M. Maurice Schumann replaced him and read M. Bidault's speech. His effort and his enthusiasm were unable, however, to catch the interest of the Assembly.

When one reads this speech, one is convinced that it was one of the best written in defense of EDC and of the European policy at large. Objections are refuted, valid arguments are brought in. The past and the future of international relations are faced. All in vain. The great debate ended up in a fight about the agenda.

A Socialist proposal, the only truly European order of the day, was rejected, 325 to 247. Being European, it was refused by the Communists and by the Gaullists; and being Socialist, it was refused by most of the Moderates. Once more, considerations of internal politics dominated the debate.

Internal politics came even more into play when the government asked for a vote of confidence on a harmless order of the day.[4] "The national assembly, referring to the declaration of in-

---

4 The M.R.P. was surprised that M. Laniel, in his speech before the vote, did not even mention the speech of M. Bidault which M. Maurice Schumann had read.

vestiture of the President of the Council, asked that the policy for a united Europe be insured and approved the declaration of the government." But this text implied a vote of confidence for the government, hence the Socialist group voted against it despite its agreement on the particular policy; 60 R.P.F. of the 79 present abstained, though the text did not even mention the EDC.

This great debate ended with the acceptance of a meaningless order of the day, by an insignificant majority: 275 (M.R.P., A.R.S., Independent, Peasant and 44 Radicals) to 244 (Communists, Socialists and 20 Radicals) and 103 abstentions (60 R.P.F., 11 Radicals, 10 UDSR). It was a vote of internal politics.

The Agony of the Treaty: November 1953–April 1954

Between the debate of November 1953 and that of August 1954, the determination of the government weakened and the moves open to the Parliament narrowed. Could the treaty have been ratified, if it had been presented and defended in the Assembly? It is doubtful. Every month, the almost irreversible trend became more obvious. Why?

The same factors which already had caused the delay of the signature, of the deposition in Parliament, and of the debate assumed now a new and accentuated character:

a) The government was less concerned with European policy in general than with the easing of international relations. On this point, when the Allies blame France for having botched the project she had proposed, it should be acknowledged that they— as much as events—contributed to this result. While a survey of interallied activity falls outside the scope of this chapter, we may note here the shift in major Allied preoccupations.

On May 11, Mr. Churchill proposed a meeting of the Big Four to prepare a conference between the three Chiefs of Government in Bermuda.

Meanwhile, in July, the three Foreign Affairs Ministers met in Washington. Mr. Dulles was convinced that the changes in Soviet policy were a result of Allied firmness and that the Conference of Four should be postponed until EDC had been ratified. M. Bidault took a contrary tactical view—that ratification would be much easier once it could be proved that a genuine understanding with the USSR was impossible. The ministers decided to meet their Russian colleagues by the end of September.

At the end of July, the Armistice was signed in Korea. This focused the next question: when will there be peace in Indochina? From that moment, M. Bidault had but one idea: though speaking about Europe, he was thinking of Asia. Delayed by the French governmental crisis in July and by the illness of Churchill, the Bermuda Conference of the Big Three could not take place until December 4, 1953. The political itinerary which started there was to end in Geneva, via Berlin. This route was required by new turns in the diplomatic agenda. To the preliminaries already set forth concerning the Saar and British participation, two other conditions had been added: conversations with the East, and peace in Indochina. This meant two other conferences: Berlin and Geneva.

b) In the meantime, internal politics strengthened the opposition to the treaty: the development was made obvious by three important votes, which carried the seeds of EDC's destruction.

In December 1953, M. Laniel was defeated for the Presidency of the Republic, because M. Naegelen ran against him until the end. M. Naegelen, a Socialist, was hostile to the EDC. The vote was secret, but we know that besides the Communist and Socialist votes, he obtained about one hundred Gaullist and Radical votes.

This was partly a vote of domestic politics. The great majority of Socialists and many Radicals voted for M. Naegelen to defeat the Conservative candidates, M. Laniel and later M. Coty. But it was also a vote on foreign policy: the Communists and a fraction of the Gaullists supported the Socialist candidate on the second vote because he was hostile to EDC.

During the following month, January 1954, M. Le Troquer was elected to the presidency of the Assembly under the same conditions. The election of his rival M.R.P. candidate, M. Pflimlin, would have been a success for "Europe." Hence the "European" Socialists and many Radicals voted for him, despite his M.R.P. label. The Gaullists and Communists voted against M. Pflimlin and for M. Le Troquer, himself rather favorable to a European policy, mainly to defeat the M.R.P. candidate, who was entirely devoted to EDC.

These developments, we recall, were initiated in March 1952, when the dissident Gaullists entered the majority under Pinay and the Socialists went over to the opposition. The trend became more marked when the orthodox Gaullists, who had remained faithful to the General, joined the majority under René Mayer in January 1953 and the Laniel Cabinet in June 1953.

Two assumptions had been quite general: 1) *that the Gaullist Rassemblement was a national, but social, movement which would incline French policy toward the left*; and 2) *that it would sacrifice its hostility to the European army, in order to be accepted within the majority*.

The opposite happened: first the Gaullists showed themselves to be quite conservative and helped to reinforce the Right in the majority and in the government. The early R.P.F. had wanted to be popular and even revolutionary, but the Gaullist parliamentary group of 1951 included mostly "bourgeois" deputies elected by Moderate voters (who had voted for the M.R.P. in 1945–1946 and were to vote for the Independents in 1953). In the second place, instead of softening their anti-European policy, the Gaullists accentuated it; because it was the only common point they still had with the General, and because this compensated him for their participation in the government against his wishes.

This double phenomenon had two consequences: first, the government's drift to the Right discouraged Leftist elements, who broke away from the majority and formed an opposition which grew constantly stronger (alongside the Communist opposition). The Socialists were the most dynamic element of this opposition, but increasingly large minorities from the Radical party and from the M.R.P. regularly voted with them against the government.

Being classical Liberals, the Radicals are socially and economically on the Right, but they tend to the Left on political and secular questions. Whenever the Right seems too "clerical" or too "reactionary," the Radical party moves toward the Left.

But if the Right influenced the Gaullists in domestic matters, the contrary happened in foreign policy. The anti-European Gaullists succeeded in weakening the pro-European feelings of the Moderates. When M. Pinay and his friends published a proclamation in November 1953, designed to win over both the Right and the former R.P.F., they carefully avoided any reference to Europe. This didn't happen by chance.

Meanwhile, a similar phenomenon occurred on the Left. The anti-European propaganda of the Communists impressed many

Socialists and even Radicals. It induced the two parties to tone down their European policy, the Socialists in order to maintain their standing with the workers, and the Radicals in order to work out an agreement with the Peasants. Besides, the following line of reasoning offered itself to the minds of many: to be anti-European is to be nationalist (like de Gaulle, Herriot, the Count of Paris . . .); the Communists are anti-European; they are consequently Nationalist (in spite of their traditional attachment to the USSR).

So that the entrance of the R.P.F. into the government majority brought about a double victory over the "Europe of the Six": a direct victory in the newly governing coalition of the Right, which was less European despite the presence of the M.R.P.; and an indirect victory by inducing the Left to form a less European (even rather anti-European) coalition, in spite of the Socialist Europeans dominating the S.F.I.O.

THE SUBSTITUTE SOLUTIONS (LES SOLUTIONS DE RÉCHANGE)

The already great complexity of internal divisions in French politics thus reached its supreme degree. Aside from the Communists, there was not one party or one mind undivided, unhesitant, untortured.

"France," wrote the Count of Paris, "has never been obliged to take such risks since the treaty at Troyes of Isabeau de Bavières, the treaty that delivered the kingdom of France to King Henry V of England."

"No vote," declared M. Jules Moch, "has troubled our conscience so much since the vote of the National Assembly of Vichy in July 1940, the vote which surrendered the Third Republic into the hands of Marshal Pétain for the Armistice with Hitler."

The doubts and anxiety of some contrasted with the hopes and certainty of others. It may be that all these elements together could be found within every mind. It was a drama of conscience for every Frenchman.

If one sought guidance from the highest authorities of the country, one found that Marshal Juin, General de Gaulle and all the generals who became famous during the last war (with one or two exceptions); the Count of Paris, heir to the Throne of France; Herriot, the patriarch of the Republic; Maurice Thorez, "the best French disciple of Stalin" [5]; Daladier, the man of Munich; M. Vincent Auriol, the first President of the Fourth Republic—all these men of experience were against the EDC.

On the other side were ranged the veteran Paul Reynaud; MM. Robert Schuman and René Pléven; M. Teitgen, President of the M.R.P.; M. Guy Mollet, Secretary general of the S.F.I.O.; M. Delbos and M. René Mayer—in short, those men who, as Prime Ministers and Ministers, were and would be responsible for France's policy. All these favored EDC.

Divided between the prestige of the men of the past and the authority of the men of the present, the French people hoped for a compromise which would satisfy all legitimate fears and desires. Uncertain of victory, both partisans and adversaries needed a compromise of such sort that the final decision on the treaty would not entail success or defeat for half the country.

These feelings were the background for the "substitute solutions" presented from both sides.

Some of these solutions sought to guarantee that the French army would continue to exist or at least would not be brutally and totally absorbed into the European Army. They were not only attached to past memories; they were also convinced that, much as the French military apparatus had suffered through the Indochinese war, it still had a certain value. They did not want to sacrifice it irreparably without knowing first what would be the real strength of the European Defense Community.

Others thought that a treaty which affected national defense so deeply could only be voted by a national majority. The French Right had not always been so patriotic—e.g., not after 1870 nor after 1940. But it was still nationalistic. To act without it now would incur lasting hostility toward the European army of those conservative forces regarded as most faithful to French military traditions.

What possible solutions would preserve both the French army and the national unity? Three were proposed:

Association Instead of Integration: General Weygand, and in a lesser degree General de Gaulle, were partisans of this solution, which would substitute for organic integration the classical pattern of allied armies. The European headquarters would be inte-

[5] In the words of his fellow-Communist Etienne Fajon.

grated, as was already the case at SHAPE, but the national armies would keep their autonomy.

This proposal was not approved by the M.R.P. nor by the S.F.I.O. Since it would revive the German General Staff, and threaten again the whole policy of European unification, it had no chance of being accepted by these parties unless the EDC was defeated.

Partial Integration: A solution advocated by some Socialists, some Gaullists, and the Count of Paris proposed to integrate armaments in peacetime, but armies only in wartime. An integrated European headquarters would be created in order to unify strategy.

To avoid the defeat of the treaty and the necessity of reopening basic negotiations, this solution proposed to eliminate those clauses concerning integration of the armies and the supranational authority, since the latter would not be necessary if the integration were limited. Such a system would also make it possible for Great Britain to participate more closely in the community.

But for this solution to be accepted by the Europeans, again, the treaty had first to be defeated.

"Loose Interpretation" solutions designed for more flexible application of the existing treaty. Some defenders of EDC, in and out of the government (MM. Bidualt and Laniel, even MM. Robert Schuman and Pléven) agreed on reducing the supranational authority of the Commissariat. That this institution should in no way become a "European Pentagon" was one point of agreement.

Another was to ease the transition to the future community. The treaty foresaw an interim period of 18 months during which the Commissariat would be represented by a delegate from each country. The new idea was to make this temporary period as long as possible, maintaining in France (and creating in Germany) a national defense ministry. Neither M. Laniel nor M. Pléven seemed hostile to this solution. But the Socialists and other "Europeans" refused to consider any solution which might be ratified without their votes.

It was M. Pinay, who, after talks outside of government channels with Generals de Gaulle and Billotte, proposed deferring any kind of supranational organization until a real political entity for

Europe could be created. The "Europeans" agreed, as they had always considered an elected political authority the first condition for a European army.

FROM BERLIN TO GENEVA

But neither partisans nor adversaries really undertook to reach a compromise prior to the parliamentary meeting of February. M. Laniel had studied the documents relating to the treaty and the substitute solutions; one of his ministers, General Corniglion-Molinier, favored dissociating the military aspects of the treaty from the political aspects. But if the EDC was much discussed at the Big Four foreign ministers' meeting in Berlin, it was largely neglected in Paris. The Gaullists, indeed, protested that the French negotiators in Berlin were acting as if French ratification were assured "against every possibility." On the other hand, the "Europeans" were disturbed by the Berlin declaration of M. Bidault "that a reunified Germany would not be bound by the EDC." M. Robert Schuman sharply protested against this statement. This was the seed of a long controversy which provided yet another point of opposition to the treaty.

At the beginning of February, while Marshal Juin declared that the treaty was "unacceptable," M. Jules Moch announced that the investigation by the Foreign Affairs Commission had revealed that, of the twenty conditions set by the Assembly in 1952, only five were completely fulfilled.

A few days later, the Gaullist group "renewed its irreducible hostility to the so-called European Army treaty." General Corniglion-Molinier echoed this hostility in the Council of Ministers on February 13: on behalf of the Gaullist ministers, he read a prepared declaration which asked for a substitute solution. The government, in the name of which M. Bidault was speaking in Berlin, remained very much divided in Paris. At the National Defense Commission, General Koenig condemned, at this time, a treaty which seemed to him "utterly inefficient from the military point of view."

A two-years old scene now was repeated. The R.P.F. opposed a debate; the M.R.P. favored it. Early in March the National Committee of the M.R.P. "insisted again that the EDC debate be started without further delay, because of the urgent need that Parliament declare itself on French foreign policy and in order to discharge French domestic policy from obligations which paralyze the functioning of the system." M. Lecourt, then President of the M.R.P. group, officially requested a debate from M. Laniel. A few days later, at the Radical Congress, M. René Mayer declared suddenly that he couldn't understand why Radical ministers remained in the government which couldn't even decide to fix a date for a debate.

In fact, the government had not yet made up its mind. The Gaullist ministers, MM. Corniglion-Molinier, Ulver and Lemaire, did not want the treaty even mentioned before the conditions were fulfilled (i.e., before the "preliminaries" were concluded). They went even further, refusing any debate before the Geneva conference. Some proposed to abandon the EDC in exchange for peace in Indochina.

The discussion continued for months under different forms. The position of M. Laniel was more simple. He stuck to his investiture declaration: "Some day, Parliament will have to take a position on the subject, namely when the Saar question is settled, the interpretive protocols signed, and the negotiations now proceeding with Great Britain concluded."

M. Bidault endeavored to speed action on the parliamentary, diplomatic and governmental levels, in order to finish, if possible, before the Geneva conference of the Big Four; the more so since a Socialist party congress was soon to re-examine the party's position.

On the parliamentary level, M. Bidault promised, in answer to the Foreign Affairs Commission, that the government would seek a vote from the Assembly on the duration of military service, on the amount of the financial contribution, and on the statute of military forces, before taking a decision at the Council of Ministers. By this expedient, Parliament could keep some rights it was afraid of losing to the Community. But now Marshal Juin publicly opposed the treaty [6] and declared himself favorable to a substitute solution (limited German forces integrated in the Atlantic Army). Next 59 Socialist deputies—more than half their total—signed a manifesto condemning the EDC. The Gaullists per-

[6] Some days later it was stated that on January 27, 1954, Marshal Juin had already written to M. Laniel that "the treaty violently offends the national feelings" and that he considered that "a categorical refusal would be better than a conditional acceptance!"

ceived, in amendments being made to the German Constitution, a possible dissociation between the treaty of Paris and the Accords of Bonn. The opposition to the treaty became much more vigorous.

On the diplomatic level, while French-German negotiations on the Saar made no progress, and while Bonn still refused to sign the additional protocols concluded almost a year before, conversations between the Six and the British began on March 26. The convention of cooperation between Great Britain and the Community was signed on April 12.

Then occurred, on the government level, a burst of fury among the adversaries of the treaty. The Ministers had been notified at the last minute that an extraordinary meeting of the Council of Ministers was to take place in order to discuss signing the convention with Britain. General Corniglion-Molinier and the Gaullist ministers protested violently against receiving an hour's notice while Parliament was in recess. Two Radical Ministers also spoke up; M. Edgar Faure declared that it was a bad time to reawaken the EDC debate, just before the Geneva conference; M. Martinaud-Deplat asserted that it would have been possible to obtain more substantial commitments from Great Britain. In reality, all this was aimed against the treaty, for if the conditions were fulfilled, the debate could start.

The partisans of the treaty knew it. "The time for consideration is over, this is the hour of decision," declared M. Teitgen, Vice-President of the Council and M.R.P. President. He insisted that Ministers who did not agree should resign, and he opposed any "new hesitation." M. Laniel now seemed inclined toward the EDC partisans, and despite the opposition of 8 or 9 ministers, the Council of Ministers authorized signature of the convention and decided "to propose in any case that Parliament fix a date for the examination of the EDC treaty."

M. Laniel gave assurances to the adversaries of the treaty: the convention with Britain would have to be approved by Parliament and the date of the debate could not be fixed before the Assembly met again. The Gaullists protested, nevertheless, against the "secrets" of M. Bidault and the *fait accompli* of the British convention which apparently only fulfilled preliminary conditions. They wondered if "new blows" of the same kind were not in preparation for the other conditions, e.g., the American guarantee and the Saar agreement. The Radical ministers expressed reservation "in substance and form." A ministerial crisis was narrowly avoided.

On the following Thursday, April 15, a new meeting of the ministers took place: a violent discussion broke out between Bidault, backed by Laniel, and Edgar Faure, backed by the Radicals and Gaullists. M. Bidault affirmed that a discussion, even if only on fundamentals, would greatly increase the chances of getting the cooperation expected from the United States. M. Faure asserted, on the contrary, that any parliamentary decision would hamper our negotiators and would reduce the chances for an agreement with the United States and for peace in Indochina. The Council of Ministers finally decided that "when the negotiations on the conditions preliminary to a ratification have been fulfilled, the government will ask the President of the Assembly, on May 18, to make the necessary arrangements so that the debate on the British and American guarantees, on the Saar agreement, on the additional protocols, and on the Bonn and Paris treaties can be started."

The resolution sought not to fix a date for the debate, but the *date on which Parliament must decide on the date of the debate.* The distinction is important. The adversaries, however, were not satisfied, and the Gaullist ministers threatened for the third time to withdraw from the government.

During this troubled week of April 1954, the Laniel cabinet was condemned. Already, even without the defeat in Indochina, EDC was dead. May 18 passed without anybody in the government thinking of asking Parliament to fix a date for the debate: Dien Bien Phu had fallen on the 13th. Minds and hearts were not in Europe but in Asia. The Laniel cabinet fell on June 12.

The Death Blow: April to August 1954

Before its fall, the Laniel-Bidault government strove during the difficult Geneva debate and the Dien Bien Phu drama to fulfill the conditions for an EDC debate. But things went from bad to worse when, at the end of April, General Eisenhower confirmed and defined the American guarantee. The Gaullists, feeling that they had been fooled, talked of withdrawing from the government. They did not find that General Eisenhower's declaration had added anything new. They maintained that neither the British convention (of which the French government had taken cognizance) nor the American declarations really fulfilled the preliminary conditions. M. Laniel refused to receive the delegation which brought their motion to him.

The Socialists, however, considered that Britain and the United States had satisfied two or three of the conditions they had set. There remained the condition of democratic control over the EDC and when, on May 4, agreement was reached on this point, the Socialist Congress was called for May 30. Their debate, awaited for two years, took place. But, too late.

THE FAILURE OF THE CONGRESS

Division had made headway in the Socialist party. On the eve of the extraordinary Congress, the great majority of the party's National Committee (21 of 31 members) declared itself again favorable to EDC. But the majority of the Socialist deputies solemnly demonstrated (58 to 104) their hostility to the treaty, asserting that none of the conditions set by their party had been satisfied. They even belittled the "agreement on a political authority, the form and application of which would be deferred until the EDC ratification." The majority motion at the party congress concentrated on these three points:

1) that the EDC was but an element in the general policy of European unification, and at the present moment the only means of avoiding the reconstitution of a free German army while creating an instrument of collective security;

2) that the EDC can have no real significance unless a close association with Great Britain, a guarantee from the United States, and democratic control be secured;

3) that on the three conditions specified above, sufficient satisfaction had been obtained.

Consequently, the party took a position in favor of ratification.

The motion presented by the minority (1215 votes) considered:

1) that the EDC treaty contradicts international socialist efforts to reach a progressive, simultaneous and controlled reduction of armaments;

2) that it sanctions, irretrievably, the present division of Ger-

many, a source of vexation, nationalism and war, and the consequent division of Europe into two blocs;

3) that it hinders negotiations between East and West;

4) that the treaty, as submitted for ratification, is more dangerous than efficacious, and that it includes no serious guarantees against eventual aggression;

5) that EDC contains the seeds and the elements of an autonomous Wehrmacht;

6) that France is justified when she opposes any form of German rearmament, for there is no risk of the allies' giving up continental Europe;

7) that the conditions set by the party for ratification are not fulfilled.

Hence the parliamentary group should refuse to ratify present projects as submitted to the French Parliament.

It is noteworthy that 47 federations voted against the treaty and only 42 for it. The latter, however, included the most important federations (Nord, Pas de Calais, Haute Vienne, Bouches du Rhône) and their influence on the Congress was decisive.

On June 9, the Foreign Affairs Commission of the National Assembly rejected the EDC by 24 votes to 18, and 2 abstentions. Six Socialists voted against the treaty and 3 for it. The decisions of the Socialist Congress thus were flouted, both on the treaty itself and on the voting discipline which the party congress had invoked. The party's Board of Directors announced that sanctions would be taken. It was labor lost. When the National Defense Commission rejected the treaty on June 18 by 29 votes to 13 and 1 abstention, 4 Socialists voted against and 3 for. Despite this new demonstration of indiscipline, the party leaders still had illusions about their ability to control the Socialist deputies. This changed with the fall of the Laniel Cabinet. Those Socialists who opposed the treaty now became the staunchest supporters of M. Mendès-France.

THE CONFRONTATION OF MENDÈS-FRANCE

The Laniel Cabinet fell on June 12, by 306 votes to 293 and 12 abstentions, after the third debate on the Indochinese situation. Besides the Socialists and Communists, 33 Radicals (among them some EDC partisans) and 44 Gaullists voted against M. Laniel.

Voting for him: the whole M.R.P., the Moderates, 35 Radicals, 11 U.D.S.R. (EDC partisans), and 24 Gaullists. But, if the Indo-chinese war killed the Laniel government, it also killed the EDC. On June 18, M. Mendès-France was invested by the National Assembly. Besides the Communist votes, which Mendès-France had said he would not count as part of his majority, he obtained 310 votes against 47 and 143 abstentions. All the Socialists and practically all the Radicals voted for him; so did 59 Gaullists (the rest abstained) and a certain number of deputies from the other parties by virtue of personal sympathy.

Mendès-France reaffirmed, as he had in 1953, his faithfulness to the Western Alliance, and declared regarding Europe that "for her friends as well as for herself, France could no longer prolong the equivocal situation which affects the interests of the alliance." To the Assembly he said:

The EDC puts before us one of the greatest matters of conscience which ever disturbed a country. It is a distressing sight—to which we cannot resign ourselves—to see the French people so deeply divided on an issue which is so closely connected with our national sensibilities. Is it not possible to set the problem objectively, and to put aside the affective elements which so often dim the real facts?

One of these facts is the necessity of Western rearmament, required by the international situation, and this has led us into considering—sore trial for the French people—the conditions of German participation in a common defense organization.

The fact that the nation is torn at such a time by passionate controversies about the forms and the institutions of this defense community; the fact that our country has resounded already for months to the great and painful quarrel which threatens to last for years, cannot be accepted by a real Frenchman, and we have to put an end to this for the sake of our national unity (applause from the Left). I appeal to the adversaries as well as to the partisans of the EDC and beseech them to give up their intransigeance, which in the end can but weaken the morale of the country and the framework of our defense.

I cannot believe that men of equal good faith, who agree on the fundamentals of the issue at large, cannot make it up with each other, even if this requires a difficult effort.

The government I wish to constitute will organize the necessary confrontation, the rapprochement which our country needs. Men and patriots of good will will be brought together and will be required, during the brief period we have to devote primarily to the settlement of the Indochinese conflict, to lay the foundations of an agreement which will be submitted to the Parliament. If these conversations prove to be ineffective, the government alone will take the responsibility.

The problem is to define the conditions which, taking into consideration the aspirations and the hesitations of the country, will allow us to create a unified national attitude, indispensable to any project of European defense. Definite proposals will be submitted to the Assembly, in any case, before the parliamentary recess.

Our allies will know, thus, that shortly they will get a clear and constructive answer from France, the answer they have waited for so long and have a right to expect from her.

To this confrontation of the rival viewpoints two members of the government—one favorable to the treaty (M. Bourgès-Manoury, Radical) and the other hostile (General Koenig, Gaullist)—proceeded without success. The two ministers endeavored to identify the general principles of the treaty which had been accepted both by partisans and opponents in good faith. But the Gaullists recalled that they were opposed to the fundamental principle of the treaty, the principle of supranationality, and that they had asked for the participation of Great Britain in the Community.

In addition, General Billotte delivered a statement to Mendès-France, in the name of the A.R.S. (dissident ex-Gaullists), excluding any supranational authority and limiting this authority "to a political meeting of the Chiefs of Governments." Two other deputies, MM. Bonnefous (U.D.S.R.) and Bardoux (Peasant), handed a counter-proposal to Mendès-France, extending the community to all the Western European countries and transforming the Council of Ministers of Strasbourg into a political organism which would have the power of decision. Finally, six Moderate deputies proposed to "submit the treaty to a referendum."

The Socialist party was obviously tired of the controversy, as were many of the others. When Mr. Dulles proposed, in case EDC were defeated, to restore to Germany her full sovereignty, the reception was almost favorable except among the hottest supporters of the Treaty of Paris. The adversaries concluded from this declaration that the defeat of EDC would provoke the reversal of alliances and the reconsideration of the Atlantic policy.

M. Mendès-France had warned Mr. Dulles, when he had come through Paris, that EDC could not be ratified in its form at that time. When he came back from Geneva, Mendès-France took cognizance of the documents relating to the confrontation between General Koenig and M. Bourgès-Manoury. A large survey of the arguments for and against the treaty, it was but an "academic" document, for no agreement had been reached between the two views. M. Guérin de Beaumont and M. Parodi, general secretary of the Quai d'Orsay, tried to find new protocols.

At the beginning of August Mendès-France encountered the same difficulties as his predecessors; he promised the M.R.P. that the debate would take place later that month. On what would it bear? "On the EDC," he answered, "and on other questions." "These other questions," he added, "cannot worry the 'Europeans,' but will respond to some of the fears of the adversaries of the treaty." But this did not at all calm the anxiety of the Gaullists: "The foundation of our agreement with Mendès-France," they recalled, "excludes any solution which could divide the French people"—i.e., in their minds, it excluded the EDC debate altogether.

The duel between the M.R.P. and the R.P.F. threatened to break out again. But this time, the M.R.P. did not participate in the government—its greatest mistake. Even when it had participated in the government, it could not prevail; outside the government, the party was powerless. The parliamentary game continued without them.

On August 11, 12 and 13, Mendès-France presented "his" solution to the members of the government. The main idea consisted in the suspension of any clause of supranationality for eight years. During this period, the Council of Ministers of the Community would have to decide unanimously on appeals presented by a member State against decisions of the Commissariat. Each country would have the right of veto. In another of the seven amendments, he proposed to limit integration to the covering forces, i.e., to the forces stationed in Germany. Thus, there would be no European army but only air forces, on French territory.

Three Gaullist ministers—General Koenig, MM. Lemaire and Chaban-Delmas—nevertheless resigned. The parliamentary group approved them "for having refused to sanction modifications of questionable value, which do not change anything in the supranationality principle; nor in the narrow framework of the Community of Six." Three other Gaullist ministers—MM. Fouchet, Ulver and Catroux—remained within the government to see how the situation would develop after the Brussels conference.

But neither would the "Europeans", mainly in the M.R.P. and S.F.I.O., defend the Mendès-France solution. When the Brussels conference at which Mendès-France presented his "protocols" to the other EDC signatories had started and was already in difficulty, two articles, one by M. Robert Schuman and the other by M. André Philip, publicized their view that the compromise presented by M. Mendès-France was unacceptable. "The right of veto is too great and the whole system would be paralyzed," wrote Schuman, "the treaty is emptied of all its substance." "Any breach in supranationality," wrote Philip, "any renunciation of military and political integration, would create a unanimous opposition of the Socialists to a text thus mutilated."

The parallelism of these two articles, as well as the moment chosen for their publication, indicated that a joint campaign against Mendès-France had been undertaken by the partisans of the treaty. At least, this was the view taken by Mendès-France himself. Witnesses affirm that when he learned of the articles at Brussels, he felt that he had been stabbed in the back. First forsaken by the anti-Europeans, now attacked by the Europeans, he now refused any new concession and resigned himself to the defeat of his compromise and of the conference.

There were still very few EDC partisans who believed that an amended treaty was the only way to avoid a complete rejection. Many were convinced that Mendès-France had presented his compromise in the hope of having it refused at Brussels. Wasn't this the "something else" which he had promised the M.R.P.? Nevertheless, the M.R.P. had the feeling of having been fooled.

THE CRIME OF AUGUST 30TH

The compromise of Mendès-France having failed, the only step remaining for him was to submit the treaty as it stood to the National Assembly. The partisans of the treaty recognized, finally, that ratification would be difficult and proposed in extremis various means to save it. It was, as always, too late. The government no longer wished to negotiate. What would be its attitude during the final debate?

The answer was simple: the government could only be neutral. Otherwise there would not be *any* debate, for the good reason that there would not be any government. The adversaries of the treaty would rather force the resignation of their deputies and, if necessary, the fall of the government. So clear was this situation that the Council of Ministers decided a vote of confidence would not be required.[7]

The government remaining neutral, what would be the attitude of its chief, Mendès-France? He was in a queer situation. He could not completely support a treaty which he partly disapproved and wanted to modify; nor could he refuse to take some interest in a treaty which engaged the fate of the nation, as he had said.

Mendès-France promised only that he would make a loyal and complete report of the negotiations at Brussels. But when, on the eve of the debate, he made his report to the parliamentary commissions, his audience inferred that he had concluded that the treaty would be rejected. On August 26, Mendès-France declared himself favorable to any other form of German rearmament than the one involved in EDC. Why, then, did he not take a clearer position against the treaty in the Assembly? Mendès-France could only have done so at the risk of being abandoned by those ministers who favored ratification [8] after he had already lost its strongest adversaries. Thus, until the very last minute of this agony, the Presidents of the Council remained the victims and prisoners of a divided government.

The day before the debate, General de Gaulle, the Count of Paris, and M. Vincent Auriol expressed anew their hostility to the treaty. The French Union Assembly, an advisory body representing the French overseas territories, expressed an opinion unfavorable to ratification. This was the case also for all the commissions of the National Assembly.

Feeling that defeat was almost certain, the defenders of the treaty tried the impossible: to postpone a debate they had so often requested. A motion of adjournment was prepared. It asked

[7] He would have requested one, declared M. Mendès-France, if his propositions had been accepted in Brussels. Failing this, the government was not able to exert on the deputies the pressure which results from a vote of confidence.
[8] After the defeat of the treaty, MM. Claudius Petit, Bourgès-Manoury and Emile Hughes handed in their resignations, which they would have done earlier if M. Mendès-France had declared himself against the treaty.

for postponement of the debate to a certain date, and the re-sumption of negotiations with the Five on a protocol of application. Threatened by this prejudicial motion, the adversaries of the treaty decided to oppose the "preliminary question," which, if voted, would lead to a possible postponement of the old debate. Thus, as soon as it started, the debate was concentrated on a question of procedure which covered in reality a problem of substance. This was argued about long after the debate was over. But nobody had been fooled in the end. The partisans of the treaty complained that they couldn't speak; they even talked about violence. The adversaries recalled that they had asked for the "preliminary question" only after the prejudicial motion by the defenders of the treaty themselves. The polemics were as violent during the session as they were later behind the scenes. Days passed and the conditions in which the vote occurred were forgotten. Only the results were important; they are shown below. The treaty had been rejected.

Parliamentary Vote on EDC

Parliamentary Groups	Total Members	Against	For	Abstained	No Vote
Communists	95	95			
Progressists	4	4			
Socialists	105	53	50	1	1*
Radical Socialists	76	34	33	2	7†
U.D.S.R.	19	10	3	1	5
M.R.P.	89	2	80	4	3
Overseas Independents	15	3	11	–	1
Republican Independents	54	12	36	1	5
Peasants	27	6	20	–	1
A.R.S.	33	16	14	2	1
Social Republicans	73	67	2	–	4
Without party (Gaullists)	12	7	1	1	3
TOTAL	602	309	250	12	31‡

* M. Le Troquer, who presided, did not vote.
† Including M. Fabre, absent on leave.
‡ Including 23 members of the government.

The "Europeans" never forgave M. Mendès-France what they called "the crime of August 30." Six months later, they overthrew him, ostensibly on his North African policy, but in reality because they considered him responsible for the defeat of EDC.

Conclusion

The EDC treaty was a victim of time. Time accentuated the conflicts inherent in the policy of European integration and in France's domestic politics.

The partisans of an integrated Europe of Six had recognized this and felt compelled to put "the cart before the horse." They sought to build military integration before economic unification, and before political integration was even begun, so that German rearmament could be incorporated within a European construction.

Oppositions of various kinds joined against the treaty; that of the Nationalists, hostile to *any* European construction; that of the Gaullists, who rejected specifically an integration among the Six; and that of the Communists, hostile to any kind of West German rearmament.

Except the Communist party, which exerts strict discipline of action, all the groups were deeply divided. There were Nationalists, Pacifists, Europeans and Neutralists in each. Every group was divided against itself and every deputy, at one moment or another, doubted his own personal convictions.

A European conscience, above particular political convictions, had formed itself slowly. But it was not strong enough to constitute a kind of supra-European party which could have prevailed over the existing structure. The traditional categories—social, political, religious—won. Thus, the force of this complex problem in an almost anarchical political context undermined three governments and led to a fourth which had finally to sacrifice the treaty altogether.

The construction of Europe should have had, as a basis, a stronger France. This its partisans in the M.R.P. and S.F.I.O. had understood, but these two parties were not able to achieve it. During the first legislature, they did not succeed in achieving their social and economic policy. During the second, they split. The weight of the conservative forces became, then, more and more significant.

The decline of European unification started on the day when,

for domestic political reasons, the Socialists deserted the majority;
the day when the Right, Gaullists and Moderates, entered into
the governmental majority with all their votes and their influence.

The "Europeans" of every political or intellectual cast forgot
that, even if their ideal was revolutionary, the reality was not.
They did not remember (or remembered too late) that in foreign
policy as in domestic policy, nothing new, nothing great, can be
built on social and economic conservatism, that is to say, without
the real approval and active participation of the nation. This is
true for the past, as it is for the future.

8 : The Postmortems

(from August 30 to vote of December 30, 1954)

STANLEY HOFFMANN

Time has the reputation of maturing minds and resolving differences. But in the case of EDC, time damaged the parliamentary situation and the treaty's chances. It also welded the Community's friends and foes into surprisingly compact blocs. Each of them had adopted a kind of minimum code of arguments which were acceptable to the entire group. As if they had agreed to do so, they both limited their attack or their defense to the treaty's technical substance, i.e. to its provisions. They did not go beyond. Only thus could such blocs be formed.

The treaty's enemies, disagreeing as to the merits of integration *per se*, were chiefly divided between those who opposed the very principle of rearmament defined in the treaty, and those who opposed German rearmament (or rather, to use a cliché, between nationalists and neutralists, not to mention the Communists who will not be dealt with here). But they all agreed at least in attacking the EDC as a case of inappropriate rearmament and integration. It revived a barely disguised Wehrmacht;[1] its institutions

---

[1] Reports of MM. Jules Moch and Max Lejeune; their speeches and that of M. Triboulet, August 28 and 29, *J.O., Assemblée Nationale*,* pp. 4379–4401; pamphlet "Contre le traité actuel de la C.E.D. pour la liberté de vote et l'unité fraternelle du parti" published at the end of March 1954 by the opponents of E.D.C. on the S.F.I.O.

* Hereafter referred to as *J.O., Ass. Nat.*

were so unbalanced that Germany would have the most weight;[2] and they were so unwieldy that the French army, the French Union, the nation's economy and public authorities would be disorganized.[3] The treaty's supporters, who disagreed about the future of European integration, as the debates of 1952 and 1953 had revealed, rallied to the defense of what survived the demise of the draft treaty for a Federal political community in the debate of November 1953. This survivor was the common defense system. They presented it as the best possible scheme because from a military standpoint, it provided France with serious guarantees vis-à-vis Germany,[4] and because, from a political standpoint it was better to keep Germany in the rigid framework of EDC than to let her free in the looser system of a Seven, Twelve, or Fifteen-Power Europe.[5] This was also the only system possible because France had no majority for any other plan, and would be isolated if she were to dismiss the present one.[6] In each camp each group developed its common theme in its own way; but the theme was strong enough for the coalition to appear harmonious and well-disciplined.

The collapse of EDC disturbed this harmony. The government's choice of a substitute solution resulted in the two blocs' dissolution, but did not build up new ones. The purpose of this chapter is to describe that dissolution. This time each faction kept to its own theme: a sophist's controversy followed a religious war. Their attitudes towards the new treaty make it, therefore, possible

---

[2] Reports and speeches of M. Lejeune and P.O. Lapie; M. Jacques Bardoux to the Commission des Affaires Etrangères, Monde, April 1, 1954; M. Maroger, "Construction européenne", Revue des Deux Mondes, April 15, 1954; M. Leo Hamon, "Les fausses consolations", Monde, August 29, 1954, after the Brussels Conference.

[3] Report of General Koenig; speeches of MM. Brusset and Apithy, J.O., Ass. Nat. p. 4405 and p. 4419; report of the "journée d'études des fonctionnaires sur le traité de Paris" entitled "La C.E.D. et la Communauté française", May 1954.

[4] Speeches of the supporters of E.D.C.: MM. René Mayer and Alfred Coste-Floret on August 29, 1954, J.O., Ass. Nat., pp. 4445–4451; MM. Reynaud, Mollet and Teitgen on August 31, J.O., Ass. Nat., pp. 4477, 4483, 4494.

[5] "Douze lettres sur la C.E.D.", published in pamphlet form by the European Movement in April 1954, p. 20.

[6] See the "libres propos" of M. Etienne Borne, Monde, January 6, 1954, and of M. Alfred Coste-Floret in the issue of March 25; and René Courtin, "Responsabilités françaises", in Courrier européen for March–April.

to distinguish the groups which had been mixed together for so long, as well as the reasons which had determined each decision for or against the dead treaty.

First Discords (August 31–September 20)

THE SUPPORTERS OF EDC

The treaty's rejection did not by itself bring about the dissolution of these blocs. But it did some harm to their solidarity. As long as no new proposal which could break it up was made, the pro-EDC bloc had no reason to collapse. Indeed, all the arguments its members had put forward before the vote of August 30, in a warning mood, were used again during the three weeks of intermission in a mood of recrimination and anxiety. They refused an uncontrolled rearmament of Germany. They were afraid of the freedom of action Germany had recaptured and which could lead her to deal directly with the American Republicans,[7] to practice a balance-of-power policy,[8] or to yield to temptation from the East.[9] Above all, they were disturbed by France's internal and external situation: would not France be pushed into a reversal of her alliances, by the likely absence of a majority for any other technique of rearmament,[10] and by the collusion between a government which had refused to take sides and the neutralists, [11] the fellow-travelers,[12] or even the Communists? [13], [14]

But though the supporters of EDC went on as if nothing had changed, they could not suppress some disagreements about the future. Now that EDC was dead, they had to answer two ques-

[7] Statement of M. De Felice to *Combat* on September 1, 1954.
[8] Communiqué from the Executive Commission of the M.R.P. September 2.
[9] Manifesto of the Executive Committee of the French Organization of the European Movement, September 3; "L'occasion manquée" by André Siegfried, *Figaro*, September 9; "Nos actes nous suivent" by Rémy Roure, *Figaro*, September 14.
[10] MM. Teitgen, Pinay, and Mollet, *J.O., Ass. Nat.*, pp. 4484, 4485, and 4497; Ch. Ronsac in *Franc-Tireur* on September 1.
[11] Raymond Aron, "Le choix n'est pas encore fait", *Figaro*, September 6.
[12] R. Duchet, in *France indépendante*, quoted by *Monde*, September 7.
[13] Pierre Brisson, "Rabâchage", *Figaro*, September 4; "Où en est-on?" *Ibid*, September 13; and "Dire et faire" *Ibid*, September 18.
[14] Thierry Maulnier in *Figaro*, September 2; Maurice Schumann in *Paris-Presse*, September 3.

tions which they had pushed aside in order to save their unity, as long as the treaty had not been voted on: the question of their attitude towards a different defense system, and the question of the future of European unity. It became immediately clear that there were two answers to the first one: some said that any new solution which would, partly at least, appease the opponents of EDC, would be unacceptable to EDC supporters;[15] but some stated that, in order to avoid the evils which were so much feared, they should not reject in advance a possible compromise as long as it would not lead to an unrestricted rearmament of Germany.[16]

The reactions to the second question are even more revealing. Already during the debates of August, the EDC supporters, except for the Socialists, had mostly spoken about EDC only. In the remaining part of their speeches, the only aspect of the European ideal which they stressed had been the repressive one: how to make Germany harmless. The Socialist leader, M. Guy Mollet, was the only one who emphasized the constructive aspect: how to get beyond the idea of sovereignty. The gap grew wider from then on, between those whom the ruins of EDC hypnotized and those who tried instead to dig the positive European ideal out from under those ruins, and who rejoiced because that ideal was no longer forcibly mixed up with EDC, as it had been ever since the prospect of a political community had been buried. The former swore that they would not give up the construction of Europe,[17] but they acted as if the mix-up went on: a defense system which would give the same guarantees to France would have to be established first. The latter believed that the military community was

---

[15] See the speech given by M. de Menthon in Strasbourg on September 10, *Monde*, September 21.

[16] The European Manifesto of September 3, (see note 9), signed by the EDC Supporters of the Right, of the M.R.P., of the U.D.S.R. and certain Radicals, (of which six were former Présidents du Conseil), was not signed by those of the S.F.I.O. nor by M. René Mayer. The three outgoing pro-EDC ministers declared themselves shortly afterwards favorable to a "realistic solution". Other notable EDC supporters followed them, (H. Frenay, "Nous ne ferons pas la politique du pire", *Monde*, September 7; editorial of *Franc-Tireur*, September 8; de Félice, "La défense de l'Europe à l'Assemblée de Strasbourg", *Monde*, September 15.

[17] Declaration of the Executive Commission of the M.R.P., *Monde*, September 3.

merely a lesser aspect of the real problem: the creation of a larger unit including several nations.[18]

Whereas the former refused any compromise in the military field, the latter were not yet all ready to accept one. The kind of Europe which they wanted to achieve was still Europe with supra-nationality; now, it was obvious that the new defense system would be less supranational than EDC: hence several hesitations.[19] And besides, were not two of the most ardent defenders of supranationality—MM. Schuman and Philip—the ones who on August 19th had denounced the French protocol of Brussels because it cut down the dose of it in the EDC?[20]

The die was not cast yet. But something was already breaking. The terms "Cédistes" [supporters of EDC] and "Européens" were no longer synonymous. From August on, some people were "Cédistes" above all and others were chiefly "Européens". Raymond Aron wrote that the fanaticism of EDC supporters would be as objectionable as their breaking up.[21] On September 20, only the convergence of two different kinds of fanaticism—the fanaticism of EDC's guarantees and the fanatacism of supranationality —could have prevented the break-up.

THE OPPONENTS OF EDC

After the treaty's end, one could have expected the disagreement between the enemies of Germany's rearmament and the adversaries of the specific EDC kind of rearmament to break out in the open. But it didn't. Perhaps they were embarrassed by the Communists' vote on EDC, or maybe they did not want to undermine the French Premier, whose internal action they approved and who, so they hoped, probably shared their hostility to German rearmament. The members of the first group proclaimed that it was merely the "present" remilitarization of Germany they objected to, and asked only that the Soviet Union's intentions be tested for the last time. Moreover, among those who took such a line, a

---

18 Emile Gabel: *La Croix*, September 3; Rene Courtin, "Espoirs et craintes des Européens", *Figaro*, September 15; speech of Guy Mollet to the Consultative Assembly of Strasbourg, *Monde*, September 21.

19 Especially with M. Mollet (see Jacques Fauvet, *Monde*, September 16 and M. Jaquet in *Populaire*, Sept. 21).

20 *Figaro* and *Franc-Tireur*, August 19.

21 "La fin de la C.E.D. ne doit pas être la fin de l'Europe", *Figaro*, September 3.

division appeared. Those who claimed that Russia should be approached at once before the vacuum was filled were isolated and did not seem too confident in their own proposal.[22] The others came out for an immediate drafting of a substitute defense system which should, however, be put into effect only if a previous Big Four discussion had failed.[23]

Furthermore, though on the subject of Germany's rearmament the inevitable discord, light as it was, could be heard, the agreement of both groups of EDC's opponents on the method of future European construction in general, and on the main features of a new defense system, remained unperturbed. The common fight against EDC had brought about a lasting merger between those men who had been against any type of supranational system from the start, and those who, on the contrary, had rejected EDC only because they thought that supranationality had been insufficiently and clumsily applied in its strictures. Supranationality appeared temporarily impracticable to the latter, and remained anathema to the former.[24] All preferred the method of association: they asked for full English participation [25] and they suggested a military confederation for the limitation and control of armaments, with close military integration.[26] This was their common answer to what one of them called "the Europe of ideologists, lawyers, and McCarthys." [27]

Insofar as they all wanted to loosen the bonds between France and Germany, they remained united. But a cleavage became apparent since some of them wanted to do so without breaking completely away from Germany, or breaking Germany away from

[22] France-Observateur on Sept. 9, strongly requested M. Mendès-France "not to go to London"; but the editorial writer of Combat was more embarrassed (Jean Fabiani, September 4); two of the main commentators of the Monde suggested the same procedure, without giving the impression that they believed it to be applicable. (Sirius, Sept. 1; Maurice Duverger, Sept. 9).

[23] Statements by MM. Barrès and Bouret in France-Observateur, Sept. 2; bulletin from abroad, Monde of Sept. 18, "L'Europe sans la supranationalité".

[24] See the report of M. Jules Moch and his speech of August 28.

[25] For the refusal of the "anticédistes" to discuss a military solution limited to the Six, cf. MM. Debré, Triboulet et Bonnefous en Strasbourg, Monde, September 19.

[26] Statement by General Billotte in Information, Sept. 3; M. Bardoux in Information, September 7; Pezet, "Wehrmacht ou non", Information, September 10.

[27] Maurice Duverger, "Construire l'Europe", Monde, Sept. 8.

the Atlantic Alliance; whereas the others did not rule out such extreme possibilities.

THE MENDÈS-FRANCE PLAN

At that moment, M. Mendès-France proposed his substitute plan. He had not given up what he had tried to achieve with his Brussels protocol: to conciliate the two camps. Nor had he given up the numerous ideas of both groups which were found in the protocol.

The principles of his plan were similar to those of the anti-EDC forces. On the military front, the "political technique" of EDC was on the whole discarded. There was no longer a *Commissariat* responsible for European defense. The main provisions for integration "from the top" were abandoned: those whose enactment had been entrusted to the Ministers' Council or to the *Commissariat* (the common budget, the duration of conscription, the promotions, the establishment of common rules on the armed forces' personnel, on their discipline, punishment and pay, etc.) as well as those which had already been written into the treaty (the European officers' schools, integrated territorial districts). Like EDC's opponents, M. Mendès-France believed that integration "from the top" in the six-power framework and under EDC's regulation was both dangerous as a principle [28] and unconvincing in detail.[29] On the political, economical, and social front also he thought that looser links between France and Germany were a justifiable necessity. Western European Union which includes Great Britain is "a frame in which a more homogeneous and better organized continent will be built".[30] By crossing out the famous article 7 of the Bonn treaty (reunification of Germany), he showed again as he did at Brussels that he was willing to run the risk of greater political latitude for Germany, as long as France also recovered more freedom of action.

But in the details of his plan, he took into account several pro-EDC arguments. He wanted to prevent the alliance of the fanati-

[28] See particularly *J.O., Ass. Nat.*, p. 4647 on the necessity of English participation.
[29] "En fait, c'était un état-major allemand sans le mot"; *ibid.*, p. 4648; See also pp. 6814 and 6915.
[30] *J.O., Ass. Nat.* p. 6884. See especially his speech and his "order of the day" in the debate in Nov. 1953.

cism of guarantees with the fanaticism of supranationality by removing any justification either of them could have. The new defense system should provide roughly the same military guarantees as EDC, through the use of supranationality and integration in very different fields. Supranationality was no longer an instrument for merger, but a technique of control. Integration was no longer a political weapon, but a military method; it was no longer applied "from the top", but "from below" (increase in J.A.C.E.U.R.'s powers, as regards the armed forces' deployment, regional distribution, training and exercises and, especially, logistical support). Thus,[31] M. Mendès-France believed that "the dangers so many Frenchmen were afraid of when the creation of an independent German army was mentioned a few months ago" [32] had been eradicated. The EDC supporters' requirement, a strong link between Germany and the West, could be met by purely technical means. In the non-military field, he promised permanent efforts for a "gradual" construction of a United Europe, which would cease to be a mere catch-word.[33] There he did not mind applying a larger measure of supranationality in more specialized areas than the broad military one. He suggested the use of the Coal and Steel Community, and the "establishment of similar organizations".[34] Hence, his plan for an armaments pool as an economic scheme. Moreover, if supranationality should conflict with the broader framework of a seven power Europe, bi-lateral or multi-lateral agreements could be negotiated in order to insure the former's victory.[35]

Finally, M. Mendès-France stressed a new element: possible bargaining with the East. The supporters of EDC had picked out only one side of EDC's international significance: the Atlantic one, i.e. the strengthening of the Western camp. The foes of EDC had been even more restrictive in order to save their unity. All their discussions had been from the standpoint of Franco-German relations. M. Mendès-France's approach was quite different. He

[31] Also on the means of maintaining the attitudes of the EDC on the level of the integration of forces, (cf. *J.O., Ass. Nat.*, p. 6815) and on the limitation of police and gendarme forces.

[32] *J.O., Ass. Nat.*, p. 6840.

[33] *J.O., Ass. Nat.*, p. 6817.

[34] *J.O., Ass. Nat.*, p. 6884.

[35] *J.O., Ass. Nat.*, p. 4652.

described his system as one which would not prevent a lessening of East-West tension or would indeed make *détente* possible by reinforcing the West (EDC supporters had already emphasized that.) [36] He also asserted that the new scheme would facilitate *détente* by its provisions on armaments' limitation and control.

Thus, M. Mendès-France's Strasbourg speech of September 20 put in new terms the old problem of European defense, and took up the two themes which had been left out by both camps during the EDC controversy: the future of European unity, and the effect of the military scheme on future relations between the two world camps. The final dissolution of both the pro-EDC and the anti-EDC camps came as a direct result of these three problems' conjunction. Let us look now at the result.

An Autopsy of the Pro-EDC Forces

AGREEMENT SURVIVES ON ONE POINT

All EDC supporters remained united on one point: the replacement in the defense system of a technique of political integration with a process of military integration weakens the bonds between Germany and the West. "The creation of a national German army with its High Command and its autonomous administration . . . exposes us . . . to the political danger which the integration system provided by EDC was designed to rule out".[37] When M. Mendès-France showed that this High Command would not enjoy greater military independence than in EDC, he did not reassure EDC's supporters on the political aspects of the problem.[38] Indeed, they believed that the loss of EDC's political safeguards might have three bad results. In the first place, the *Wehrmacht's* reappearance was a threat to German democracy.[39] Secondly, it might lead to collusion between the Soviet Union and

[36] See, for instance, the "douze lettres" noted above.

[37] Ch. Ronsac, *Franc-Tireur*, Sept. 21. See also Pineau, "La preuve du dilemme", *France-Tireur*, Sept. 24.

[38] See the motion of EDC supporters in the October debate; three of them asked for integration measures from the top (*J.O.*, *Ass. Nat.*, pp. 4644–4645). See also the motion on foreign policy by the Congress of the U.D.S.R., *Monde*, Nov. 2.

[39] Mollet, *J.O.*, *Ass. Nat.*, p. 4643; Teitgen, p. 4635; Legaret, p. 6702; Gaillard, p. 6935.

Western Germany, which would now be rearmed, sovereign, and less closely connected with the West, and which could expect no benefits from the West and many from the Russians. The combination of the Soviet threat and the German danger remained the most widely used argument (not only in the ranks of EDC's supporters.)[40] Thirdly, the functions assigned to the Western European Union seem to be based on mutual distrust, whereas integration from the top should have promoted a spirit of association and confidence. This change, by favoring nationalistic grievances, might undermine the whole new system. The "community of action" was missing.[41]

But the common front of EDC's supporters broke down on all other points where they split into three groups. The conjunction of fanaticisms did not occur, or rather it took place in one of these groups only.

THE "ULTRAS"

Paradoxically enough, the new agreements which reduced supranationality's importance were rejected by a group which had emphasized, between November 1953 and August 1954, that EDC's supranational Commissariat would not be more than an administrative body and that most of the important decisions would be made by the Minister's Council, where one could expect the French to use their right of veto for the preservation of their interests.[42] This argument had been one of the barely audible variations of the pro-EDC common theme. Here is another paradox: the new agreements, which gave precedence to military considerations, were often criticized by a group whose main argu-

[40] Pinay, speech given at Vivonne, *Monde*, Sept. 21; Maurice Schumann, articles in *Paris-Presse*, Sept. 24, Dec. 17, and *J.O., Ass. Nat.*, p. 6717; Bourgès-Manoury, *Combat*, Oct. 7; Reynaud, *J.O., Ass. Nat.*, pp. 4575, 4669, 6761; Maurice Faure, p. 6721; Chastellain, p. 6928.

[41] Schuman, *J.O., Ass. Nat.*, p. 4630. See also Reynaud, p. 4669; Pflimlin, p. 4675; M. Faure, p. 6721; Christian Pineau: "De l'intégration à la coalition", *Franc-Tireur*, Oct. 8; René Courtin: "Les Européens devant les actuelles negociations", *Figaro*, Oct. 21; Raymond Aron: "L'accord de Londres", *Figaro*, Oct. 4; "Les accords de Paris", *Figaro*, Oct. 25.

[42] See the articles by Jacques Fauvet, *Monde*, Feb. 5 and March 18, 1954, on the arguments of M. Pleven and M. Bidault; *L'Eveil de l'Europe*, July 1954, (article by J. Mallet: "L'armée européenne: pourquoi?", p. 31); the speech of M. Alfred Coste-Floret, August 29, 1954.

ments, based on fear of German militarism, developed all the themes of militant nationalism. Not only the political safeguards kept by France, but also the specifically military ones, are said to be much lesser than in EDC. Only integration from the top could protect France against the superiority or dynamism of Germany's military machine.[43] The "ultras" stressed the inefficiency of all controls and they pushed the argument so far that it ruled out any supranational institution in its sweep: the more supranational the institution, the heavier the damage.[44] They forecast an armaments race between France and Germany [45] and deplored Germany's newly-won right to build military airplanes and some additional types of warships, its apparent right to import atomic weapons,[46] and its obvious right to revive its war-industry.[47] They claimed that the new system gave an aggressive taint to the Atlantic defense system [48] and that the unilateral character of Dr. Adenauer's pledge to refrain from the use of force for the unification of Germany [49] only makes this taint worse. But the German danger was not their only source of complaint. They also bitterly criticized England's privileged position in WEU [50] and the increase in J.A.C.E.U.R.'s powers which, they said, puts French security into foreign hands.[51]

Paradox number three: this group had given strongest support to the draft treaty for a political community prepared by the European *ad hoc* Consultative Assembly in 1953. This draft provided both for an extension of the community's jurisdiction to new areas, especially economic,[52] and for considerable, though tempo-

---

[43] de Chevigné, *J.O., Ass. Nat.*, pp. 6755–6756; see also Reynaud, p. 4567; Pleven, p. 4673; Schuman, pp. 6718–6719.

[44] A. Coste-Floret, controversy over the business of armaments, *J.O., Ass Nat.*, pp. 6672–6675. See also Teitgen, p. 4636; Simonnet, pp. 4639–4640; de Chevigné, p. 6756.

[45] Teitgen, *J.O., Ass. Nat.*, p. 6752; de Menthon, p. 6839.

[46] A. Coste-Floret, *J.O., Ass. Nat.*, p. 6771.

[47] P. Abelin, *J.O., Ass. Nat.*, pp. 6792–6793.

[48] Schuman, *J.O., Ass. Nat.*, pp. 6717–6718.

[49] A. Coste-Floret, *J.O., Ass. Nat.*, p. 6776.

[50] Teitgen, *J.O., Ass. Nat.*, p. 4635; Simonnet, pp. 4638–4639; de Chevigné, p. 6755; A. Coste-Floret, p. 6776.

[51] Teitgen, *J.O., Ass. Nat.*, p. 4635; Gaillard, p. 6935.

[52] See the M.R.P. motion at the end of the 1953 debate in the Assemblée Nationale: the limitations of the sphere of political authority would only be temporary.

rary, curtailment of supranationality in its institutions. But when it came to W.E.U., the members of this group were the least ready to admit that the new organization could be useful and the most violently opposed to "the bad principle of associated Europe" [53] (as compared to integrated Europe). All they were willing to see in it was England's political domination, Anglo-American arbitration,[54] a revival of the hackneyed alliance system, and Germany left out in the cold.[55] However, when they mentioned their own objectives, they were strangely vague and asked for a return to integration, but did not say how.[56] Sometimes they were surprisingly close to the method of gradualism put forward by all the other pro-E.D.C. forces and by M. Mendès-France himself.[57] They seemed to be caught in a vicious circle.

Finally, as regards negotiations with the East, they were deeply suspicious. They were afraid that it could endanger Europe's defense and integration (which they seemed to cling to, even if they did not like the methods used for it).[58] Moreover, they said that they were skeptical about such negotiations because Germany would take part in them, and, as M. Alfred Coste-Floret has asked, "What can one expect from a five-power conference with a nation which has territorial claims?" (cf. note 53; another argument which unwittingly smashes EDC as well.)

However, there is one explanation for these paradoxes, for the group's refusal to vote the new treaty, and for its enthusiastic support of EDC: a limitless faith in the magical virtues of a legal formula—integration of a political community. The kind of integration they sponsored was not a technical means for the solution of Western Europe's specific problems, but a kind of religious ideal which should be embodied as fast as possible in a "fraternal Federal community." (cf. note 57). Now the integration and federation they dreamed of could be real and effective only at the cost of a complete overturn of the nations' social fabric, which would

[53] A. Coste-Floret, *J.O., Ass. Nat.*, p. 6777.
[54] Reynaud, *J.O., Ass. Nat.*, p. 6760; Gaillard, p. 6935.
[55] Reynaud, *J.O., Ass. Nat.*, p. 6761; Pléven, article in *Le Petit des Côtes du Nord*, reprinted in *Monde*, Jan. 1, 1955.
[56] Motion of the National Committee of the M.R.P., *Monde*, Nov. 16; A. Coste-Floret, *J.O., Ass. Nat.*, pp. 6770 and 6777; Gaillard, p. 6935.
[57] Teitgen, *J.O., Ass. Nat.* pp. 6750–6751; Reynaud, p. 6761. They enumerate the steps to be taken.
[58] Mutter, *J.O., Ass. Nat.*, p. 6882; Gaillard, p. 6936.

be both dangerous and hardly acceptable by these nations' authorities. If, on the other hand, one wanted to soften these dangers and this resistance, one would have to establish institutional safeguards, vetoes, checks and balances, which would reduce integration to a sham.[59] Instead of choosing between the two kinds of integration, a maelstrom or a lie, the bulk of the Mouvement Républicain Populaire rallied to the *ad hoc* Assembly's ambiguous plan, thus running both risks simultaneously. M. Bidault, however, was Foreign Minister, and could not escape. He had to choose, and he seems to have secretly given up real integration. Hence, on the one hand, his rejection of that Assembly's plan and his efforts for a compromise plan between association and integration in the political field; and on the other hand, his attempt to water down political integration in EDC proper. [60] Unfortunately, on the first front, he succeeded only too well in crossing out integration and no kind of European community was ever mentioned again, whereas he utterly failed on the second front to modify the EDC treaty which was left alone in a now hostile setting like an isolated bridgehead. The impetus which carried the other members of the group beyond EDC towards the Six-Power Federation was therefore broken and they had discovered that their love for a supranational authority with both undefined powers and unlimited jurisdiction was absolutely unshared. Their ultimate objective having evaporated, they were forced to make a defensive retreat with disastrous results. The ideal they were trying to achieve became more and more distant as they agreed to weaken the legal process which had been designed for its realization. In praising the veto instead of integration, they played into the hands of the enemy. On the other hand, they did not dare speak up after November 1953 for the only aim they had set their hearts on: the Six-Power Federation. But, since they refused any compromise after they ceased to have political power, they had increased that very isolation which explained their tactics

[59] *Cf.* Duverger, *Monde*, Nov. 18, 1953, denouncing the wordiness of many "European" professions of faith.

[60] On the first point, see in *Année politique 1953, passim*, the Conferences of European States; Fauvet, *Monde*, Sept. 23, 1953. On the second point, for the additional protocols and the attempt at reinforcement of the Atlantic character of the EDC (which foreshadows the Brussels protocol), see J. J. Servan-Scheiber: "La nouvelle conception française", *Monde*, Jan. 20, 1953; and the *Monde* of April 25, 1953, after M. Bidault's speech at the Eiffel Tower.

more than if they had spoken frankly. An outspoken debate would have forced them to realize the dilemma hidden in the myth of integration, and would have brought them closer to other "Europeans".[61]

For this panacea, contradictory as it was, was still supposed to work magic. First they believed that in the balance between present-day Germany's virtues and vices, only this formula could put the decisive weight in virtue's scale; any other kind of rearmament would be decisive in the opposite way. This, of course, showed unlimited trust in a legal method, but unlimited distrust of present-day Germany; [62] and this distrust made them reject the new plan which they accused of perpetuating distrust.[63] If they couldn't have total supranationalism, it was total nationalism they wanted.

Secondly, this cure-all would make not only watchfulness, but also diplomacy, unnecessary for France, because it would solve the international problem of Germany as well. EDC had been conceived in terms of a rigid international situation which it was intended to solidify even more in order to make the temptations of the Russian siren harmless. EDC was to establish between Germany and the West a "definitive" bond which would dispel the nightmare of reunification.[64] This explains M. Alfred Coste-Floret's words quoted above. It was assumed that no other system could achieve these results and that negotiation was both unnecessary under EDC and dangerous without EDC. The dream of a "Six-Power Europe" was, in a way, isolationist and parochial; it neglected the problems existing in the rest of the world, it skipped the problem of Europe's division, it stemmed from an obsession with Franco-German problems alone.

Because the "ultra-Europeans" had preferred a kind of escapism to the solution of so many difficulties, the return to reality has been hard on them. There is always something painful about falling from the top of an ivory tower.

[61] Cf. Joseph Folliet in *La Croix*, Nov. 17. The "ultras" stood on grounds which were "mythical and mystical . . . grounds exceptionally mystifying".

[62] M. de Chevigné, *J.O., Ass. Nat.*, p. 6756, even supports the idea that an integrated structure would create a group spirit sufficient to compensate for the material inferiority of France.

[63] De Menthon, *J.O., Ass. Nat.*, p. 6839.

[64] Simonnet, *J.O., Ass. Nat.*, pp. 4640–4641; A. Coste-Floret, p. 6777; Chastellain, p. 6928. Reynaud, statement in *Le Monde*, Sept. 26.

THE "EUROPEAN" CONVERTS

Another group of EDC supporters came out for the new agreements under what seemed to be just as paradoxical circumstances. Those who now rallied to integration from below were those who had most strongly asked that integration from the top be applied unrestrictedly in the defense system (see below, note 70). This explains the reluctant character of some of the converts' acceptance.[65] But the explanation they have given of this apparent change makes it possible to have a better understanding of their support of EDC.

Unlike the "ultras" they barely referred to the purely military safeguards for France. Though they may not have been completely convinced by M. Mendès-France's argument on this point, at least they did not stress it.[66] There are numerous reasons for this silence. They had some confidence in Germany.[67] They did not believe that even the most perfect type of defense system could, all by itself, regenerate a German nation whose democratic elements would have been in the sidelines before the system's enactment. Also, they thought that the new formula (which could be improved through a return to integration "from the top" in respect to armaments [68]) was quite able to keep Germany on the Western side in spite of its imperfections. Furthermore, some of these converts (the Socialist supporters of EDC) had never been highly enthusiastic for EDC. [69] In the beginning they had hesitated between two mutually exclusive methods—both different from EDC: integration without limits and vetoes, or a looser scheme with full English participation. For a long time, they had tried to get both,[70] but they failed and had to be satisfied with make-

[65] Notably that of M. Robert Schuman, *J.O., Ass. Nat.*, p. 4631; speech at Hanover, quoted in *Monde*, Oct. 31.

[66] See, however, the editorial of *Franc-Tireur*, Dec. 24, and the speech of Maurice Faure, *J.O., Ass. Nat.*, pp. 6720–6721. But neither M. Schuman nor M. Mollet speaks of it.

[67] Jaquet and Le Bail, *J.O., Ass. Nat.*, pp. 6745, 6754–6755.

[68] Jaquet, *J.O., Ass. Nat.*, p. 6747; Mollet, p. 6921.

[69] E. Roche, *Franc-Tireur*, Sept. 29; R. Schuman, *J.O., Ass. Nat.*, p. 6810.

[70] The motion adopted by the Assembly, Feb. 27, 1952, noted two demands; in the November 1953 debate, MM. Mollet and Jaquet protested against the excessive role of the Council of Ministers in the EDC, at the same time demanding a solid contract of association with Great Britain, for national defense

shifts. It is therefore not surprising that after the fall of EDC M. Mollet and the Socialists tried to reach fully one of their two objectives (British participation), while obtaining still a minimum of supranationality.[71] Moreover, all these "Europeans" wanted to avoid a break-up of the Atlantic alliance. Finally, their conversion was made easier by the reappearance of the "European" element.

Indeed, unlike the "ultras" again, the converts were most clear and insistent in their emphasis on European integration.[72] They claimed that the new agreements contained real prospects of integration,[73] because they shared M. Mendès-France's preference for gradual construction "with carefully and wisely planned steps,[74] and for concentration on the economic tasks.[75] These new prospects which M. Mendès-France reintroduced in the non-military field have had two very important results.

In the first place, they brought out in the open again the disagreement between the "ultras" and the "converts" concerning the future of European unity. As long as they had fought for the defense system only, this opposition had been concealed (and the limitation of the fight had been intended to conceal it). The converts (including M. Robert Schuman who, with the Coal and Steel Community, had selected the "functional" method for European construction), worked on the assumption that the individual nations of Europe could no longer solve their common problems, especially the economic ones.[76] Therefore, they could not but reject the idea of a supranational political community which would leave all real power to the nations' governments

---

is not in their eyes a simple specialized field like coal and steel. This distinction facilitated the acceptance of M. Mendès-France's point of view: less supranationality in national defense than in the technical sectors.

[71] See his article in *Populaire*, Sept. 30.

[72] René Mayer: "Après le déluge" (continued), *Monde*, Sept. 29; R. Schuman, *J.O.*, *Ass. Nat.*, pp. 6809–6810; Mollet, p. 6921; Delbos, p. 6876.

[73] Executive Office of the French Union of Federalists, *Monde*, Oct. 19; Paul Coste-Floret and Pflimlin in the National Committee of the M.R.P., *Monde*, Nov. 16.

[74] Le Bail, *J.O.*, *Ass. Nat.*, p. 6753.

[75] For the succeeding steps in this matter, see: Jaquet, *Franc-Tireur*, Oct. 28 and *J.O.*, *Ass. Nat.*, p. 6746; René Mayer in the *Revue de Paris*, Dec. 1954; The resolution of the Executive Commission of the M.R.P. of Bas-Rhin, *Monde*, Nov. 14.

[76] A. Philip: "L'Europe unie et sa place dans l'économie internationale", 1953.

under the cloak of integration. When the Socialist leader, M. Guy Mollet, states today [77] that real integration can be achieved only in specialized areas, and between different nations, he remains faithful to his past attitude. He has always been opposed to a Six-Power Federation, he refused to sit with the constitutional committee of the *ad hoc* Assembly,[78] and to accept the latter's plan, which he accused of creating a pseudo-federation.[79] On the other hand and inversely, the wall which had divided (on the only problem discussed at that time) the moderate EDC supporters and the moderate EDC opponents vanished with the same stroke. They were opposed on the defense system, but not on anything else. As they were all set against confused integration in over-extended areas, they were able to agree on specific measures of real integration. Both M. Soustelle, a leading Gaullist, and M. Mollet spoke in favor of a supranational armaments pool. Ever since advance in the non-military field became possible again and in order to resume it, the functional supporters of EDC could, without shedding too many tears, make the necessary concessions on the only obstacle which had prevented it—the defense system.

Contrasting again with the "ultras", the "European converts" were not frightened by the prospect of negotiating with the East. They all claimed that the problem of Western defense must be solved first (or else negotiations would be delayed once more)[80] and that the East-West discussion should not harm European construction.[81] Freedom for Western Europe comes before the unification of Germany.[82] But under these circumstances, and within these limits—which greatly narrow the negotiations' object —they felt that a conference should meet.[83] In their opinion, no

[77] *Combat*, Dec. 20, 1954.
[78] *Populaire*, Feb. 28, 1953.
[79] Other Europeans who had come to that point of view had made similar reservations about this project: M. Defferre, René Mayer and Maurice Faure in the Nov. 1953 debate, M. Schuman shortly afterwards, *Monde*, Feb. 20, 1954.
[80] M. Faure, *J.O., Ass. Nat.*, p. 6722 and Mollet, pp. 6922–6924.
[81] Schuman, *J.O., Ass. Nat.*, p. 6809.
[82] Mollet, *J.O., Ass. Nat.*, p. 6823. Here the Socialist supporters of EDC remained constant: in 1953, the motion adopted by the Congress of the S.F.I.O., and the Socialist motion in the autumn debates of the Conseil de la République and the Assembly, demanded both the European army and negotiation.
[83] Le Bail, *J.O., Ass. Nat.*, p. 6752; M. Faure, p. 6722.

type of European integration and defense system can do more than prevent such inauspicious solutions of Germany's international problems as would turn her into the world's master or make her an aide of the Russian bloc. These are no solution in themselves, nor do they exempt the West from diplomacy. Thus, this new element introduced by M. Mendès-France made conversions easier by revealing that the two groups of EDC supporters were not of the same mind on the possibility of a prolonged diplomatic stalemate and on the risks of a negotiated improvement of international relations.

THE "ATLANTIC CONVERTS"

A third group of former EDC supporters should be mentioned. They talked little, but they counted a lot. Among the 287 deputies who voted for the new London Agreement, 148 had voted against the previous question (i.e., for EDC) on August 30. Not more than 80 or 90 of these 148 belong to the "European converts" group. The newspapers Le Figaro and L'Aurore can probably be considered the mouthpieces of the others.

They cared less about the details of the defense system and the methods of European integration than members of the two other groups. They believed that the military safeguards France received in the new system were less favorable than those of EDC.[84] They therefore refused to blame those deputies who, during the debate of October 1954 in the National Assembly, refrained from approving them because they had expected "other guarantees".[85] They also stated that the new plan involved a retreat on the subject of European integration. But all this did not prevent them from thinking like the European converts that a united Europe "can be attained tomorrow only from the base provided by the Paris agreements".[86]

Indeed, what they mostly cared about was the strengthening of the Western powers which they had already seen as the principal merit of the EDC. They considered the twelve German

[84] L. Gabriel-Robinet, Figaro, Dec. 24; Paternot, J.O., Ass. Nat., p. 6925.
[85] L. Gabriel-Robinet, Figaro, Oct. 13.
[86] Raymond Aron, "Quelques faits et quelques mots", Figaro, Dec. 27. See also Brisson, Figaro, October 25; Pinay at the Congress of Independents, Monde, Dec. 10.

divisions to be neither useless nor dangerous, but necessary.[87] Therefore, these Atlantic supporters turned against the "ultras", when the latter's attitude in the December debate on ratification seemed to imperil the agreements and play into Moscow's hand. [88] This also explains why many deputies from the opposition rushed to the government's support in the final ballot.[89] The pelasure of having escaped from a reversal of France's alliances made them breathe sighs of gratitude towards M. Mendès-France.[90]

But the French Premier had not presented the international problem in the same terms as EDC's supporters. Now for the Atlantic politicians ratification was supposed to ward off the Eastern threat and certainly not to be the first step toward an appeal to the authors of this threat. Their gratitude, therefore, never did appear without a great measure of distrust, both because of what M. Mendès-France's new presentation left out as compared to the old one, and because of the new things he brought in. On the one hand, the lack of any reference to the Communist danger in the preliminary statement to the ratification bill as well as in M. Mendès-France's speech did not pass unnoticed.[91] On the other hand, the Atlantic supporters said that any invitation to the East for a lessening of the world's tension would undermine the West. They did not believe in the success of negotiation and in the merits of "notarial documents".[92] Thus, they feared that M. Mendès-France had not rescued the Atlantic Alliance for good

---

[87] Raymond Aron: "Après le débat, avant le vote", *Figaro*, Oct. 11; Bergasse, *J. O., Ass. Nat.*, pp. 6926–6927.

[88] P. Brisson, *Figaro*, Dec. 25; R. Lazurick, *Aurore*, Dec. 25.

[89] On December 30, eight Independent deputies, four Independent Peasants, one Peasant and two members of the A.R.S. who had voted against the new agreements on Dec. 24, after having voted against the previous question on August 30, finally voted for the motion.

[90] See notably, after the interview given by M. Mendès-France to *U.S. News and World Report*, R. Aron: "Continuité de la politique exterieure de la France", *Figaro*, Sept. 29; after the London Conference, the congratulations of M. Duchet, *Information*, Oct. 5; L. Gabriel-Robinet in *Figaro*, Dec. 24, and R. Bony in *Aurore*, Dec. 31.

[91] L. Gabriel-Robinet, *Figaro*, Dec. 31.

[92] Raymond Aron: "Ni refus, ni annexion", *Figaro*, Dec. 2; "Subtilités inutiles," *Figaro*, Dec. 8. See also his series of articles on the enemies of coexistence, notably those of Nov. 4 and 8 in *Figaro*.

and that the crisis had only been delayed.[93] Like the "ultras", they recriminated against his new outlook, hoping that the old would become fashionable again as soon as possible and fearing that a negative decision would be a much greater triumph for that new "soft" outlook they deplored. The rearmament of Germany and European integration are here elements of a militant conception of the cold war.

Finally, these three groups all made their decision on the new agreements out of loyalty to EDC. But their support of EDC had had different motives and different points of emphasis: first draft of a Six-Power, supranational and political Europe; a stage in the functional organization of Western Europe; a military system for a reinforcement of the West, etc. EDC meant different things to different people, and gave three different answers to three different hopes. Every coalition is a misunderstanding.

An Autopsy of the Anti-EDC Forces

The common front of EDC's opponents, barely cracked in the first three weeks of September, did break apart after the Strasbourg speech. But its dissolution came more slowly. Whereas EDC's supporters were already split in the beginning of October, only a small part of EDC's opponents had left their common front at that time. On October 12, only 41 of the non-Communist deputies who had voted for the previous question (i.e. against EDC) on August 30, refused to vote for the new agreements which were approved by 178 anti-EDC representatives. But on December 30, there remained only 107 of these for ratification; 112 voted against it, abstained or did not take part in the final vote.

THE TOTAL NATIONALISTS

Among those who had dissented at once were the nationalists who opposed any kind of rearmament of Germany and any type of European construction. At the time of their fight against EDC they had nevertheless contributed within the "National Committee for Defense of French Unity and of the Unity of the

[93] Pierre Brisson, *Figaro*, Dec. 21, suspected a governmental attempt at reconciliation with "the small group of flatterers (thuriféraires) whole-heartedly attached to Left Wing totalitarianism."

French Union" to the assembly line of substitute proposals. Now, even though they could hardly "tell why the Paris and London agreements did not correspond exactly to the principles they had defined themselves" [94] they voted against the new system. With their back to the wall, they had to say why.

The reason is to be found in their refusal to accept any German participation in Western defense which would not be discriminatory. They could only approve German mass formations placed at the allies' disposal in North America,[95] or of a *Landwehr* (without an air-force) mobilized on the spot and . . . buried in concrete resistance nests.[96] They considered Germany as dangerous as the USSR and therefore any non-discriminatory defense system as an evil. Consequently, M. André and M. Aumeran found in the agreements a number of vices which the "ultras" also saw in them. The arguments of nationalism—total or conditional—are not inexhaustible. The checks are inefficient: [97] Germany may either join Russia or attack it in order to achieve her unification [98] (which they claim, not unexpectedly, to be dangerous for "her neighbors and for peace"); the privileges granted to Great Britain are unacceptable.[99] As for the German divisions, they are deemed to be both dangerous and archaic, with more passion than logic.[100]

Since nationalism here is total, it is also aimed against any kind of European integration. M. Pierre André, who had been an enemy of the Schuman plan, repeated that France should not take the road to European unity as long as the French Union had not been buttressed, North Africa not welded to the mainland, and metropolitan France had not succeeded in achieving military, economic and financial reform.[101] This was a low class burial.

POINTS ON WHICH THE OTHER EDC OPPONENTS REMAINED UNITED

The other foes of EDC, i.e. the great majority of them, had succeeded in agreeing on the general outlines of a military and politi-

[94] Billotte, speaking to M. Pierre André, *J.O.*, *Ass. Nat.*, p. 6799.
[95] Aumeran, *J.O.*, *Ass. Nat.*, pp. 6691–6692.
[96] P. André, *J.O.*, *Ass. Nat.*, p. 6802.
[97] Aumeran, *J.O.*, *Ass. Nat.*, p. 4580.
[98] Aumeran and P. André, *J.O.*, *Ass. Nat.*, p. 6693.
[99] Aumeran, *J.O.*, *Ass. Nat.*, p. 6692; de Villeneuve, p. 6928.
[100] Aumeran, *J.O.*, *Ass. Nat.*, p. 6691 and P. André, pp. 6799–6802.
[101] *J.O.*, *Ass. Nat.*, p. 6804.

cal substitute solution. When M. Mendès-France's plan became known and later to a large extent adopted, their agreement survived. And, until after the October debate of the National Assembly, all EDC opponents except the total nationalists concentrated their arguments on the new agreements' substance and on the "European" developments proposed by the French Premier. As in the past, they left aside the international aspects.

They approved the new military scheme because it did away with EDC's main defects: it did not give up as much sovereignty,[102] it preserved the integrity of the French army and of the French Union,[103] it prevented exaggerated interference in the French economy.[104] Above all, it made it impossible for Germany to become preponderant, because it discarded "the so-called technique of political integration," [105] and because it included Great Britain.[106] Thus, they did not believe, as EDC's supporters (both the "ultras" and the "converts") did, that the political dangers of rearming a divided Germany were inversely proportional to the degree of integration "from the top" which existed in the defense system. Hence, their warnings to the Premier in order to prevent him from reintroducing too large chunks of supranationality in further agreements.[107]

Their congratulations extended also to the new conception of European unity.[108] They believed that it would allow a more harmonious advance, because national feelings would no longer be neglected.[109] (Technocracy, which political integration was accused of leading to, was condemned not only by the right-wing

[102] Soustelle, *J.O., Ass. Nat.*, p. 6622; Max Brusset, *Combat*, Oct. 7; Moro-Giafferi, *J.O., Ass. Nat.*, p. 6874.
[103] Soustelle, *J.O., Ass. Nat.*, p. 6696. See also L. Noël, p. 6705; Barrachin, *Combat*, Dec. 11.
[104] Lapie, *J.O., Ass. Nat.*, p. 6681.
[105] de Pierrebourg, *J.O., Ass. Nat.*, p. 4579.
[106] *Monde*, Oct. 1: Bulletin de l'étranger, "Un pas formidable"; Robert Lacoste in the National Council of the S.F.I.O. of Oct. 11, *Monde*, Oct. 13; Daladier, *J.O., Ass. Nat.*, p. 4675; L. Noël, p. 6705.
[107] Except on the matter of the armaments pool. See Palewski, *J.O., Ass. Nat.*, p. 4670; Soustelle, p. 6696.
[108] Loustaunau-Lacau, *J.O., Ass. Nat.*, p. 4633; Bardoux, p. 6695; Lussy, "Les Européens sans Europe", *Journal du Parlement*, Dec. 30.
[109] Isorni, *Le Monde*, Oct. 26, opposed a "Europe of nations" to a "denationalized Europe"; Billotte, *J.O., Ass. Nat.*, p. 6640.

foes of EDC, but also by the Socialist and Radical-Socialist [110] opponents of EDC, as well as by the "European converts" who had always demanded democratic checks on the specialized communities they advocated.) [111] The anti-EDC forces claimed that gradual transfers of sovereignty would be more easily accepted if the ideal were more modest [112] and the framework larger. One should therefore concentrate on the economic and social tasks.[113]

Thus, the foes of EDC remained united for a certain revival of nationalism. It was indeed the feeling which dominated the debate (only the converts did not display it); but it was also able to inspire the most contradictory actions. This will be obvious again if one looks at the points on which the anti-EDC front broke down.

THE MODERATES

Indeed, when it came to approving the new scheme's immediate enactment (and not as in October, merely its principles) they clashed on the very question which their agreement against the provisions of the EDC treaty had allowed them to push aside: the evaluation of the world situation. It was not just, as among EDC's supporters, a quarrel between those who thought that it was not fitting for the West to beg for an improvement in East-West relations and the others—a minor dispute among people who all believed that Germany's rearmament was inevitable and that the Russian danger was at least as big as the danger of rearming a divided Germany as long as she is linked to Western Europe. The disagreement here is on a basic issue: the ranking of dangers.

One group of EDC's foes shared completely the Premier's and the "European converts'" outlook. Like the converts, they stated that the Russian threat was the bigger one.[114] Like the converts and Mendès-France, they claimed that insofar as sufficiently close bonds continue to unite Germany to the West, the poisons which

[110] Moch, *J.O., Ass. Nat.*, p. 4382; A. Gourdon in *Le Jacobin*, Sept. 24.
[111] *Cf.* a speech by G. Mollet at the European Conference of the Socialist Internationale, *Monde*, Feb. 28, 1954, and his statement to *Combat*, Dec. 20.
[112] Soustelle, *J.O., Ass. Nat.*, p. 4623, denounced the dream "of a European nation which history did not create and which it would be dangerous to suppose all made".
[113] Lapie, *J.O., Ass. Nat.*, p. 6682; Bonnefous, pp. 6834–6835.
[114] Billotte, *J.O., Ass. Nat.*, pp. 4666 and 6640.

are active in Germany will be neutralized. Their only disagreement with the converts concerned the character of these bonds. The moderates believed that EDC's political integration, far from insuring the victory of the German democratic elements, would destroy them, because it would give back to Germany the temptation of, and an opportunity for, hegemony; [115] technical integration instead should make anti-democratic forces powerless. [116] But both the moderates and the converts believed that there were already healthy elements in Germany and that they would survive the enactment of the new rearmament scheme. This is where they differed from both the "ultras" and those EDC opponents who voted against ratification.[117] Here, therefore, the revival of nationalism (whose rationale and effects on Germany's nationalism are certainly disputable [118]) is reduced to no more than a cautious reaction. "European converts" and conciliatory EDC foes are separated only by divergent evaluations of the importance of national feelings, and by different bets on the chances of quick and lasting unity in the Europe of 1954.

The "European converts", the French Premier, and the moderates agreed not only on the order of the dangers, but also on the future developments of Atlantic policy: ratification must lead to negotiation.[119] A rejection of the agreements would make negotiations impossible, for it would cause a crisis in the Atlantic Alliance, outside of which France could not act.[120] On the contrary, the agreements' adoption would make negotiation easier than if EDC had been adopted, because they established looser bonds between Germany and France. In EDC France would have risked "being driven into high gear" because of Germany's terri-

[115] Stibio, "Après la bataille", *Journal du Parlement*, Dec. 29. Lussy, article quoted in note 108.

[116] Billotte, *J.O., Ass. Nat.*, pp. 6642–6643; *Monde*, Bulletin de l'étranger, "L'alliance maintenue", Oct. 5; Bonnefous, *Combat*, Dec. 18.

[117] Billotte, *J.O., Ass. Nat.*, pp. 4666 and 6642; Corniglion-Molinier, p. 6862 which emphasized this difference.

[118] M. Faure, *J.O., Ass. Nat.*, p. 6721; Klaus Jacobi, "Germany's Great Old Man", *Foreign Affairs*, Jan. 1955.

[119] The appeal for negotiation made by M. Mendès-France thus brought about the support of several hesitant opponents of the EDC: notably that of M. Jules Moch, *J.O., Ass. Nat.*, pp. 6737–6745.

[120] Moch, *J.O., Ass. Nat.*, p. 6741 (see also the extracts from his answer to letters he had received, quoted by A. Wurmser in a violent article in *Humanité*, Jan. 8); Bonnefous, p. 6741; Corniglion-Molinier, p. 6882.

torial claims in Eastern Europe: [121] it would have been difficult for the French to stop Germany's eventual moves since EDC reduced France to the status of a member of a European community. Some latitude for maneuvering and negotiating seemed indispensable to those who did not believe that Germany could be imprisoned in Western Europe forever, no matter what kind of a prison it is. This is the last reason for this group's hostility to EDC, and its last argument for Western European Union,[122] an argument which has probably been decisive in the conversion of important anti-EDC Socialists.

THE REBELS

There is one group left: the group of those who, after having opposed EDC, refused to consent to the new treaty's ratification, but whose arguments are more far-reaching than those of the total nationalists'.

Basic disagreements between political forces which have, nevertheless, common objectives, are like deep-rooted incompatibilities between people who are obliged to live together: they remain concealed as long as possible. The clash between the rebels and the moderates, though close to the surface, had been avoided in October; [123] it came out in the open only afterwards. Some rebels, before they denounced ratification in bitter terms,[124] had even seemed to accept German rearmament after the Strasbourg speech.[125] The reason for these hesitations was that it was becoming impossible to go on expressing both loyalty to the Atlantic alliance and hostility to Germany's rearmament. It had been possible under EDC, as such *political* hostility could still be stated merely in terms of criticisms of EDC's *technical* provisions. But

[121] Bonnefous, *Combat*, Dec. 18; Marcellin, *J.O., Ass. Nat.*, p. 4672. See the objections of Guy Mollet, *J.O., Ass. Nat.*, p. 6921 (greater independence toward the U.S. in the EDC).

[122] It had already been explained by MM. Billières and Bonnefous in the Assembly in Nov. 1953.

[123] *Cf.* the significant order of the day of M. G. Palewski, *J.O., Ass. Nat.*, p. 4644.

[124] See M. Duverger, *Monde*, Jan. 1955; Fabiani, *Combat*, Dec. 24, 25, 29, and 31, 1954.

[125] M. Duverger: "Le moindre mal", *Monde*, Oct. 10, "The fight against German rearmament seems, alas, to be virtually at an end." In the same vein, Fabiani, in *Combat*, Sept. 21. The neutralists were the only ones who did not hesitate. (*France-Observateur*, Oct. 7.)

since the new treaty brought ample satisfaction on the only points which EDC's foes had seen fit to attack in the past, the would-be rebels were now obliged to consider openly a substitute *policy*, not just a substitute defense system, and to realize how irreconcilable it was with Western policy. No wonder that some of them made up their minds against ratification at the last moment only.

In the eyes of the rebels, the greatest threat to peace was not the division or weakening of the Western nations, but the division of the world and the tension between the East and the West—something the other groups considered as mere symptoms of the world's woes.[126] It follows that everything that could increase such division and tension or impede their attenuation should be prevented, even if the price one has to pay for it is very high. Today, the danger takes the form of a divided Germany's rearmament. Though the new system is better than EDC, the only difference will be that in the balance of Western Germany's good and evil forces, the weight the Allies will put in the scales of danger will not be as heavy as the weight called EDC. But it will still be put on the wrong side of the scales. One should therefore not be surprised to discover that the rebels meet the "ultras" on the familiar ground of chauvinism,[127] even though the latter attack the new system only, while the former reject all systems.

The weight of W.E.U. is undoubtedly lighter than the weight of EDC. But, said the rebels, it could have been lighter still. The rebels did not refrain from objecting to the new rights the French Government had to yield to its allies and to Germany in exchange for the concessions it got from them. They resented the greater opportunities for direct contacts between the Germans and the Americans provided by JACEUR's increased powers.[128] They protested against the postponement of the determination of maximum strength for the police forces and home guards.[129] They emphasized that Germany receives greater facilities to make certain types of armaments and to buy weapons abroad.[130] They stressed that an agency for armaments production would be neces-

[126] Lebon, *J.O., Ass. Nat.*, pp. 6693–6694; Sirius, "Quel est le pire", *Monde*, Dec. 24.

[127] Soustelle, *J.O., Ass. Nat.*, p. 4624.

[128] *Ibid.*

[129] Noël, *J.O., Ass. Nat.*, p. 6706; Daladier, p. 6763; Herriot, p. 6811.

[130] Badie, *J.O., Ass. Nat.*, p. 6658; Daladier, p. 6763; Moro-Giafferi, p. 6875.

sary in order to restore Europe's independence from the United States, but they complained that this would be much more difficult to establish once France could no longer threaten to deny or to delay ratification.[131]

Furthermore, even if that weight were lighter, it would still be decisive. First, because from a military standpoint no legal framework would be strong enough to keep Germany's rearmament within limits. The checks would be lifted and France's right of veto would be just as useless as it has proved to be in NATO's councils against the rearmament of Germany. The whole trend would be speeded up by the armaments race which, according to the rebels' prophecy, would now take place between the East and the West.[132] Germany's military might would therefore outgrow France's forces, especially as the French have their hands tied by their difficulties in overseas territories.[133] Secondly from a political standpoint also, Germany's remilitarization would be a threat to peace. Whatever the formula, it would increase tenfold the evil influence of Germany's anti-democratic forces,[134] and kill the liberal forces if they really exist. Indeed, all the rebels did not appear to believe that they do exist, and the old argument against "eternal Germany" [135] has been stated by some of them with many historical references and even more vigor than by the total nationalists. Like these, and like the "ultras", the rebels criticized the aggressive aspect given to NATO by the coming entry of a Germany which claims her borders of 1937.[136] They feared either

---

[131] Soustelle, *J.O., Ass. Nat.*, p. 6697; Daladier, p. 6762.

[132] Soustelle, *J.O., Ass. Nat.*, p. 6698; Noël, pp. 6700, 6706; Palewski, p. 6757; Herriot, p. 6811; Vallon, p. 6872; Liautey, p. 6920.

[133] Soustelle, *J.O., Ass. Nat.*, p. 6819 and "La réponse du bouc émissaire", *Combat*, Dec. 27; Moro-Giafferi, *J.O., Ass. Nat.*, p. 6875; Palewski, p. 6937.

[134] Palewski, *J.O., Ass. Nat.*, p. 6759; Denis, p. 6769; Herriot, p. 6810; Vallon, p. 6872; Cl. Bourdet, at the meeting organized by the Peace Movement on Dec. 6, *Humanité*, Dec. 27; Léon Hamon, "Il ne faut pas jouer la détente sur un pari", *Monde*, Dec. 28; Sirius, "Le pas est franchi", *Monde*, Jan. 1, 1955.

[135] De Pierrebourg, *J.O., Ass. Nat.*, p. 4580; *Loustaunau-Lacau*, p. 4633, ("Germany is a kind of poisoned cake"); Lebon, p. 6694; Soustelle, pp. 6700–6701; Daladier, p. 6764, (. . . "A Germany which it was hoped was a new Germany and which, in the end, is always the same old Germany"); Moro-Giafferi, p. 6875; Liautey, p. 6920, ("for the Germanic people, Right is founded on Might alone which fashions and transforms it").

[136] Soustelle, *J.O., Ass. Nat.*, pp. 4625 and 6698–6699; "Vers le pire", *Monde*, Dec. 17; Vallon, p. 6872.

that Germany would set off a new world war [137] or that she would go over to Soviet Russia.[138] Thirdly, they felt that the discussions with the East, which the French Government wished to hold, would be impossible or very dangerous for the West if they are to be undertaken only after ratification. The reason is that Germany will then be part of the West (Soustelle, cf. note 138), an argument used elsewhere. Like the "ultras" the rebels feared that Western Germany might succeed in exploiting the East-West rivalry.[139]

But there is something which separates completely the rebels from the total nationalists and the ultras. The rebels proposed a substitute international policy. If the greatest danger for world peace is the remilitarization of a divided Germany, and if European integration could only make it worse instead of dispelling it, negotiation between the great powers for a common settlement of the German problem should be undertaken at once before ratification. This argument is of course worlds apart from the ideas of the "Atlantic converts" which the "ultras" approved. But there is a very great gap even between this idea and M. Mendès-France's thesis, shared by the "European" converts and the anti-EDC moderates, who all put Western unity (i.e. strong links between Germany and the West) before Germany's reunification. The negotiations the latter favored after ratification could hardly deal with anything bigger than some kind of armaments limitation and control on both sides of a persistent iron curtain, since they decided that the fundamental principles of Western policy should remain unquestioned, even by a Big-Four deal. M. Mendès-France's silence on the chances of German unity, combined with his refusal to accept Germany's neutralization, is eloquent enough. But the rebels, who do not give precedence to maintaining these Western principles, want much broader negotiations.

Now, what exactly should be the scope of this sweeping and immediate discussion? It does not appear that the rebels were all of one mind in this respect, and that the substitute policy they

[137] Against the East, (Soustelle, *J.O., Ass. Nat.*, pp. 4625 and 6700; Loustaunau-Lacau, p. 4632; Denis, p. 6768); or even against France, (Moro-Giafferi, p. 6875; Lebon: "Et demain", *Monde*, Jan. 6.)

[138] Palewski, *J.O., Ass. Nat.*, pp. 4671, 6759, and 6937; Soustelle, p. 6700; Daladier, p. 6762; Denis, p. 6768.

[139] Palewski, *J.O., Ass. Nat.*, p. 6889; Sirius, "Quel est le pire",*Monde*, Dec. 24; Hamon, "Ratification, négociation et position française", *Monde*, Dec. 7.

would like to carry out is the same for all of them. Only some of them took the reunification of Germany as their objective (and they did not indicate what conditions they would propose or accept in order to reach it). Moreover, many of those who did ask for it said so in oblique terms.[140] They asserted that they wanted an international compact safeguarding German unity,[141] or they deplored that the thesis of a protracted partition appears to "begin to be accepted" (Hamon, *cf.* note 139). The other rebels, however, avoided any kind of open or implicit reference to reunification. Instead of defining these aims, they expressed vague though emphatic hopes of disarmament,[142] or used obscure terms like "modus vivendi between the East and the West",[143] or pressed for a return to the Potsdam system [144]—a much more revealing clue. Many of them insisted that Germany should remain an object of four-power administration [145] or claimed that the Western powers and the Soviet Union should sign a common peace treaty with Germany before giving sovereign rights back to what is just one fragment of the former Reich.[146]

Some doubts can therefore be raised about the rebels' unity. There may be a crack in it which leaves on one side those who see danger only in Germany's division, and on the other side those who see it in Germany's very existence. The former, who put their hope in a new Germany, want to free her from partition and from domination by blocs, so that she may prosper at last. Reunification is their cure-all. (They are similar to the "ultras", whose cure-all is called integration. The remedies are mutually exclusive, but the diagnosis is the same.) The latter, who conserve their fear of "eternal Germany", try to revive an international control of France's neighbor which would be kept powerless. They are not

[140] Denis, *J.O., Ass. Nat.*, pp. 6768 to 6770; Vallon, p. 6872; Minority of the Socialist Party, (Coffin Report) at the Congress of Suresnes, *Monde*, Nov. 12.

[141] General de Gaulle's statement of December 4, *Monde*, December 7; Palewski, "Ratification et mise en application", *Monde*, Dec. 8; see also Palewski, *J.O., Ass. Nat.*, pp. 6889–6890.

[142] Loustaunau-Lacau, *J.O., Ass. Nat.*, p. 4633; Bardoux, p. 6696; Herriot, p. 6811; Caillet, p. 6880. But Palewski points out that disarmament is an effect, not a cause, p. 6838.

[143] Soustelle, *J.O., Ass. Nat.*, p. 4626.

[144] Palewski, *Monde*, Nov. 10; Daladier, *J.O., Ass. Nat.*, p. 6764.

[145] Vallon, *J.O., Ass. Nat.*, pp. 4671 and 6874; Capitant, *Monde*, Nov. 10; Laffargue, article quoted.

[146] Liautey, *J.O., Ass. Nat.*, p. 6920; see also Palewski, p. 6759.

total pessimists moved by an anti-German feeling as strong as the total nationalists'. Hence their reluctance towards reunification prospects; it is strongest among those who least believe in Germany's democratic potentialities. (*Cf.* note 135). But as they are more logical and socially less conservative than the total nationalists, they end up by treating Soviet Russia as a lesser danger, and even as an occasional safeguard. And they ask for Franco-Russian reconciliation which, they say, is far more urgent than Franco-German reconciliation.[147]

However, the event which could test and break the rebels' unity (a united, but neither neutralized nor disarmed Germany) is at present still a remote contingency.

Conclusion

Four problems had been inextricably mixed together in the EDC controversy.

The Technical Problem: What system would make the rearmament of Germany less dangerous for France and peace? During the EDC fight, it was this problem only—the narrowest one— which determined Frenchmen's choice of camps. The EDC supporters thought that there was no escape from the yoke of reciprocity: transfers of sovereignty were the only guarantees, and therefore integration "from the top" was the best formula. The danger of German supremacy in the affair was to be avoided, either by the very virtues of integration, or by the institutional exceptions to integration. The foes of EDC thought that a merely technical integration could restore greater freedom to France's diplomacy and greater prestige to France's nationalism without unshackling Germany's diplomacy or letting Germany's nationalism loose. Germany would be dangerous only if she could use her army unrestrictedly, or if her army could dominate her.

The Far Broader Problem of European Integration: The autumn debate showed the disagreement among EDC's supporters to be stronger than the common bond created by the brotherly fight for EDC. It also proved that the general agreement on the method

---

[147] Soustelle, *J.O., Ass. Nat.,* pp. 4624 and 6699–6700; Lebon, p. 6694, (Union of two nations against the Germanic danger).

to be followed (which had been reached by those EDC supporters who wanted specialized and gradual integration, and by those EDC foes who stood for closer association and limited contracts between European nations) was more important than the particular disagreements which could break out about the pace of European advance and about the dosage of supranationality to be used at each step. When supranationality becomes a technical procedure instead of a political dogma, compromises are possible.

The More Complicated Problem of International Relations Which Conditions All the Others: Here the main cleavage appeared among EDC's enemies. But those who tried or hoped for a united Germany unconnected with either bloc, or even for a revival of big-power rule, were a minority. A far greater number (all EDC's supporters and many of EDC's opponents) believed that the only reality for a long time was the cold war. Realism, therefore, required that the nightmare of Germany holding the balance of power be avoided, and the dream of a swift reconciliation of the antagonistic Great Powers be abandoned. The more spectacular controversies were the more superficial ones. On the most serious problem the measure of agreements was the greatest. This does not mean, of course, that the winning camp was free of minor quarrels between those who asked for nothing but situations of strength, those who would like to mitigate the cold war once these situations were established, and the total nationalists (who had also chosen the Atlantic alliance but whose hostility to Germany prevented them from accepting their choice's implications). However, the very fact that the question of international relations, hushed up during the EDC debate, dominated the discussion of W.E.U. and that a majority of both friends and foes of the new system made efforts towards a negotiated relaxation of world tension, showed that in a few months attention had turned from the purely Atlantic aspect of the problem to a new phase: the relations to be defined between the two power blocs. Ratification of either EDC or WEU nevertheless meant the end of diplomatic immobility in Europe.[148]

[148] However, the discretion of supporters of "parallel" negotiations and the confusion of supporters of "previous" negotiations on their aims, befogged the discussion in the Assembly in contrast to the clarity of the debate in the Chambre des Communes.

The Problem of Germany: Lastly, there is one problem which is at the core of all three others, and which haunted the French during the whole controversy on EDC and W.E.U., even though it is not much more than a reflection of past agonies. Just as the alignments for and against EDC in the National Assembly had been determined by the technical problem of defense, the alignments for or against W.E.U. were commanded by the problem of Germany. Here again, the end of EDC brought some revelations with it. It showed that there are three groups of Frenchmen. Some look forward to a golden age which some panacea would establish; those are the ones who believe in reunification or in political integration. Some look backward to a bloody past and hold that the only solution to the problem of Germany lies—let us be frank—in repression: genuine discrimination or guardianship by the big powers. The others, who expect only a gradual solution of the problem, and who want to promote both Western security and world peace, try to bind Germany to her Western neighbors, but do not entertain illusions about the miraculous and eternal character of such bonds, whatever stuff they are made of, in the present state of world affairs.[149]

[149] Last note, on internal policy. We cannot help being struck by the tendency of Parliament (as a mouthpiece for the country in this respect) to divide itself on each new question into multiple groups, never the same. Each of the four problems which arose brought out four different splinterings into small groups. And whatever the question at stake, a solid majority could not be obtained except at the price of really smothering the other questions.

RETROSPECT
AND
PROSPECT

9 : Reflections on France in the World Arena

DANIEL LERNER

> I beseech our allies and compatriots to be careful: a serious
> foreign policy issue should not become a matter of domestic
> political passions. Let us abstain from such over-simplified and
> untrue slogans. . . .
>
> Vincent Auriol
President of the Republic,
(21 April 1954)

Ideology is a degenerate form of political discourse. Between persons and events it interposes a screen of prefabricated vocabulary. It constricts flexible judgment of changing circumstances within the doctrinaire bonds of a political "line". Thereby it produces a systematic distortion of reality. When ideological conflict is prolonged and intense, confusion tends to be compounded by self-righteousness. The partisans begin to see error as knavery and opponents as traitors. Such, as Raymond Aron has indicated, was the case of EDC. That a decision of such gravity should be debated at length was natural. That the policy debate should degenerate into an ideological quarrel which, over four long years, increasingly divided and embittered the participants was unnecessary. The outcome was confusion and distrust in France, in the United States, and between these indispensable allies.

In America attention had been focused on the goal of European Community, hopes for its achievement had been pinned on EDC, and the issue had been dramatized in the grand manner, *au tragique*. Its defeat in the Assemblée Nationale produced a shock in political and intellectual circles, for the moment of "agonizing reappraisal" now seemed to have arrived. The larger American public was confused. As French perspectives on EDC had never been explained by the government or the press, many Americans with reasonable information and good will could not see why the French rejected this hopeful step toward a United Europe, which would dissolve traditional antagonisms on the Old Continent and give it the means for a fresh start. Those other Americans who view Europe with little interest and less sentiment took the defeat of EDC as only another example of malignant perversity. The vote of 30 August 1954 seemed likely to widen a growing breach between France and America into proportions of major political consequence for the Atlantic system.

American confusion reflected, in a certain measure, the confusion that reigned in France itself during the debate. Recall that EDC was, in origin, a French creation. Recall that during the early years of the debate, as M. Stoetzel has shown, public support of the project was widespread. As late as 1953, a substantial majority of Frenchmen expressed approval of American efforts to help unify Western Europe. An IFOP poll reported that, after the Marshall Plan, this was the most approved of American activities —and more popular indeed among the French elite than among the general public:

American Efforts to Unify Western Europe [1]

	Approve	Disapprove	No Opinion
Public	56%	20%	24%
Elite	77%	12%	11%

Small wonder that the American public was confused when, barely a year later, loud complaints against "American pressure" began to be heard as a principal reason for opposition to EDC.

The flow of public oratory had shifted, but even the French public was not clear on what had happened and why. Nor is it quite clear today. A fortnight after the historic vote of August 30th, the Institut d'Etudes Européennes undertook a systematic inquiry on the question: "Why did EDC fail?" We have by now

[1] Institut Français d'Opinion Publique, *Sondages* (1953), No. 2, p. 74

interviewed in detail over 1,500 leading spokesmen for the principal sectors of French society. Our study is in midpassage, but the absence of consensus at the summit of political life is already clear. M. René Pléven attributes the defeat to superior propaganda by the *Anticédistes* and failure by the *Cédistes* to gain the required number of Socialist votes. M. Joseph Laniel ascribes the outcome to the action of the Gaullists. M. Georges Bidault sets the defeat in a different frame: the opposition to all change by "static France" and the specific opposition to EDC by M. Mendès-France. These men headed the French government during the EDC period. Throughout the *milieux dirigeants* there is a marked lack of agreement on cause and effect. This is reflected in the confusion that prevails among the larger public.

This book was undertaken as a step toward clarification. Our aim has been to disengage the themes of the debate and to discuss them in greater depth, with more light and less heat, than was possible during the controversy and its immediate aftermath. The authors, who include prominent partisans on both sides of the issue, have here laid aside their preferences in a common effort to seek enlightenment. This concluding chapter seeks merely to underscore several points that seem important in the perspective of a friendly American observer. In this perspective France figures as a vital center of the Western civilization and of the Western system of power designed to defend it. Clarity between Frenchmen and Americans on their common goals, and on optimal ways of reaching those goals, is essential to the healthy functioning of that system.

An impression gathered from interviews among the *milieux dirigeants* is that their explanations of the EDC defeat may be misleading by their precision. Retrospection often tends to clothe the past in false clarity. The EDC debate involved many problems of great complexity during a period filled with events whose meaning was obscure at the time. The wisdom of hindsight counsels caution in these matters, particularly since two of the major consequences predicted during the debate have in fact rather produced their opposite. An argument against EDC was that it permitted the rearmament of Germany. But no sooner was EDC rejected than a new program—the Accords of Paris—set the rearmament of Germany into motion. Or again, a persistent argument against both EDC and the Accords of Paris was that such action by the West would make negotiations with the East difficult or impossible. But no sooner were the Accords of Paris ratified than the USSR undertook major negotiation with the West—first by initialing the Austrian peace treaty, next by participation in a Big Four conference at Geneva.

One type of oversimplification that strikes a foreign observer is the French tendency toward explanations that are wholly contained in the universe of internal events. The effort to comprehend foreign policy decisions in *any* country requires a context in which "internal" and "international" events endlessly interact and reciprocally influence each other. It is no less true in France than elsewhere that national sovereignty has been compromised by the facts of life in a bipolar arena of world politics. The current arena of world politics requires many "international decisions" to activate policies that exceed the independent capacity of any single nation.

Hence it has not been possible to explain the defeat of EDC solely in terms of: (1) the parliamentary maneuvers in the Assemblée Nationale; or (2) the weakness of the Executive branch of the French government (either under Laniel or under Mendès-France); or (3) the influence of the "interest groups" upon the votes of deputies; or (4) the action of propaganda and public opinion. Each of these factors doubtless played a role, although the roles assigned to them by our interviewees are often incompatible and sometimes contradictory. If the defeat of EDC was decided wholly by parliamentary maneuvers, as many affirm, then public opinion had no great significance. Naturally this does not prevent partisans of both positions from claiming that "public opinion was on our side" and attributing to the other side the evil intention (or at least the evil effect) of confusing public opinion.

Moreover, even when handled consistently, the domestic factors do not account for the defeat of EDC in strict empirical fashion. The *internal* order of events appears inadequate to explain a decision of this magnitude. Consider the various efforts to correlate the parliamentary vote with the regional distribution of "European" sentiments. This is a domain in which French observers, with an excellent research tradition in political geography, usually make very acute observations. On EDC, however, none of the major hypotheses corresponds to the observable facts.

One such hypothesis is that EDC was killed by the French interior, the *départements* known as *le Centre*. This view, expressed by President Pléven among others, corresponds to the American dichotomy between "isolationist" Middle West and "internationalist" coastal states. It rests on the theory that interior regions form insular political judgments, whereas border regions reflect their constant contact with the outer world in a greater political "internationalism". On many French issues, this theory has some explanatory value. But it is clearly refuted on EDC by the actual distribution of parliamentary votes. As is shown by Map A below, the tallies for border *départements* and *le Centre* were as follows:

Parliamentary Votes on EDC

Number of Departments

	For	Against	Abstained	Total
Border Départements	15	20	4	39
Le Centre [2]	6	6	3	15

[2] *Against:* Allier, Creuse, H. Vienne, Puy de Dôme (absolute majority); Cher, Nièvre (relative majority)
For: Cantal, H. Loire, Vienne (relative majority); Dordogne, Saône, Loire (absolute majority)
Abstained: Charente, Corrèze, Indre

The facts, then, clearly refute both parts of this hypothesis. The border departments of France divided, but with a distinct majority voting *against* EDC. Hence the "internationalist" perspectives of the border areas, whatever may be the case on other issues, did not operate on EDC. So, too, the "isolationist" departments of the center divided with arithmetical precision. While *le Centre* is not precisely defined in French political geography, a glance at Map A shows that these proportions shift even further counter-hypothesis (*for* EDC) if one adds the next "ring" of departments to the central core.

A second hypothesis, suggested by President Bidault, is that the cleavage of "European" sentiment followed the line which divides "static France" from "dynamic France". In this dichotomy, which corresponds to the American distinction between the progressive industrial North and the backward agrarian South, static France fears competition and distrusts the strange whereas dynamic

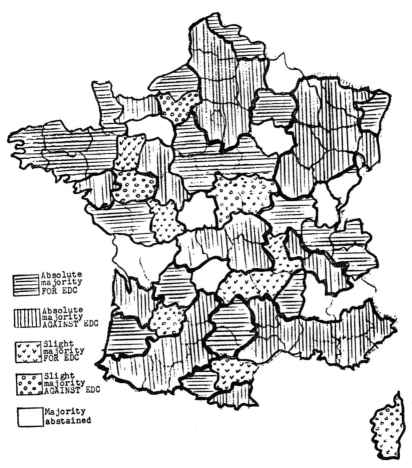

MAP A

PARLIAMENTARY VOTE ON EDC

30 August 1954

Absolute
majority
FOR EDC

Absolute
majority
AGAINST EDC

Slight
majority
FOR EDC

Slight
majority
AGAINST EDC

Majority
abstained

PARLIAMENTARY VOTE ON EDC

30 August 1954

(WITHOUT COMMUNISTS)

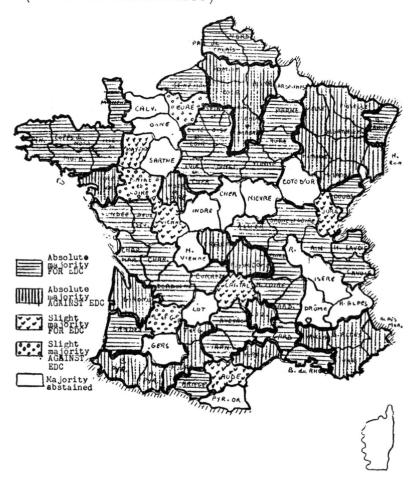

MAP C

SOCIALIST VOTE ON EDC (94 DEPUTIES)

30 August 1954

FOR EDC

AGAINST EDC

MIXED

France welcomes new ventures as opportunities for growth. The alleged role of the "underdeveloped areas" in defeating EDC is examined in the chapter by M. André Philip, who divides static from dynamic France along a line drawn from Rouen to Marseille: northeast lie the pro-Europeans, southwest the anti-Europeans. While such a schema may correspond to the voting pattern of the Socialist labor federations, it does not correspond at all to the regional distribution of votes in the Assemblée Nationale. As the map shows, the industrial northeast in fact voted predominantly *against* EDC whereas the underdeveloped southwest voted largely *for*. If a line can be drawn at all, it would tend to cross the map in the opposite direction from the line Rouen-Marseille. This is equally true when we plot the EDC votes of the Socialist deputies only, as is shown on Map C. But if the Rouen-Marseille line is false, its traverse is meaningless. Nor has another line been detected that will be both true and significant as an explanation of these voting distributions.

A third main regional hypothesis holds that EDC sentiment can be analyzed as a simple function of hostility toward Germany. This derives from a theoretical proposition contrary to the "cosmopolitan border" theory, according to which contact multiplies cordiality. The present hypothesis stresses the case where contact multiplies hostility. On this view, those regions would be most intensely opposed to EDC which had suffered the most from German military power in the past. The facts suggest that, whatever the weight of anti-German sentiment among the public, it was not the significant factor in the regional distribution of parliamentary voting. The map shows, indeed, that the most solid regional bloc of votes *for* EDC is Alsace-Lorraine, which has been the historic route of German invasion and has suffered more directly than any other region of France from the German armies.

Supporters of these regional hypotheses often state, when the facts disconfirm their views, that the true regional pattern has been obscured by the monolithic bloc of 100 Communist votes which tend to obliterate regional differences. To determine the weight of this factor, we recomputed the distribution of parliamentary votes on EDC without counting the Communists. The results, presented in Map B above, demonstrate that the subtraction of Communists produces only limited changes in the regional disorder. None of these changes, however, alters the regional portrait of Map A in such fashion as to support any of the above hypotheses.[3]

Our interest goes beyond the negative testing of important hypotheses. The inadequacy of the hypotheses is itself the essential point. For they indicate that the traditional universe of internal French politics, and the new universe of political sentiment evoked by EDC, simply do not coincide. More was involved. Every writer in this book, whatever his views on EDC, insists that something profound in the French conscience was activated by this prolonged controversy. The retrospective effort to force the results into conventional categories of exegesis only reduces the EDC decision to a wilful act that seems to justify the diagnosis of "parochialism" (*politique de clocher*) often made by foreign observers. For such explanations ignore the larger world by which the politically-relevant segments of French society were influenced, in many cases decisively.

This shows in the inconsequential handling of "foreign influences" on EDC during and since the debate. Instead of discussion situating France in the current arena of world politics as a whole, there was a series of disjointed notes on each country in its turn. With respect to EDC, the whole structure of international politics was reduced to four main slogans: 1) "German menace"; 2) "American pressure"; 3) "British abstention"; 4) "Soviet refusal to negotiate". When handled in this itemistic fashion, without any more comprehensive context, several of the factors appear to be incompatible. For example: it may be true to assert that "British participation" in EDC might have reduced the "German menace"; but would British participation have made negotiations with the USSR easier—or harder? Or again: can those who desired "British participation" consistently complain of "American pressure", when increased British participation was among the objects that American pressure sought? Or finally: given the well-established British position on continental commitments, can those who made "British participation" a condition of French ratification have been thinking at all of world political realities?

The curious structure of the post-mortems reflects the weird

[3] These statistical studies were made by the Institut d'Etudes Européennes in cooperation with the French Political Science Association. To its executive officer M. Henri-Gréard, and to M. Jourdan for preparing the maps, we extend our thanks.

logic of the debate itself. Spokesmen for either side used an amalgam of arguments that were often incompatible and sometimes contradictory. Or, on the contrary, both sides made use of the same proposition to prove opposite points. An instance is the theme of German rearmament: *Anticédistes* justified their opposition by their hostility toward the re-creation of a Wehrmacht; *Cédistes* justified their support of the treaty on precisely the same grounds (insisting that the way to avoid an autonomous German army was by creating an integrated European army). In the next debate, on the Accords of Paris, the same theme recurred with new variations. Embittered *Cédistes* declared that those who had rejected EDC on the false slogan "No Wehrmacht!" now were preparing to ratify a treaty which did, in fact, recreate the Wehrmacht.

The inconsistencies of the debate suggest that the explicit themes were mainly important as a rationale and a resonance. Opponents and proponents could agree on the undesirability of a new Wehrmacht and on the desirability of negotiations with the USSR. Neither side could demonstrate that from either premise his conclusion must follow. For both sides drew their conclusions rather from profound preferences that are often refractory to the demonstrations of logic. In this sense, the defeat of EDC reflected an extra-rational act of *will*. No single factor counted so much as the new image of France's place in the world defined by the ensemble of the project. To the familiar sense of France as a great autonomous *présence* in the world, EDC opposed the strange new vision of France as a cog in the wheel of Europe. It was this vision that was being rejected by many of those who opted against EDC. Vincent Auriol, retiring President of the Republic, spoke of "a mutilated nation in a mutilated Europe". President Robert Schuman told me that the one strong thread which bound together the diverse strands of anticédisme was the feeling that *"la France serait diminuée"* (France would be diminished).

The imagery of EDC is a subject that remains to be explored. It is in no sense pejorative to suggest that sentimental, or extra-rational, features played a larger role than has been allowed by most commentators. Public opinion often expresses itself most profoundly in responding with vague and diffuse images to the more articulated propositions of political debate.

An aspect of the EDC image that evoked profound reactions of this order was supranationality. Messrs. René Mayer and Mendès-France (arch-adversaries over EDC as over other issues) nevertheless find themselves in rare agreement on the proposition that "it is not possible to make the French swallow more than a certain dose of supranationality per generation". Indeed in his autopsy of EDC, which was squarely based on this proposition, M. Mayer differed from M. Mendès-France mainly on the question of who invented the formula.[4]

One may well ask why it is that in France, the nation that invented modern internationalism and formulated the cosmopolitan conception of "the rights of man" (not merely Frenchmen), this parochialization of sentiment should now be so widespread. It is a question worthy of serious study why Frenchmen, who once spoke so confidently in the name of all humanity, now reject the more limited challenge to identify themselves as "Europeans". One order of inquiry, in terms of the French psyche, would lead us into a discussion of "national character". Such analysis would take into account the characteristics which the French frequently attribute to themselves, among those notably their "individualism" and their "skepticism". The trait of *méfiance*, which is a common French stereotype of the French, indexes a high degree of defensiveness. Of this the French are keenly aware; an instance, when asked *"Comment va?"*, is the mocking reply *"On se défend!"* The manifestation most striking to foreigners is extreme verbal aggressiveness, a familiar mechanism whereby threats and challenges in the environment are exorcised rather than interiorized.

The relevance of such a self-system to political behavior becomes apparent precisely when a nation is confronted by a historic challenge to redefine itself in new and unprecedented dimensions. EDC was perceived as a challenge of this magnitude—namely, to incorporate French identity into European identity. The European idea was handled easily, given the magnificent French gifts of verbal facility, so long as it remained on the doctrinal level. When presented as a demand for action, however, with specified time and place dimensions, it ran headlong into French percep-

[4] René Mayer, "Réfléxions sur le Supranational", *La Revue de Paris* (December 1954), p. 14.

tion of the whole non-French world as "the outside". Hence, there hovered about EDC from the start, increasing as the years passed and positions became rigidified, an air of unreality.

The more so as EDC turned the European question on its military side. The specific problem it posed was self-defense, defined as the defense of continental Europe. But, for very many Frenchmen, Europe does not figure as a realistic component of the "self". Nor, for very many, has defense figured as a real priority. Indeed, much of French postwar opinion has been characterized by selective inattention to the military order of world problems. One question in our interview schedule asked elite Frenchmen: "Do you think France should undertake to manufacture atomic weapons?" The responses, despite an extended Cabinet debate and two major statements by President Faure on the subject, have been meagre and evasive. A French colleague, reviewing these responses, commented: "For us the atom bomb is something that explodes in the Pacific or in Siberia; it seems fantastic to discuss actually making one in France".

Public attention in France has been focused less easily on problems of national military posture than on nuances of personal ideological posture. There has been very little discussion, for example, of the fact that metropolitan France has but two armed divisions in being. The "exciting" postwar debates have turned rather on the sequence of slogans coined by the ideologues: extremism (*jusqu'au-boutisme*), privatization (*je m'en foutisme*), displacement of hostility (*"U.S. go home!"*). We do not exaggerate the importance of these catch-words; we do note that privatization of attention and neutralization of purpose are widespread among the intelligentsia and observable also among the other French elites today. Among our interviewees, only 1 out of 50 mentioned war when asked: "What are the great problems of the world in 1955?" The French are surely no less aware of the risks of war than others; but since they now feel less capable of dealing with it than was historically the case, they avert their gaze.

From the sense of impotence, or diminished potency, follows the widespread propensity among French spokesmen not to focus their political thinking on a world arena in which the decisive criteria of power have been military, i.e., thermonuclear. In consequence, the demand posed by EDC, that Frenchmen henceforth think of self-defense as incorporated in the defense of Europe, seemed *unreal.* In the course of the four-year long debate, as is revealed by every chapter in this book, the military defense of the continent barely figured as an issue at all. Temperatures rose rather over the general ideology of European unity.

When the discussion descended from this high doctrinal level, the particularities were debated rather according to the segmented and incompatible perspectives of class and interest groups. The politicians spoke largely in terms of their prerogatives. The views of top business spokesmen on the economics of a "common market" were often predictable from the industry for which they spoke. The soldiers justified their opposition to EDC, often explicitly and in public, in terms of their unwillingness to put into unknown hands control over their own promotions. Few voices were heard loud and clear in the land which evaluated EDC in terms of the military responsibility of France within the Western system of defense.

This much said, let us turn from the psychic order of inquiry. While psychic mechanisms operate among the French as among all other peoples, top political decisions are based on a net evaluation of many factors, to which preferences often must yield priority for the sake of rational choice. Rationality still operates at the level of French policymaking; and if the ravages of privatization and neutralization are visible among the French elites today, the "unreality" of the European idea to many Frenchmen can also be explained on quite rational grounds. Indeed, the rejection of EDC can be compatible with a realistic assessment of the French position in the world arena today. To state these terms in a sentence: In the bipolar phase of the nuclear epoch, the French have in fact *not been responsible for their self-defense,* whether the self be conceived as wholly French or partly European.

The basic fact of international politics for France, during the past decade, has been the American "atomic guarantee" of continental Europe. The defense of France, as of all Europe lying West of the invisible "bomb line" that divides Germany, has been located in those bomber bases equipped with nuclear weapons which the Americans have installed at strategic places around the world. The local headquarters of continental defense has been NATO; but, though NATO has a Paris address, in its council the French compose one voice among many.

NATO expresses a relatively new state of affairs in modern history. The traditional balance of power in Europe, with its strategy of shifting coalitions, was operated by autonomous nations seeking relative advantages through their own foreign ministries and general staffs. The new structure of European politics, under NATO, is already quite different. All member nations have ceded part of their capacity, and most of their responsibility, for self-defense to a common headquarters. NATO is the only agency which takes responsibility for defense of the *whole* continent conceived as a single military terrain. SHAPE is the sole headquarters on the continent with the capacity to use nuclear weapons in case of military need. This delegation of responsibility was carried still further in the EDC treaty, which proposed to integrate European troops into a single military formation and European armaments into a single weapons-system.

There are several ways of reacting to such a new situation. Each can be justified as both rational and moral. Hence no clarification is gained by assigning pejorative labels. To represent faithfully the nuances of perspective would require a gallery of political portraits. But we sketch the attitudinal profiles of pre-EDC France in terms of three main postures: internationalist, neutralist, nationalist. The crudity of these categories is suggested by one analysis, which identifies five quite distinct varieties of neutralists—and there are others.[5]

EDC ruptured this array of attitudes as it did the traditional boundaries between parties and regions. Some internationalists opposed EDC either because they wanted a more cosmopolitan conception than the Europe of Six—i.e., the Europe of 7 (W.E.U.), or of 15 (Council of Europe), or of 18 (O.E.E.C. and E.P.U.)—or because they preferred the Atlantic conception to any purely continental plan. This view was expressed in the warning of Pierre Dieterlen against merely "raising parochialism to the European scale". Other interrnationalists supported EDC precisely as a means of securing the continental sector of the Atlantic system. On a contrary hypothesis, some neutralists (the "third force" variant) supported EDC as a means of disengaging Europe from Atlantic control. But other neutralists (the "pacifist" variant) rejected all military projects and joined in a common opposi-

[5] L. de Sainte Lorette, *L'idée d'union fédérale européenne* (Paris, Colin, 1955), pp. 180–2.

tion to EDC with the nationalists (who were not, earlier, their natural allies).

There is no simple hypothesis that neatly correlates the general political attitudes of Frenchmen with their specific net judgments for and against EDC. But we are in a better position to locate the spinal column of these attitudinal structures if we differentiate Frenchmen according to their focus of attention. Many commentators have observed that the EDC "debate" consisted of separate monologues—people talking past (rather than to) each other. Most talked around the specific issue of EDC to other, more or less related, problems that preoccupied their attention and prefigured their perception. *The* issue was military organization for continental defense. Hence we start by noting, as a key differential in attention patterns among Frenchmen, their awareness of the military facts of life in our time.

One type of Frenchman had been able to internalize the fact that Europe had become a single military terrain and to perceive the consequence that henceforth France was no longer defensible along the traditional political lines of national boundaries. Ground defense of France now begins at some point east of the great North German plain. Air defense of France, which hinges upon the location of systems for warnings and alerts, now begins even closer to the Eastern source from which the only hostile aircraft could arise over the continent. A Frenchman seriously concerned with military security would perceive the defense of France and Europe as orchestral, and would put a high value on having the best possible array of instruments. He would note that EDC proposed a weapons-system with certain specific military advantages. For one, it provided a channel whereby armaments could be suited to the specific technical requirements of continental defense, such as aircraft whose flight-to-target lasts five minutes rather than fifteen minutes. This was important to Europeans in 1950 (and may, for certain limited purposes, still be). Aircraft that become effective only a quarter-hour after their departure may be useful for the defense of continental North America. They would be quite inadequate for the defense of continental Europe, over which enemy bombers could be flying a few minutes after their departure. A Frenchman alert to the military facts of life would be bound to support some type of continental defense—and, on this basis, probably some type of continental economics and even of continental politics. French military leaders who opposed EDC in detail (e.g. Marshal Juin, General Koenig) were careful to couple their opposition with alternative proposals designed, while preserving their prerogatives, to safeguard the basic idea of continental defense.

Another type of Frenchman, reflecting on EDC, has the specific problems of military defense less sharply at the focus of his attention. Such a man might acknowledge that France no longer has a completely independent capacity to defend herself. But from this he might rationally derive either of two very different lines of policy, the choice being shaped by his proximate interests and ultimate goals. If he were especially concerned with the future stature of France in a world of super-powers, he might urge leadership of an effective European Community as a way to replace her diminished national capacity. By promoting European integration, France's position at the head of the larger community would be earned by initiative and agility. Such a Frenchman would not necessarily endorse EDC—but he would be *likely* to, even if its technical arrangements seemed less perfect than he might wish. On a long view of the historical process implied by his own policy, he would not permit controversy over details to obscure the symbol of his main goal, namely "Europe." [6]

Still another Frenchman, perceiving that France no longer has an independent *capacity* for self-defense, might conclude that France need no longer take *responsibility*. Since her security is guaranteed by the American "bomb line", France might better expend its energies on other matters. Although the final style of European defense must be orchestral, France might better play solo elsewhere while she can. Rather than search for new leadership in Europe, he might prefer to ensure French leadership in those places where it actually exists. "After all," he might say, "there is still a French Union, and the problems we face in Indo-China and North Africa are largely military. Hence let us not merge our army, which is a key instrument of our national policy, into some amorphous European army whose operations we can only influence but not control." [7] Even the Sixth Additional Proto-

[6] Former Prime Minister René Pléven, who sponsored the original EDC treaty, told me that its defeat was largely due to the narrow terrain on which the debate was contained. The great symbol of "European Unity" faded from the scene.
[7] Paraphrased quotation from recent interviews with respondents of this type.

col of 24 March, 1953 did not obviate the fear that the French *présence*, once deprived of a national army, would be fatally weakened in her overseas territories.

This reasoning could lead rationally to a vote against EDC and would, on other issues, entail policies that are anti- or at least non-European. The man who prefers a familiar France to a future Europe, a national army to a continental army, would be likely to perceive the prospects of a continental economy in a similar manner. The line could be: let us rather devote our resources to strengthening what we have, metropolitan France and the French Union, than commit ourselves to the European system of production and consumption proposed in these new "pools" and "common markets."

The foregoing represents a "nationalist" (or "anti-internationalist") as opposed to "European" line on EDC. Its vitality derived from a single fact: that, so long as they were living under an American guarantee, the French faced no urgent practical need to expend their resources on defense. It was natural, in such circumstances, that some French leaders should have chosen to focus their efforts elsewhere. This was, indeed, the theme on which M. Mendès-France closed his final speech on the eve of the fateful vote:

> "We are faithful to the alliance which gives us our security and our conception of the alliance is a cordial cooperation between associates equal in rights who debate together their common interests, while each remains judge of his essential and vital interests . . . The primary task that the French government should accomplish to strengthen the community of western nations is first the internal reconstruction of our country." [8]

This was a clear-cut choice between alternative policies. The EDC issue involved, at bottom, a decision on how the French budget should be spent. The priorities formulated by Mendès-France favored civil rather than military expenditures. This was a perfectly realistic assessment of the facts of bipolar life, including the role of the atomic guarantee. Any policy is a choice between ways of "getting around" facts, and the choice at this level is shaped by one's image of a desirable future. The preference of

[8] P. Mendès-France, *Gouverner c'est choisir. Sept mois et dix-sept jours* (Julliard 1955), p. 112.

many Frenchmen, on the EDC issue, for a national rather than a European solution, was perfectly comprehensible.

It was on this point that a serious failure of communication between France and the United States occurred. The "European" solution had been highly publicized and approved in this country; but scant attention was paid to the "national" solution and its appeal to very many Frenchmen. Few understood that it was precisely the American guarantee which gave France security at minimal cost and made possible the rejection of EDC on rational grounds of self-interest. Failing this, many Americans could not understand why their support of EDC seemed to some Frenchmen a puerile game of giving with the right hand and taking with the left. For it was clear among French political leaders that EDC, while presumably requiring no formal increase in France's military budget, would by remilitarizing Germany put them in a competitive position that inevitably would divert large shares of their limited resources to military purposes. Hence it seemed to them unreasonable to demand French expenditures for a defense which was already guaranteed—and which a French contribution could not significantly improve.

Nor was the position much clarified by insisting, as many "European" spokesmen in France and America did, that the material contribution was less important than the symbol of French will to sustain a common defense. We do not minimize the importance of such symbols in international life. On the contrary, we suggest that they are too important in their own right to parade in the pretentious costume of military divisions which, moreover, also involve men and money. Had the real stakes been clearly formulated, the anguish might have been reduced.

What EDC asked Frenchmen to do was, for the sake of an invigorating symbolism of the common will, to obscure the historic identity represented in its national army and to divert a substantial part of its resources from development of the French economy. This was a lot to ask of any nation; and there were reasonable grounds for responding to such a demand one way or the other. Grateful recognition of American aid was not a reasonable ground, for gratitude is not an appropriate political emotion. It has, in any country, little weight in decisions on the national budget. Indeed, American support of EDC was not wholly unrelated to the desire to reduce American troop commitments (and taxpayers' burdens) on the European continent. Had Americans understood this better, they would have felt less hostility at the end. Indeed, they might have committed less emotion to the project from the very beginning.

The American commitment reflects a confusion in public opinion that can be attributed in considerable measure to the Department of State. But for a reason wholly different from the usual charge, after the EDC failed, that they had "guessed wrong". It is too much to ask of *any* reporting system that it guess right on all such issues. If the American Embassy in Paris was wrong on the outcome of EDC, so indeed were many French political commentators and experts.

The important American mistake was "guessing wrong" not at the end but rather at the start. This was the error of permitting EDC to become, and to endure through four years as, a high doctrinal controversy over the basic symbols of French identity. Rigid State Department support of EDC helped to sustain an acrimonious quarrel which intensified ideological differences, defined certain attitudes that might better have remained amorphous, and pushed French partisans into extreme positions. No American purpose was served by the cleavage among Frenchmen over their most bitter choice since the surrender of France to Hitler by Vichy (according to Jules Moch), or its surrender to Henry V at Troyes (according to the Count of Paris). Said Mendès-France: "EDC puts before us one of the deepest matters of conscience which ever disturbed a country". Jacques Fauvet, veteran of parliamentary rhetoric, found the deputies in this case genuinely "tortured". André Philip saw the "fundamental personality traits" of Frenchmen laid bare. Even my austere colleague Raymond Aron, recollecting in tranquillity a full year after the quarrel ended, concludes that Frenchmen had not been so deeply divided "since the Dreyfus case". The long-term effects of this schism remain to be seen. An immediate consequence was "*l'immobilisme*", which hampered French leadership from taking effective action on many other domestic and international problems, while not settling the EDC issue either.

To implicate American policy in all this is, however, a different matter than the angry charge that "American pressure" killed the EDC. This charge seems to me untrue. It would be a much sadder day for France than it is in fact, if "American pressure" in this sense really had played the decisive role. While the leaders of any nation may be annoyed by pressure from what they regard as "the outside", no top policy with consequences as important as those of EDC for France is made on the basis of whether or not they have been annoyed. Those who exaggerate the theme of "American pressure" might do better to reflect on the theme of the American guarantee.

A less dubious comment on American intervention is that it would have been more effectively applied in persuading the French government and parliament to confine the EDC debate within its proper limits. The reasonable procedure was to debate EDC as a problem in the organization of continental defense and to reach a decision on this issue rapidly. In the limited measure that American policy was able to, but did not, prevent the debate from becoming a bitter ideological controversy, it shares responsibility for its unhappy consequences in French politics. In the larger measure that it encouraged American opinion to perceive this organizational problem as a high moral issue, American policy again committed a grave error.

Our interest here is not to score easy victories over the past, but rather to learn from EDC errors how Western policy may operate more efficiently in the future. An important lesson can be drawn from the failure of the American threat to undertake an "agonizing reappraisal" if the French rejected EDC. France rejected EDC nevertheless. As America could not make such a threat effective even when its "atomic guarantee" was the sole deterrent to potential Soviet aggression, obviously the type of thinking that underlay this threat had better be shelved as the world approaches weapon-parity and—more remotely—a new phase of potential multipolarity. Threats will surely not work when the nations of Europe (or some non-American combination of them) develop an effective capacity for defending themselves.

"Agonizing reappraisal" failed because it was a bluff, and was widely recognized among Frenchmen as a bluff. The American commitment to Europe is much too great to be easily revised. To mention only the crudest military stakes: some of the air bases which activate the American "atomic guarantee" are located on French territory in North Africa. More important: continental Europe is one sector of the American world-map in which a "little war" would, under all foreseeable conditions, trigger the Big War. In the bipolar world area America, too, finds its power of unilateral decision severely limited.

Moreover, besides being a bluff, this was a threat. Reappraisal implied that the guarantee might be withdrawn and France left defenseless or, perhaps worse, dependent upon a European defense system based in Germany. The implication was that the French would have no alternative but to ensure their security by ratifying EDC. Instead, some French spokesmen turned the threat into a boomerang by reaching for the other horn of the dilemma—namely, by a campaign for negotiations guaranteeing its security by agreement with the Soviet Union. (An extremist minority in the Assembly even took up the Communist slogan of a *renversement des alliances*.)

This was agile diplomacy. But the adroit maneuver was of minor importance, for it too was merely a bluff. The United States cannot leave the Western system simply by threatening to do so. Neither can France. Both France and America are bound together in the Western system by ties knotted with ideological sentiment, social institutions, economic interest, and military interdependence. However, certain consequences were entrained by the French maneuver that indicate how risky a game is bluffing between allies. Three consequences are worth noting:

(1) A new anti-EDC coalition emerged which had not previously existed in postwar France. This was a coalition led on one side by the Communists and on the other by the Anti-Internationalists. The Communist interest was obvious and followed logically from its permanent alliance with the Soviet Union. The Anti-Internationalist position, stated simply, was that if the United States demands too high a price (supranationality) to defend us against potential Soviet aggression, then our best bargaining strategy is to forestall any such aggression by negotiations with the USSR. We need not exaggerate the permanence of this coalition, but neither should we underestimate its potential influence upon French policy in the near future. One of our interviewees has said that "the anti-EDC coalition was valid for one day only" (meaning 30 August, 1954). This forecast seems to me lacking in foresight. The coalition may again become active, and its influence may increase each time that it is reactivated, whenever future American policy attempts to *bluff* France into a bipolar dilemma.

(2) The next effect of the propaganda campaign hooked to the Soviet horn of the bipolar dilemma was to weaken the sense of the USSR as the major adversary that confronts the Western world. While the opponents of EDC were advocating immediate negotiations with the Russians, they naturally were no longer able to speak of Russia as the main danger. The slogans of negotiations were taken up and repeated by the Assemblée Nationale, by the press, and by the public (in demonstrations where Gaullists shared with Communists the platform of a common opposition to EDC). It was natural that all these voices busily speaking of possible "Soviet negotiation" should, at the same time, stop speaking about potential "Soviet aggression". The controversy, then, had the paradoxical effect in France of weakening the image of precisely that potential aggressor against whom EDC had been conceived in the first place.[9]

(3) In the measure that the image of the USSR as the danger weakened, in just this measure the image of Germany as the adversary was strengthened. The most striking shift in French political opinion was the increasing hostility toward Germany during the latter years of the EDC debate. Starting from a relatively low point in the traditional *mésentente*, French attention (hence hostility) to Germany grew steadily through the four years and reached a crescendo by the time EDC was rejected. This was a natural public response to the continuous repetition of the twin themes that the Soviets were to be negotiated with, but the Germans were to be distrusted and feared. Hence, the final paradox of the EDC controversy, which had been dedicated as a cornerstone of European construction, was that it aggravated the pathology that constitutes a major resistance to any sort of integration. It is not too much to say that the net effect of the EDC episode in France may have been a net decrease in the immediate psychic potential for a European Community.

One lesson of these unsought consequences is that, even in a bipolar world, power is qualified by purpose. Instead of talking so much about "psychological strategy", America might do better to practice consistently the main features of such a strategy: namely, by avoiding propositions which call the very existence of the West-

[9] Former Premier Georges Bidault, with this sequence in mind, told me that negotiation with the East entails the risk of "the disintegration of internal French opinion".

ern system into question; by keeping out of ideological controversies infused with moral judgments; and by conducting diplomatic relations with allies in terms of specific and limited problems which have to be met. A reasonable politics of persuasion seeks so to define any specific issue that the common purpose may more readily be perceived. When this happens, the joint power is equitably shared without sermons. But this will require recognition that the post-war period has ended, and with it the validity of a policy developed at a time when America was the only effective power in the West. In a world of several potentially independent powers, new policies will be needed whose efficacy derives from a genuine sense of community.

The lesson for France seems equally important as weapon-parity is attained and thermonuclear development takes a course that may lead to a new multipolarity in the world arena. France may not be able, in the near future, to rely so heavily upon external protection as was possible during the EDC period. Then, a "nationalist" French policy on European defense was made possible by the atomic guarantee based on clear weapon-superiority in the hands of a friendly America. But what was rational for Frenchmen during the past decade may not be feasible during the next decade. For we are entering a new phase of the nuclear epoch, in which the main condition will be the attainment of weapon-parity between America and Russia.

In this new period, French policy will be shaped partly by estimates of the time required to attain full parity between America and Russia, partly by the reactions to this new situation among the other powers.

With regard to the stockpile position, effective parity probably has been achieved. It only takes a determinate number of nuclear weapons to insure the capacity of any nation for total destruction of any other; beyond this number it becomes a waste of resources to manufacture additional bombs. There will doubtless be continuing efforts to improve the hydrogen bomb and to develop some new Weapon X, but this becomes a task of secondary priority once the capacity for total destruction exists. At present, American superiority hinges mainly upon its capacity to *deliver* destruction— in the old military phrase "to get there fustest with the mostest". The safe assumption is that the USSR will before long catch up in this capacity as well. The American slogan of "instantaneous and massive retaliation" was one way of declaring that the world has already moved into the phase of weapon parity.

Once the bipolar capacity to deliver total destruction exists and is recognized, however, then the American "bomb line" no longer serves its former function as the *absolute* guarantee of European territory. It may be true that America still has, and for some years will continue to have, the power to destroy the Soviet Union immediately after an attack. Such retaliation would not be much help to Europe, which might well be destroyed by the first offensive blow. Until now the Soviet Union has not had this capacity and perhaps does not yet quite have it; but within a brief period the Soviet capacity to destroy Europe totally will exist.

In this new phase, then, Europe will remain partly dependent, but cannot rely exclusively upon, the American guarantee. The luxury of being able to rely upon others for defense of the continent, leaving oneself free for other tasks, is likely to vanish. The future calls for a comprehensive "system" of defense, in which American strategic and logistical power will be coordinated with massive contributions from the European nations.

This is the challenge posed to France and Europe in the post-EDC phase, and it entails some hard choices. To make their contribution to the Western system of defense, the European nations would have to reconsider their military budgets and therewith the program of industrial development on which they are engaged. This raises again the issue of EDC, but in a different form and with higher stakes.

Britain is already well advanced on a long-term program of nuclear development for industrial uses. M. Francis Perrin, High Commissioner for Atomic Energy, has announced that by 1957 France will have in operation a factory capable of "important" production.[10] There is no reason to doubt that an autonomous Germany will undertake a nuclear reconversion of its industrial plant. The smaller nations of Europe also have a common stake in industrial development through the research center at Geneva. The question now is: How long, and under what system of mutual agreements, will Europe be permitted to develop its nuclear resources exclusively in this fashion?

The debate on this question began in France immediately fol-

[10] *Le Monde*, 23 March 1955, p. 1.

lowing the British announcement of their intention to produce the hydrogen bomb. Practically all commentators expressed the sense that France must, willy-nilly, be led by the course of events into the development of nuclear armaments. This view was made explicit in a major statement by Prime Minister Edgar Faure:

> "If things continue there will be a sort of demarcation line between the noble and powerful nations which have thermonuclear means, and the inferior nations, not from the moral viewpoint but in the sense of power, which have none. I should say that I am putting to myself the question of knowing if France should resign the right that it has always had, to rank in the first category. I have the intention of examining this question shortly, in collaboration with ministers I have especially charged with this study. I believe that I will dismiss the negative solution, that of resignation . . .
>
> "Whether France will follow this course more vigorously or will seek a European formula with certain powers to facilitate progress, that is not decided. The government will deliberate. France cannot rest in a category of 'declining great powers' by reason of this new criterion." [11]

But one month later, on 14 April 1955, M. Faure announced: "We do not intend to devote research to the creation of an H-Bomb or other bomb. It is after long reflection that we have decided to orient ourselves in this way and I think that this choice will not prevent France from maintaining her place as a great power." [12]

It is relevant to observe that this decision was based upon a plan established by M. Gaston Palewski, Gaullist parliamentary leader, who had been a major adversary of EDC. Current French nuclear policy doubtless reflects his estimate that the American "atomic guarantee" still remains effective; hence that France may reasonably devote its limited nuclear resources to modernizing its economy rather than its defense. At least for the immediate present.

It seems probable, however, that a French decision to proceed with the manufacture of nuclear armaments will not be indefinitely postponed. It may be delayed, despite the British decision to produce a bomb now, for a few years. But there is likely to be an "agonizing reappraisal" of French policy when Germany and others begin to come into possession of their own thermonuclear

[11] *Le Monde*, 18 March, 1955, p. 1.
[12] *Le Figaro*, 14 April, 1955, p. 1.

technology. (Even the current ban on German ABC weapons may not long outlive Chancellor Adenauer.) The logic of international politics, M. Faure suggested, does not permit a nation which has been great to decide, as a matter of policy, that it will no longer be great. Since political greatness today is defined primarily by the capacity to produce and deliver nuclear firepower, the question before France will soon become how to develop nuclear weapons most efficiently.

Three main courses seem open to France: no action, independent action, cooperative action. For the moment the official course appears to be *no* action, but the implication is clear that this is a temporary policy that will have to be modified. France is not weak enough to forego permanently all nuclear armament; nor is France strong enough to operate a complete nuclear program of her own. The former course would retire France from the arena of world power long before her time; the latter would drain French resouces of men, money, and materiel beyond all reasonable relation to total capacities and real needs. France may be obliged, in consequence, to choose the cooperative course.

A large hurdle on the cooperative course is the Franco-German relationship. It would be presumptuous for an American observer, even a deeply friendly one, to offer gratuitous solutions of this problem. Indeed, it is not theoretical solutions that have been lacking, but rather the perception of common need and benefit that would make any solution acceptable. Such a perception may be in the making as one looks to the thermonuclear future. Neither country can now afford to develop its *own* complete weapons-system; but still less can either afford to remain outside of *some* complete weapons-system. As the moment of decision approaches, France will once again confront a debate on the familiar themes of the EDC period; German danger, British participation, American pressure, Soviet negotiation. These are the constants of the French position in a world where no nation can any longer be a policy-island. Until France comes to satisfying terms with these issues, there can be no unity in Europe nor stability in the Western system.

One may hope that the obscurantist schisms of the EDC period will be avoided in the debates ahead.[13] An essential lesson is that

[13] Since these words were written, a year ago, two alternative proposals for pooling nuclear resources have in fact been presented to France and Europe.

EDC was but one of several routes to the goal. It may be that the way of supranational institutions has been closed for our generation. Other ways to European cooperation, perhaps less dramatic but more feasible, lie open. Indeed, the most durable foundation for an eventual new-style Community may, in the post-EDC epoch, be an actual old-style coalition based on the enlightened self-interest of all parties.

If the spectres of ideology can be laid, there will be clearer sights on a rational course, which seeks maximum value at minimum cost. A rational course would be cooperative Franco-German thermonuclear development within the complete weapons-system of the Western fraternity. A way must be found. But where there is a will, there are many ways. Can we draw from reflection on EDC the lessons which are essential to the future of the West?

The one called Euratom proposes a supranational community on the EDC model. The OEEC plan proposes a more conventional type of intergovernmental association. The great debate on these alternatives merits our attention. D. L.